Praise for *Touc...*

"A high-quality account of the soldiers who became leaders in the Gilded Age ... rousing and vibrant." —*Akron Beacon Journal*

"An extraordinarily lucid and richly researched history ... Perry provides letters, diaries and other sources to bring military and political details to life." —*San Antonio Express-News*

"One of those rare histories that combines impeccable research with an imminently readable and often lighthearted style. With keen insight and details he draws readers into a time we have forgotten." —*The Pegram Advocate*

"*Touched with Fire* sheds new light on these Gilded Age presidents and makes for a vivid reminder of what a truly great generation can accomplish." —*Warren Tribune Chronicle*

"[An] elegantly written, educational, and entertaining study." —*Military Heritage*

"Perry offers detailed accounts of these future Presidents' wartime exploits. The chronicles of the various battles are particularly good." —*Library Journal*

"Perry, a wry storyteller, delivers the regimental-level detail that buffs crave while dusting events with the skepticism that presidential electoral campaigning invites." —*Booklist*

"Solid, informative ... [Perry] knows his territory and his people, and has a readable journalistic style." —*Publishers Weekly*

"A well-crafted survey of five presidents ... [Perry] writes fluently and memorably ... does a good job of giving a you-are-there account of the presidents' season under fire and of drawing attention to often overlooked figures." —*Kirkus Reviews* (starred review)

"A new approach to Civil War history, and Perry pulls it off extremely well. He cleverly combines war with politics, revealing how wartime experiences, blended with strong personality ambition, helped shape political futures." —*Military Officer*

"Here is history as it should be written. In *Touched with Fire*, Jim Perry, one of America's great political reporters, proves once again that fiction cannot compete with carefully researched, masterfully told, and eminently readable history." —Mark Shields

"I highly recommend *Touched with Fire* to anyone interested in supplementing or challenging his view of American history." —John S. D. Eisenhower, author of *So Far from God* and *Yanks*

TOUCHED WITH FIRE

Five Presidents and the

Civil War Battles That Made Them

✳ ✳ ✳

JAMES M. PERRY

B

PublicAffairs

New York

Book design and composition by Mark McGarry, Texas Type & Book Works
Set in Monotype Bell

Library of Congress Cataloging-in-Publication data
Perry, James M. (James Moorhead).
Touched with fire : five presidents and the Civil War battles that made them /
James M. Perry.
p. cm.
Includes bibliographical references and index.
ISBN 1–58648–240–2 (pbk)
1. Presidents—United States—History. 2. Presidents—United States—Biography.
3. Soldiers—United States—Biography. 4. United States—History—Civil War,
1861–1865—Biography. 5. United States—History—Civil War, 1861–1865—Campaigns.
6. Grant, Ulysses S. (Ulysses Simpson), 1822–1885—Military leadership. 7. Hayes,
Rutherford Birchard, 1822–1893—Military leadership. 8. Garfield, James A. (James
Abram), 1831–1881—Military leadership. 9. Harrison, Benjamin, 1833–1901—Military
leadership. 10. McKinley, William, 1843–1901—Military leadership. I. Title.
E176.1.P474 2003
973.7'3'0922—dc21
2003046625

10 9 8 7 6 5 4 3 2 1

For Peggy

Through our great good fortune, in our youth our hearts were touched with fire.

CAPTAIN OLIVER WENDELL HOLMES, JR.
20TH MASSACHUSETTS VOLUNTEER REGIMENT.

Contents

Introduction

FOR A NATION that has always been a little dubious about the role of the military in a democratic society, the United States has been conspicuously generous in sending a long line of soldiers and sailors to the White House.

George Washington, truly the great man in the American Revolution, was elected president twice and served eight years in office, reluctantly, setting an impossible standard for all those who followed. He was a great general and a great president. One other combat-tested president emerged from the Revolutionary War—James Monroe, who was wounded while taking part in Washington's daring Christmas night attack on Trenton and Princeton.

The War of 1812 yielded two soldier-presidents, Andrew Jackson and William Henry Harrison. The War with Mexico produced two more, Zachary Taylor and Franklin Pierce. The Spanish-American War gave us Theodore Roosevelt, and World War I produced Harry Truman.

Seven future presidents served in uniform in World War II,

most notably Dwight Eisenhower, the architect of the Allied victory in Europe. Only three of them were actually involved in day-to-day combat, all of it with the navy in the Pacific: John F. Kennedy, whose torpedo boat was sunk; Gerald R. Ford, who picked up ten battle stars for his time on an aircraft carrier; and George H.W. Bush, whose torpedo bomber was shot down.

But it was the Civil War, the most wrenching of all U.S. wars, that produced the most presidents with combat experience—five in all, two of whom survived rebel gunfire only to be struck down in office—and it is safe to say that none of them would have been elected president if it hadn't been for their wartime performances. Ulysses S. Grant, of course, was paramount, the general who won the war for the North. The others were Rutherford B. Hayes (the only president other than Monroe to have been wounded in action), James A. Garfield, Benjamin Harrison, and William McKinley.

Americans have never known anything like the Civil War. Two million men wore the Union blue, and 360,000 of them died; another million wore the Confederate gray, and 260,000 of them died, representing, altogether, 2 percent of the combined population, North and South. If 2 percent of the U.S. population were to die in a war today, the historian James M. McPherson has reckoned, the number of American war dead would add up to more than five million.

Veterans of all of the wars the United States was involved in were deeply touched by the experiences they had shared. Washington's officers wept when he said good-bye, and they organized the first veterans' organization, the Society of the Cincinnati, to pass their memories down, generation after generation. World War II veterans have attended thousands of reunions for all the regiments, divisions, air squadrons, and ships they served with. Tom Brokaw has called them "the greatest generation," a designation that tends to overlook the ragged soldiers who served with Washington and Knox and Lafayette and the men who fought in so many bloody battles with Grant and Sherman and Sheridan.

Washington's men created a nation; Grant's men kept it from breaking apart. They were great generations too.

The five Civil War presidents never doubted they had been part of a major historical event. They and two million others in their generation had put down a bloody rebellion and saved the Union, and nothing else could ever mean more to them than that.

The five soldier-presidents were all westerners for their time, Midwesterners for ours, from Illinois, Ohio, and Indiana, and they fought most of their battles in the western theater, so often neglected by historians dazzled by Lee's campaigns in the east, at such places as Fort Donelson and Chickamauga and Resaca. They all believed the tough, long-striding western soldiers could march longer and fight harder than the pale city boys from the east.

Grant, the West Pointer, was the only professional among the five. The rest were all civilian volunteers with no military training of any kind. Hayes and Harrison were hardworking lawyers; Garfield was a college president and a state senator. McKinley, the only one who served as an enlisted man, was a teenager.

Other than McKinley, who had studied briefly at Allegheny College, they were all college graduates—Grant (West Point), Garfield (Williams), Hayes (Kenyon College and the Harvard Law School), and Harrison (University of Miami in Ohio).

McKinley was too young to be married, but the others were all married to women of considerable character. Grant's wife, Julia Dent, was just as muscular as her husband and could ride a horse just as capably; she and her husband were attracted to each other in a powerful, physical way. Hayes's spirited wife, Lucy Webb, is best remembered as "Lemonade Lucy" for banning spirits in the White House. But she was much more than that. She and the children regularly visited Hayes and his regiment when they were in camp, and the soldiers loved and admired her. She was a fierce supporter of the Union cause and sometimes wished she could fight at the front herself. Garfield's wife, Lucretia Rudolph, known to her friends as "Crete," had a great deal to bear, for her husband, her "dear Jamie," was a notorious womanizer. Her letters to her philandering husband are wise and eloquent. As a young woman, Harrison's wife, Caroline "Carrie" Scott, was fun-loving and flirtatious; she brought a little warmth into his dour Presbyterian soul. Harrison's letters to Carrie show a romantic, even earthy, side to his character that hardly anyone else ever knew existed.

All of these future presidents were aggressive, sometimes impetuous, soldiers. They had nothing but contempt for commanders who were overly cautious. In his early campaigns, Grant grumbled about his slow-moving superior, General Henry W. "Old Brains" Halleck. Garfield and Hayes in particular viewed almost all West Point generals with suspicion. Garfield firmly believed that some of them, because they were Democrats, were traitors. He had his own frustrating times with General William S. "Old Rosy" Rosecrans. Hayes was unhappily linked for months with Colonel Eliakim P. Scammon, a very indecisive West Pointer from Maine. West Pointers, Garfield and Hayes agreed, tended to be autocratic and tyrannical, little understanding that running a volunteer army was a lot different from running a professional one. West Pointers, in their defense, believed that these civilian generals were often more interested in advancing their political careers than in defeating the enemy. Garfield was the sort of general they had in mind. Harrison didn't have any special problems with West Pointers—he was a rigid disciplinarian himself—but he did have a colorful and long-standing feud with one of his commanding generals, his "incubus," the incompetent William W. Ward, a lawyer like himself as well as a heavy drinker.

McKinley was too young to be looking very far into the future, but the rest all had political connections. Grant owed his West Point experience to the congressman who gave him the appointment. Another congressman helped in getting him into the Union army as a colonel and in winning his promotion to brigadier general. Hayes had been the city solicitor in Cincinnati, Garfield was a state senator, and Harrison held a statewide elective office, reporter of the state supreme court.

Political ambition and a good war record took all five of these men a very long way.

What helped all of them as well was the fact that they were generally seen as fairly down-to-earth fellows. Grant is remembered, famously, for meeting Robert E. Lee at Appomattox Court House dressed in what he called rough soldier's garb. Lee was wearing his finest dress uniform. It was no accident; that's the way Grant wanted to appear on the biggest day of his life.

Garfield was a schemer, but his men knew little of that. They revered him, and the boys in the 42d Ohio were sorry to lose him when he moved on to bigger things after his successful campaign in the Big Sandy Valley in eastern Kentucky. Hayes was a first-rate regimental and brigade commander, with perfect instincts for leading civilian volunteers. He listened to his men and cared for them; they, in turn, cherished him. He fought in a dozen battles—he actually saved the day for Sheridan at Opequon—with a ferocity that is hard to reconcile with anything in his life that led up to the war or that followed it. Because of his stern and unforgiving demeanor, Harrison was never a popular figure with the men who served under him. But because he was a courageous leader in battle—he and his men turned back John Bell Hood's furious charge at Peach Tree Creek—they came to respect him. They called him "Little Ben," and in time they called him that with something approaching affection. McKinley—"Mack" to his fellow soldiers—could be both effervescent, in the way of most teenagers, and serious and religious. The boys in the 23d Ohio never forgot his reckless ride to bring them hot rations at Antietam, the war's bloodiest day.

Grant emerged from the war as the first soldier in history to command more than one million men. Hayes, Garfield, and Harrison completed their military service as generals, but they had done almost all their fighting as colonels. McKinley, only eighteen years old, entered the army as a private; he was mustered out as a twenty-two-year-old major.

None of them has ever been ranked as an outstanding president, although every now and then a historian tries without much success to put a gentler spin on Grant's record in office. In defense of all of them, it should be remembered that this was the Gilded Age when change was sweeping the country and when presidents really weren't expected to do very much about it. Even so, Hayes had his defining moments in office, and McKinley established the United States as a world power. Hardly anyone defends Harrison, grandson of another soldier-president. No one has even bothered to type up his Civil War letters, most of them written in pencil and now fading away in the stacks at the Library of Congress.

Garfield remains the mystery man. He was probably the smartest of the lot; he was also the most devious. But because he died from an assassin's bullets only four months after taking office, we will never know what kind of president he might have been.

We remember these Civil War presidents, when we remember them at all, as serious older men, with long beards and starched collars. But surely that's not how they thought of themselves. Once they were young and virile and full of martial spirit. They were the boys in blue, and they saved the Union in the one time in their lives when their hearts were touched with fire. That is the story this book will tell.

Chapter 1

APRIL 12, 1861

AT 4:30 A.M. on April 12, 1861, Lieutenant Henry S. Farley, an artillery officer in what would soon be the Army of the Confederate States of America, fired an old coast-defense mortar at Fort Sumter in Charleston harbor. Witnesses, holding their breath, watched as the shell, its red fuse burning brightly, gracefully made a path across the dark sky. It exploded directly over the fort defended by Major Robert Anderson, United States Army, and his garrison of nine officers and seventy-four enlisted men.

It was the opening shot of the Civil War, the War of the Rebellion, the War Between the States, the war that has held millions of Americans in thrall ever since. Because it was the first war in which news was rapidly relayed by the telegraph—the "lightning," soldiers and newspaper reporters called it—word of what had happened soon spread throughout the nation.

No one reacted to the news with more interest than five men from the Midwest who would soon join the Union army, lead men into combat, win good notices in the newspapers back home, and eventually march all the way to the White House. They were

Ulysses S. Grant, thirty-eight years old, from Galena, Illinois; James A. Garfield, twenty-nine, from Hiram, Ohio; Rutherford B. Hayes, thirty-eight, from Cincinnati, Ohio; William McKinley, eighteen, from Poland, Ohio; and Benjamin Harrison, twenty-seven, from Indianapolis, Indiana. It is hard to imagine a more unlikely collection of future presidents.

Grant, who would become the greatest soldier of them all, was palpably a failure. He had failed as a potato farmer in Missouri (he called his farm house "Hardscrabble"), his fortunes reaching such a low point that he was reduced to selling firewood on street corners in St. Louis. He had given up the farm and tried bill collecting, a job for which he was wholly unsuited, and he had failed at that too. He finally had been forced by his declining, even desperate, circumstances to move his wife, Julia, and their two children to Galena and to take a job as a clerk in the leather and harness shop owned by his father, Jesse (but operated by his brothers Orvil and Simpson). He hated every minute of it.

But, of course, he was a West Point graduate (ranking in the bottom half of his class academically), and he had served with some distinction in the War with Mexico. He had left the army after fifteen years' service—resigning his captain's commission—in 1854. When the news of the bombardment of Fort Sumter swept Galena, townspeople remembered that Jesse Grant's son Ulysses, his clerk at the harness shop, had once been a soldier, Galena's only professional warrior.

The second evening after the news came to town, almost everyone assembled at the court house. "Although a comparative stranger," Grant wrote in his memoirs, "I was called upon to preside; the sole reason, possibly, was that I had been in the army and had seen service. With much embarrassment and some prompting, I made out to announce the object of the meeting. Speeches were in order, but it is doubtful whether it would have been safe just then to make other than patriotic ones."*

---

* See bibliography at back of book for sources.

The evening ended with Grant calling for volunteers to fill a 100-man company as the local answer to President Lincoln's call for 75,000 young men to serve for ninety days. "The company was raised and the officers and non-commissioned officers elected before the meeting adjourned," Grant wrote. But the old West Pointer, expecting bigger things to come his way later, declined the captaincy. One thing he was sure of—his clerk's job in his father's shop was over. "I never went into our leather store after that meeting, to put up a package or do other business," he said.

Grant's West Point credentials were significant. At the top command level, the Civil War was a West Pointers' war. Historian T. Harry Williams figures that West Pointers commanded both armies in fifty-five of the sixty biggest and bloodiest battles, and in the remaining five a West Pointer commanded one of the armies.

When the war began, only 440 West Pointers were serving in the Union army. Scores more, led by Robert E. Lee, had defected to the new rebel army. Of the more than 500 other West Point graduates who had left the army for jobs in the private sector and who now sought a role in the Union army, 115 reentered the regular service, and 393 accepted commissions in the volunteer regiments being organized in the loyal states. Grant wanted one of those jobs.

After several disappointments, he was given command of the 21st Illinois Volunteers and sworn in to three years of federal service at Mattoon, southeast of Springfield, the state capital, on June 16, 1861. He and his troops set off together on July 3 for the slave-holding state of Missouri and for the history books.

The West Point professionals commanded the armies, but it was the amateurs—thousands of them—who led the companies and the regiments and the brigades and the divisions.

James A. Garfield, the most complex and, in his calculating, devious way, perhaps the most intriguing of all these future presidents, was at his place in the legislative hall of the Ohio state senate in

Columbus when one of his fellow senators burst onto the floor to announce, breathlessly, that the rebels had opened fire on Fort Sumter. A woman in the gallery cried out, "Glory to God!"

Garfield's family home—a log cabin—was in a tiny village called Orange, near Cleveland (then a town of no more than a dozen dwellings), in the swampy, remote Cuyahoga River valley. His father, Abram, had died when Garfield was three; he and his older brother and sister were brought up in something very close to stark poverty by their mother, Eliza. The family was comforted by its attachment to the Disciples of Christ, a newly organized religious sect that believed the Bible was the only authority on questions of faith and personal conduct (but that gave its members wide latitude in interpreting what the words really meant).

Garfield recalled years later that his friends at school taunted him for being fatherless and for being poor. In August 1848, when he was sixteen years old, he ran away to nearby Cleveland and found work on a canal boat, the *Evening Star*, owned by a distant cousin. He was a "driver," meaning he worked the tow path making sure the horses minded their business. The job lasted six weeks. He came home, not feeling very well, and was nursed back to health by his mother, a warm and understanding woman. Thereafter, he took up schooling more seriously, attending Geauga Academy, a Baptist institution in nearby Chester, while teaching in district schools in the summer to pay for tuition and room and board.

It was also about this time (1850 and 1851) that he discovered the opposite sex. While teaching at Warrensville, he became enamored of one of his pupils, Mary Hubbell. Garfield's friend, Corydon Fuller, said Miss Hubbell was "witty and apt at repartee," but, as far as he could tell, "had no serious thoughts on any subject." He advised Garfield that the girl was not suitable. Garfield agreed, but ending the relationship was easier said than done. "I feel myself in a dilemma," Garfield responded. Although he and Miss Hubbell weren't officially engaged, he noted, most people who knew them thought they were, or should be. "Of all characters in society,"

Garfield said, "none is more despicable, heartless, and truly deserving the frown and contempt of all good men and women, than the man who wantonly trifles with the affections of a woman." But if he did the right thing by her, Garfield wondered, would he "curb my career and fasten a clog to my improvement?" James Garfield, at a fairly tender age, was already ambitious. He did drop Miss Hubbell, but not for several months, by which time they were both students at a new school, the Western Reserve Eclectic Institute in Hiram, southeast of Cleveland. Known as the Eclectic then, it is Hiram College today.

He was baptized, head to toe, in the Chagrin River, making a commitment to Christ and to his mother's church, the Disciples of Christ, which ran the Eclectic. And Miss Hubbell was soon succeeded in his affections by a much more suitable young woman, Lucretia "Crete" Rudolph, whose father, Zeb, was a prominent member of the Disciples and a trustee of the Eclectic. Miss Rudolph, a dark, handsome, serious girl, was also a student at the school.

Although he was never ordained as a minister, Garfield did some serious preaching, beginning in late 1853 or early 1854. In his first sermon, he startled his devout audience by comparing the life of Jesus Christ to the life of Napoleon Bonaparte. After all, he said, Napoleon rose from obscurity, climbed to great heights, was banished, and then returned triumphantly to Paris, almost as if he was rising from the dead. "At the conclusion of the service," one witness reported, "the attention was intense and the stillness most profound."

It is always hard to know just how deeply Garfield felt about some things, including the teachings of his church. Garfield really came first, and it was his own ambition that led him eventually to a school that most Disciples would have considered dangerously secular, Williams College in Williamstown, Massachusetts. As soon as he arrived on the little campus—he was surrounded by the first mountains he had ever seen—he reported to the home of the college's president, Mark Hopkins. There, he was given a brief entrance exam—answer a few questions on geometry, translate a few passages from Latin and Greek texts. He did well enough to win admission and was placed in the junior class.

In 1854 Williams was a small, struggling school, and Hopkins was an effective but eccentric teacher (he once boasted he had never been interested in reading books). Even so, Williams was a lot more stimulating than the Eclectic. At Williams, Garfield became a prime debater and something of a literary figure. For the first time, he began considering the great issues of the day seriously; it was while he was a college student that he developed his strong distaste for the institution of slavery, noting in his journal that "I feel like throwing the whole current of my life into the work of opposing this giant Evil. I don't know but the religion of Christ demands such action."

Garfield was a big, powerful man, and it was at Williams that his boisterous personality—something akin to Lyndon Johnson's—first began to emerge. He was not an outstanding student, but he was a man to be reckoned with on campus. He even found time to carry on another romance, this time with Rebecca Selleck, a member of a Disciples of Christ congregation near Williamstown, although he was officially engaged to Crete Rudolph back in Hiram. He had the nerve to write Crete about Rebecca, saying he was only dallying with her because she reminded him so much of his own true love. Crete, a smart young lady, was not fooled or amused (but she did forgive him, and they would be married in 1858).

He returned to Hiram after his graduation from Williams and in no time at all was president of the Eclectic. His opponents said he had used devious means to topple the favorite for the job to get it for himself—the kind of criticism that would dog him throughout his life. Then he did something else that shocked the Disciples, who didn't believe that religion and politics should be mixed—he ran on the Republican ticket for the state senate, and won. So by the time he was twenty-nine, this young man, reared without a father in a log cabin in an Ohio backwater, was both a college president and a member of the state senate, where he was widely seen as "a coming man." It is no wonder that one of his biographers was Horatio Alger.

When he heard the news that Sumter had been fired upon, Garfield knew that, sooner or later, he would have to go to war. So did his fellow senator and roommate—they shared the same bed in a Columbus rooming house—Jacob Dolson Cox.

They called on Governor William Dennison on Sunday morning, April 14, to talk about Ohio's response to the firing on Sumter. Later that day, Garfield wrote his friend and greatest admirer, J. Harrison "Harry" Rhodes, a teacher at the Eclectic and eventually Garfield's successor as its president. "I am glad we are defeated at Sumter," he said. "It will rouse the people. I can see no possible end to the war till the south is subjugated. . . . Better lose a million men in battle than allow the government to be overthrown." Garfield said he and Cox had agreed to join the army "if it be necessary."

"The situation hung upon us like a nightmare," Cox remembered. The two roommates had been thinking about war for weeks, staying up late into the night reading military manuals and histories of Napoleon's campaigns. Garfield had concluded from that brief investigation that it didn't take a whole lot of specialized knowledge to lead an army. West Pointers, he felt, didn't have much on him. "Pluck," he wrote, was what it would take, not "military science." Cox was the first to sign up, and in no time at all—much to Garfield's amazement and possible consternation—he was wearing the star of a brigadier general in the Ohio Volunteers. Garfield believed he deserved no less. A phrenologist, he recalled, had felt the bumps on his head and declared that they were the kind you would find on a general's noggin.

"I have offered the governor my services in any capacity he may see fit to appoint me," Garfield wrote Harry Rhodes on April 17. "He may not require me to enter the army now, he may not at all. It is thought by some that a brigadier generalship will be assigned to me, but this is not probable. . . . I would do nothing wrong or rash, but there is something due to the state from the position I hold."

Instead, Governor Dennison recruited Garfield for some secret maneuvering. Hearing that Illinois had more muskets in its armory than it could use, Garfield was dispatched to Springfield to procure the overstock for Ohio's volunteers. At the same time, Dennison asked him to do what he could to convince the governors of Illinois and Indiana that troops from all the valley, or midwestern, states should be commanded by Ohio's highest-ranking soldier, Major General George B. McClellan.

"I am to open negotiations with the governors of Illinois and Indiana," he wrote Harry Rhodes, "with the design of obtaining permission to divide the forces of the Union into two grand armies, all east of the mountains to be called the army of the East and to take charge of Washington and the sea coast, and another to be called the army of the valley, who shall take the whole line of coast from Pittsburgh to Cairo, and shall open a way down the Mississippi River." McClellan, he noted, was the obvious choice to lead the army of the valley. "It will be a work of some difficulty to get all the states of the valley to submit to the leadership of Ohio. I am to try my power of diplomacy to effect this purpose."

He had no trouble with the muskets. He told Governor Dennison that he had shipped them by rail from Lafayette and Indianapolis for 55 cents per hundredweight. He also reported that he had talked to Governor Richard Yates of Illinois, who was in "hearty concurrence" with McClellan's role in the west and the two-army strategy. The muskets, obsolete as they surely must have been, were a help. The two-army idea—sound in theory—languished.

Ohio's early regiments elected their own officers, and Garfield now sought to be elected colonel of one of them. He tried the 7th first, then the 19th. He lost both times. Furious at the results, he concluded there had been a conspiracy to deny him what he so obviously deserved. "Unscrupulous men," he said, wanted him "out of the way."

Starting with the 23d Regiment, field officers were appointed by the governor. That meant that Garfield could now turn to his

patron, Governor Dennison, in full expectation of being named to a
high command, thus avoiding the grubby necessity of campaigning
for votes. The governor couldn't give him a general's star, or even a
colonelcy, but he did make Garfield an offer on July 27. "Can you
take a lieutenant colonelcy?" he asked.

The governor's telegram didn't catch up to Garfield until
August 7, and it wasn't until a week later, August 14, that he swal-
lowed his pride—he had already turned down a lieutenant colonelcy
once—and agreed to accept. He wrote Crete from Cleveland that he
had telegraphed the governor his decision. "I have concluded to go,"
he wrote. He said he was waiting in his hotel room for the governor's return telegram, instructing him when and where to report.
He signed it, "With kisses for yourself and Trot," Trot being the
Garfields' nickname for their only child (more would come later),
one-year-old Eliza Arabella, and the cherished subject of many of
their letters. Crete replied the next day that she was "glad these terrible hours of torturing suspense to you have passed and you can lift
up your soul again to energetic action." She said she was packing a
trunk for him, but she warned that "your undershirts are getting
thin, but you will want flannel when you go out into camp." She also
figured her "dear Jamie" might need some new sleeping shirts.

Garfield was mustered into federal service at Camp Chase on
August 16, the de facto commanding officer of the 42d Ohio Volunteers. In fact, he was the only soldier attached to the regiment. It
was up to him to recruit the other 999. His first success came in
Hiram, where sixty of his students volunteered in an hour. Other
companies came from Ravenna and Ashland and Mount Ephraim.
On September 5, Garfield was promoted to colonel and given formal command of the regiment. It had taken him a while, but he
finally had achieved what he had wanted so badly back in April
when the shooting began. The boys of the 42d began drilling with
roughly carved wooden muskets in early November.

*

Rutherford B. Hayes was a classic amateur soldier, "one of the good colonels," in his own words. At the time the shooting began, he was thirty-eight years old, a married man with three young children, tending to an increasingly successful law practice in Cincinnati. Hayes was well educated, a graduate of Kenyon College and the Harvard Law School, and he had already served a term as Cincinnati's city solicitor. His uncle Sardis Birchard, the closest thing Ruddy Hayes had to a father (his own had died before he was born), thought he should stay home and take care of his family.

But Hayes, who had been a lonely, sometimes sickly boy—he was reared in Delaware, Ohio, by his Bible-reading, straitlaced mother and his mother's spinster aunt, Arcena Smith—was full of surprises. He had a romantic streak under that somewhat serious exterior, and he had dreamed for years of going off to war and becoming a hero.

On April 19, a week after the firing of the first shot, he was full of patriotic vigor. "We are all for war," he wrote Uncle Sardis, the family entrepreneur, living in Fremont. "The few dissentients have to run like quarter-horses [for cover]." Hayes's wife, the former Lucy Webb, was also raring to go. "Lucy enjoys it," he wrote, "and wishes she had been in Fort Sumter with a garrison of women."

By April 20, Hayes and most of his "cronies" were drilling and learning how to "eyes right and left" as members of a volunteer home-guard company called "Burnet's Rifles." It was composed almost entirely of members of the city's Literary Club. Hayes was the captain.

Hayes kept a daily diary for his entire adult life. Here's the entry for May 15, 1861:

Judge [Stanley] Matthews and I have agreed to go into the service for the war—if possible into the same regiment. I spoke my feelings to him, which he said were his also, viz., that this was a just and necessary war and that it demanded the whole power of the country; that I would prefer to go into it if I knew

I was to die or be killed in the course of it, than to live through and after it without taking any part in it.

Grant was a professional. He returned to the army because he felt it was his duty and because he sensed soldiering would turn out to be a better line of work for him than clerking in his father's leather shop. Hayes's thinking was entirely different. He knew nothing about soldiering—he had no idea what kind of soldier he would be—but he was a patriot, and that was enough. A thoroughly decent and honorable man, he signed up because he desperately wanted to do what he could to preserve the Union.

Hayes wrote Uncle Sardis on June 9 that he and his friend, Judge Matthews, had been notified by telegraph to report for active duty at Columbus the next day. "We are to be in a regiment with Colonel [William] Rosecrans—a West Pointer ... and a capital officer [in charge], Matthews as lieutenant-colonel and I as major."

He wrote Uncle Sardis again the next day, from Camp Jackson (soon to be Camp Chase), four miles west of Columbus, to say that his new regiment was the first in which all the field officers had been appointed by the governor. "We are the Twenty-third regiment," he wrote, "and our companies will probably be from the north."

When news of the firing on Fort Sumter came to the small town of Poland, just south of Youngstown, in the old Western Reserve in northeastern Ohio, a crowd gathered at a tavern called the Sparrow House. Charles Glidden, a local attorney, delivered a stirring speech from the front stoop and called for volunteers to serve in one of Ohio's new volunteer regiments. It was a little like a revival meeting; one after another, young men stepped forward and vowed to serve the Union. In the crowd that day were two eighteen-year-old cousins, William McKinley and William McKinley Osborne. McKinley came from a middle-class family with a strong interest in literature, education, and the Bible. He had briefly attended

Allegheny College, in nearby Meadville, Pennsylvania, before being forced to withdraw because of illness. He was bright and personable, but very deliberative.

He listened carefully to Glidden's speech and then observed the young volunteers—they called themselves the "Poland Guards"— as they drilled six days a week on a church green and in a nearby school yard. He talked things over with cousin Will, another thoughtful young man who was living at McKinley's parents' home studying for the law. He and Will followed the Guards to Youngstown and watched them set up camp. "I decided to wait and study the situation a little more carefully first," McKinley said.

In the end, they decided they had no choice. To keep the respect of their friends and neighbors, they agreed to enlist. It was "in cold blood and not through the enthusiasm of the moment," Will Osborne said. Years later, McKinley agreed. "I came to a deliberative conclusion, and have never been sorry for it."

It was a curious way for an eighteen-year-old to go to war.

McKinley and Osborne followed the Poland Guards to Camp Jackson in time to be mustered into federal service on June 11. The Poland Guards were now Company E of the 23d Ohio Volunteer Infantry Regiment.

McKinley was a very self-contained man, and he didn't like to write letters or accumulate private papers. But he did keep a diary for the first few weeks he served in the army. He took note of the regiment's major, Rutherford B. Hayes, in an entry on July 4. Major Hayes, he said, read the Declaration of Independence to the regiment. Lieutenant Colonel Matthews, who one day would be a U.S. senator and an associate justice of the Supreme Court, spoke, too, "most sublimely." The regiment was now ready to set off to war, two future presidents of the United States in its ranks.

Poor Benjamin Harrison may not have known it, but he really didn't have much choice. He was the grandson of William Henry

Harrison, Old Tippecanoe himself, who had earned so many laurels fighting the Indians and the British that he had marched all the way to the White House in 1840. For all of that, it took Ben longer to make up his mind than any of the other future presidents. And when he finally made the plunge, it took him and his impatient regiment months to get into action. But when he did, he saw more fighting and more bloodshed in a month than his grandfather had seen in a lifetime.

Harrison came from a distinguished Virginia family, once proprietors of the great Virginia plantation house, Berkeley, where his grandfather, the ninth president, was born. William Henry Harrison's father, the first Benjamin Harrison, was a signer of the Declaration of Independence. Ben's father, John Scott Harrison, hardly fit the family's aristocratic pattern. He had been given a 600-acre farm and a farm house by his father, President Harrison. It was called the Point, and it was located at the mouth of the Big Miami River in southwestern Ohio, not far from Cincinnati. Hard as Scott Harrison tried, rarely could he sell enough corn, wheat, and hay to turn a profit. He kept up appearances by borrowing money from friends and relatives. It was all he could do to send Ben, fourteen, and his older brother, Irwin, sixteen, off to Farmer's College, a secondary school, in Cincinnati in the fall of 1847.

There, the same sort of thing happened to Harrison that had happened to Garfield at Williams College—he was taken in hand by an outstanding teacher. In Harrison's case, it was Dr. Robert Hamilton Bishop, who had already served as president of Miami University in Oxford, Ohio. Bishop, a warm, kindly man born in Scotland, was revered by everyone who studied with him and, under his daily tutelage in history and political science, Ben blossomed.

John Scott Harrison had hoped to send his two boys to one of the "Yankee colleges" back east, perhaps Harvard or Yale, but he couldn't afford to do so. Instead, Ben ended up at Miami University, "the Yale of the West," the school that Dr. Bishop had run for so many years. He arrived at Miami about the same time his father took his place as a Whig congressman in Washington. The Harrison name, his election demonstrated, still carried considerable political cachet.

Benjamin Harrison was smart, quiet, deeply religious, and not very congenial. It was no doubt his good luck that he met and fell in love at Miami with Caroline "Carrie" Scott, daughter of the Rev. Dr. John W. Scott, a distinguished member of the Miami faculty and founder of its sister school, the Oxford Female Institute. Ben's "own tendencies to seriousness and reserve were completely submerged in her presence," according to Harrison's lone scholarly biographer, Harry J. Sievers. Carrie was gay and flirtatious and loved to dance, a diversion that Harrison, a stern Presbyterian, felt was against his religious beliefs. Carrie took him to dances even if she couldn't get him to the floor. Critics always complained that Harrison was a cold fish, but his warm and tender letters to Carrie indicate that there was another, more appealing, side to his character.

After his graduation—he gave a speech at his commencement about the appalling conditions of the poor in England, speculating that the mother country's "manly race" was dying out—he began studying for the law in the offices of a well-known attorney, Bellamy Storer, in Cincinnati. He was admitted to the Ohio bar two years later and married Carrie in Oxford on October 20, 1853. They eventually settled in Indianapolis and struggled for a while until young Ben entered a thriving partnership with William Wallace, brother of Lew Wallace, who would serve with distinction in the Civil War and then write *Ben Hur*.

Harrison's father, John Scott Harrison, served two terms in Congress, during which time he grew increasingly unhappy and frustrated. He flirted first with the American Party, the "Know-Nothings," and as the 1860 election approached, joined forces with the Constitutional Union Party. He was unhappy when young Ben became an active supporter of the newly organized Republican Party. Ben took his biggest political step by running for supreme court reporter, a statewide position, in 1860, and he was swept into office along with Abraham Lincoln and the rest of the Republican ticket with a plurality of almost 10,000 votes. During the campaign, Harrison discovered he had a flair for stump speeches. His loud raspy voice soared above the crowd and drew enthusiastic responses. It was always a puzzle why Harrison could touch hearts in speeches to large audiences and disappoint so many people in more intimate surroundings. His small talk, it would seem from all the evidence, was almost Nixonian.

The court reporter job was just what Harrison needed. It entitled its incumbent to publish all the decisions and opinions of the state's highest court in book form and to pocket a goodly share of the sales revenue.

Given this background, Harrison's reluctance to step forward when the shooting began was understandable. By April 1861, he and Carrie had two children and were expecting a third. In addition, they were supporting Harrison's younger brother, John, and a nephew, Harry Eaton. Their home in Indianapolis was crowded, and Harrison made ends meet with borrowed money. But with the court reporter position offering substantial income, he was on the verge of breaking clear of all these distressing problems.

So he stayed home while dozens of his friends and colleagues marched off to war. Among them were his own brother, Irwin, a lieutenant, and Carrie's brother, Henry "Harry" Scott, a private, both serving in Colonel Lew Wallace's 11th Indiana Volunteers. They celebrated when they heard that Wallace and his Indiana boys had raided rebel territory and had won a small but decisive victory at Romney, Virginia.

Lincoln's first call for ninety-day volunteers had been enthusiastically received in Indiana. But when Lincoln called for 300,000 volunteers on July 1, 1862, to serve for three years, Hoosiers were slow to respond. Eight days later, on July 9, Harrison and his friend and law partner, Will Wallace, called on Governor Oliver Perry Morton, one of the great northern war governors, to discuss some routine political matters. They found the governor deeply distressed. He walked them across the reception room to a window, through which they could see a number of healthy young men working on the construction of a new building. How could that be, the governor asked, "when the country itself is in danger of destruction?"

Morton told his two visitors that there had been almost no response in Indiana to Lincoln's call for volunteers. "The people do not seem to realize the necessities of the situation," he said. "Something must be done to break the spirit of apathy and indifference which now prevails."

Harrison figured Morton was hinting that maybe he should be the one to get things moving. "Governor," he said, "if I can be of any service, I will go." Morton quickly proposed that Harrison raise a regiment in and around Indianapolis and then let someone else take it into the field. After all, the governor said, Harrison held an important statewide office. But Harrison was canny enough to know this wouldn't do. He couldn't enlist 1,000 men for a war in which many of them might be killed and then step aside for another man to lead them.

Harrison, truly a modest man, told the governor he wasn't at all sure he was competent to lead a regiment into battle. Morton accepted that. He commissioned Harrison a second lieutenant on the spot and instructed him to begin raising a regiment. As they walked down the capitol steps, Harrison signed up Wallace as his first recruit in what would come to be the 70th Indiana Volunteers. After that, he bought a military cap, hired a fife and a drum player, and hung an American flag outside the window of his law office. It was only then that he went home and told Carrie that he had decided to recruit a regiment and to go to war.

Chapter 2

THE MAKING OF
A GREAT COMMANDER

Colonel Ulysses S. Grant did not enter the Civil War on a positive note. His first command, the 21st Illinois Volunteer Regiment, stationed at Camp Yates, near Springfield, already had earned a reputation as a rowdy bunch. "With their drinking and fighting and robbing of chicken roosts, the men were the scourge of central Illinois," Bruce Catton says. "Worse yet, they were beginning to be known as 'Governor Yates's Hellions.'"

The regiment's founding colonel, "elected by the votes of the regiment, had proved to be fully capable of developing all there was in his men of recklessness," Grant remembered years later. "It was said he even went so far at times as to take the guard from their posts and go with them to the village nearby and make a night of it."

Governor Richard Yates had seen enough. He fired the good-time colonel and gave Grant command of the regiment, with orders to whip it into shape. Grant met his hellions for the first time on June 16, 1861. Dressed in a faded civilian coat and an old felt hat, he was anything but an imposing sight. The troops hooted and jeered, and a few even jostled him. But in hardly any time at all, the boys who had been hellions began to realize that maybe they were wrong about this unimpressive figure. Maybe he was a soldier, after all.

"I found it very hard work for a few days to bring all the men into anything like subordination," Grant said, "but the great majority favored discipline, and by the application of a little regular army punishment all were reduced to as good discipline as one could ask."

Unlike the rank and file, the officers were "sober and attentive and anxious to learn their duties," he told his devoted wife, Julia. But he did regret the fact that his lieutenant colonel and his major, both devout, churchgoing men, were anything but hellions, with whom, he said, he could never have a game of euchre. "For the Field officers of my regt. the 21st Ill. Volunteers one pint of liquor will do to the end of the war."

There is almost nothing more surprising about the Civil War than the emergence of Ulysses S. Grant as a great fighting general. No one could have predicted it, and even Grant would go into his first battle uncertain of his fighting qualities. But it would be in these first encounters that he would prove to himself and to the nation of what stern stuff he was made. Belmont gave advance warning to anyone who cared to pay attention that Grant was a very aggressive general. It led to his great victories at Forts Henry and Donelson, where he burst upon the Union as a hero, a relentless soldier—"Unconditional Surrender" Grant—who would give away nothing to his enemies.

Grant's 21st Illinois was one of a number of Illinois regiments that had agreed to serve in the army for thirty days, at the end of which time the soldiers would decide whether to sign on for three years. Grant's problem was to convince these short-term soldiers to enlist for what everyone hoped would be the duration. He recruited two Democratic congressmen, John A. McClernand and John A. Logan, to speak to the regiment. McClernand led off, with a stout speech. Logan followed, with a dramatic one. Grant was then called on to speak himself. "Men," he said, in the voice of a professional soldier, "go to your quarters!" To their quarters they went; most, now sensing the importance of their cause, signed up for three years.

Grant was a direct, down-to-earth, imperturbable man, drawing on a vast amount of old-fashioned common sense. He was, of course, a West Point graduate, and he had served with some distinction in the War with Mexico, although hardly anyone could remember exactly what he had done. In that war, though, he had had a chance to observe two distinctly different generals—Zachary Taylor, "Old Rough and Ready," who never wore anything resembling a uniform, and Winfield Scott, "Old Fuss and Feathers," who never saw a fancy uniform he didn't like. Grant patterned himself on Taylor; Robert E. Lee, another Mexican war veteran, emulated Scott. The Taylor model was the perfect one for dealing with the Union's army of volunteers.

On July 3, he was ordered to move his regiment by railroad cars from Springfield, in the central part of the state, to Quincy in the west, a Mississippi River city with embattled Missouri—a border state with a militant minority favoring the Confederate cause—on the other side. But Grant had other ideas; he *marched* his men to Quincy, ninety miles of sore feet and aching backs.

The first day, the regiment marched only five miles. Grant told them they would begin marching at 6:00 the following morning. Morning came, and nobody was ready. They moved out, after eating their breakfast, at 7:00. The next night, Grant told them the same thing—be prepared to march at 6:00 the following morning. Once again, when the time came to move out, hardly anyone was ready. This time, though, Grant ordered the march to begin anyway. Half the men were left behind, furiously looking for their uniforms and shoes, their tents and backpacks. Some of them set off down the road only partly dressed, jumping up and down, first on one leg and then on the other, as they tried to get their socks and shoes on. The next morning at 6:00, every man in the regiment was ready to go. More than any other West Point general, Grant knew—almost by instinct—how to turn these Union volunteers into warriors.

Grant's regiment had just appeared in front of Quincy when he was given orders to relieve an Illinois regiment that was surrounded by rebels a few miles west of Palmyra, in Missouri. "My sensations as we approached what I supposed might be 'a field of battle' were anything but agreeable," he said in his highly regarded (but not always accurate) memoirs. "I had been in all the engagements in Mexico that it was possible for one person to be in; but not in command. If someone else had been colonel and I had been lieutenant-colonel I do not think I would have felt any trepidation." But it was a false alarm. Before Grant could cross the river, "the besieged regiment came straggling into town. I am inclined to think both sides got frightened and ran away."

The 21st Illinois marched into Missouri a few days later, first to Palmyra and then to the Salt River, about twenty-five miles farther west, where crews were rebuilding a bridge that had been destroyed by rebel bushwhackers, undisciplined marauders who specialized in burning and pillaging. There, he was told to pursue one of the rebel raiders, Colonel Thomas Harris, believed to be camped at Florida, twenty-five miles downriver to the south. Grant confessed he was nervous.

As we approached the brow of the hill from which it was expected we could see Harris' camp, and possibly find his men ready formed to meet us, my heart kept getting higher and higher until it felt to me as though it was in my throat. I would have given anything then to have been back in Illinois, but I had not the moral courage to halt and consider what to do; I kept right on. When we reached a point from which the valley below was in full view I halted. The place where Harris had been encamped a few days before was still there and the marks of a recent encampment were plainly visible, but the troops were gone. My heart resumed its place. It occurred to me at once that

Harris had been as much afraid of me as I had been of him. This was a view of the question I had never taken before; but was one I never forgot afterwards. From that point on I never experienced trepidation upon confronting an enemy, though I always felt more or less anxiety. I never forgot that he had as much reason to fear my forces as I had his. The lesson was valuable.

He and his regiment were transferred to another Missouri town, Mexico, where Grant for the first time led his ex-hellions in battalion drill. "While I was at West Point," he said, "the tactics used in the army had been Scott's and the musket the flint lock. I had never looked at a copy of tactics from the time of my graduation. My standing in that branch of studies had been at the foot of the class. The arms had been changed since then [percussion caps for flints] and Hardee's tactics had been adopted. I got a copy of tactics and studied one lesson, intending to confine the exercise of the first day to the commands I had thus learned. By pursuing the course from day to day, I thought I would soon get through the volume."

Grant was promoted to brigadier general late in July, partly because he was a West Pointer who seemed to be doing a good job with the boys from the 21st Illinois, partly because his congressman back home, Elihu B. Washburne, was pushing his cause. Grant commanded the 21st Illinois for less than two months, but in that time he turned it into one of the better units in Major General John C. Fremont's western army. It went on, without him, to compile a distinguished record in the war.

Grant was ordered to take command of the army's District of Southeastern Missouri; he arrived in Cairo, the southern tip of Illinois, on September 4, 1861. He had sold his colonel's uniform and hadn't yet received his new brigadier general's uniform, so he walked into his new headquarters in "citizen's dress."

It was here, at Cairo, out of uniform as he surely was, that the remarkable Civil War career of Ulysses S. Grant truly began.

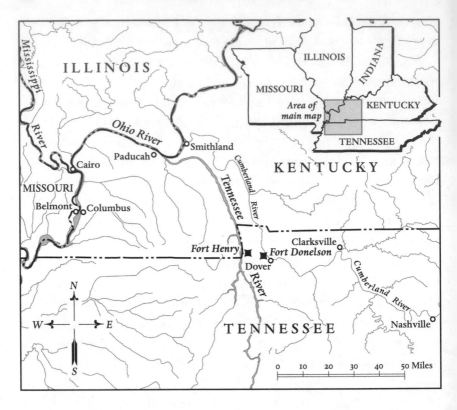

It was about this same time—September 1861—that Captain Andrew H. Foote, one of the navy's most neglected heroes, arrived in Cairo, where the Ohio River joins the Mississippi, to take command of the Union's river gunboat fleet. Foote was a wonderful character. Back in November 1856, his ship, the sloop of war *Portsmouth*, had been fired upon by one of four forts guarding the Chinese city of Canton. The forts, garrisoned by 5,000 men, mounted 176 guns. Foote asked for an apology, and when he didn't get one, he led 287 sailors and marines against the fort that had fired the shots. He held an umbrella over his head to protect himself from the fierce sun as he and his men waded through rice fields, dragging four howitzers behind them. They charged the works and routed its defenders; Foote reported they left fifty dead behind. The salty, Bible-thumping Foote and the plainspoken Grant, working together, would make a memorable fighting team, for Foote was every bit as aggressive as Grant himself.

The first gunboats to fly the Union flag were converted side-wheel steamers protected against enemy fire by heavy oak sheathing. There were three of them, the *Tyler*, the *Lexington*, and the *Conestoga*, and they did valuable service. But the fighting ships were the seven ironclad gunboats still being built (with 4,000 workers in two shipyards and countless machine shops) by James B. Eads, a St. Louis engineer, and they were big, ugly brutes—175 feet long, 52 feet wide, covered by iron plates 2 1/2 inches thick, drawing only 6 feet of water. They were armed with thirteen guns, including three powerful 9- and 10-inchers in the bow.

These gunboats gave Union commanders an immense advantage—control of the inland waterways, the Mississippi and the Ohio, the Cumberland and the Tennessee. The big ironclads couldn't move very fast—nine miles an hour was top speed—but when they reached their destination, they could let fly with a blaze of shot and shell.

On September 5, the day after Grant arrived in Cairo, the Confederate general Leonidas Polk, a West Pointer who had resigned from the U.S. Army to pursue a career in the Episcopal ministry (he had become bishop of Louisiana), made a serious blunder. He ordered one of his generals, Gideon Pillow, to seize Columbus, Kentucky, a Mississippi river city below Cairo, and to put heavy guns up on the bluffs. Until then, Kentucky had been insisting it was neutral in the war, and both North and South had respected that neutrality, waiting only for the day when one side or the other would make a fateful move.

Grant immediately sensed the significance of Pillow's decision and sent Foote's three wooden gunboats and two regiments of infantry to seize Paducah, Kentucky, thirty miles east of Cairo, an important and strategic town at the mouth of the Tennessee River, and, just above it, Smithland, at the mouth of the Cumberland River. "Grant's prompt reaction," the historian Kenneth P.

Williams says, "was one of the major decisions of the war." Kentucky, outraged by Pillow's seizure of Columbus, accepted Grant's move on Paducah and Smithland, with the result that this absolutely crucial state entered the war on the Union side.

Paducah was Grant's first victory; it was made even more memorable with the news that Brigadier General Charles F. Smith, who had been commandant of cadets when Grant was at West Point, was being ordered to take command there. Smith, a regular's regular, became the third member of what would now be the Grant-Foote-Smith partnership.

Paducah had been bloodless, but Grant wanted action. In a report to General Fremont on September 10, he said, "All the forces show great alacrity in preparing for any movement that looks as if it were to meet the enemy, and if discipline and drill were equal to their zeal, I should feel great confidence even against large odds." He said that if it were up to him, and if he were given some modest reinforcement, "I would take Columbus."

Columbus was the first "Gibraltar of the Mississippi" (Vicksburg would be the second), and with its towering cliffs, it was almost the perfect place to position artillery. There were two sets of cliffs—the "Chalk Bluffs" south of town and the "Iron Banks" north of town. The rebels built three tiers of batteries on the Iron Banks. The water battery, the one nearest the river itself, bristled with huge 10-inch Columbiads and an 11-inch howitzer. The biggest gun of all, the "Lady Polk," a Whitworth that fired a 128-pound projectile, was positioned at the top of the cliff. There weren't quite as many guns on the Chalk Bluffs, but there were enough to discourage anyone from coming very close. All in all, the rebels had 140 cannon at Columbus, making it the most heavily defended post in North America. Along with the guns, Polk had about 17,500 men, formed into divisions led by Pillow, Benjamin F. Cheatham, and John S. Brown. An old West Pointer, John Porter McCown, directed the artillery.

Gideon Pillow was the one officer in the Confederate army

whom Grant truly despised. They had served together in the War
with Mexico, at the conclusion of which Pillow had been the leader
of a cabal to discredit Scott's masterful victory; he had tried,
through various ruses, to take the credit himself. Pillow, General
Scott said, was "wholly indifferent in the choice between truth and
falsehood, honesty and dishonesty;—ever as ready to attain an end
by the one as the other, and habitually boastful of acts of cleverness
at the total sacrifice of moral character." Pillow was, in fact, a
rogue, and Grant could hardly wait to get his teeth into him.

Grant reported on September 15 that he had 13,481 men under
his command, but they were spread out at five different posts. It
was hardly enough to make much of a dent against Polk's mighty
fortress at Columbus. To make things even more annoying, an
investigative team from the House of Representatives arrived in
town late in October to question Grant about his little army. He
gave them straight answers.

"Have you any knowledge of a lot of Austrian muskets sent to
the fort at Cairo?" he was asked. Yes, he said, he did, the Austrian
muskets had preceded him to Cairo, and he didn't think much of
them. "In firing them," he complained, "the greater portion of them
would miss fire," and when they did fire, "the recoil is so severe that
it militates very much against the effectiveness of the arm."

And what about the quality of the beef that had been furnished
to him? They were "small, lean cattle—many of them cows—
which, in my judgment, would not make over 250 pounds of beef,
net weight, each, if even that," he replied. Did he consider the beef
unfit for the use of the army? "Most decidedly." And what did he
plan to do about it? "Throw them back upon the hands of the con-
tractor, and refuse to receive them from him."

On November 2, Grant was ordered by Fremont's headquarters
to make a series of demonstrations on both sides of the Mississippi
to discourage Polk and Pillow from sending reinforcements from
Columbus to other Confederate commands. In addition, the next
day Grant was ordered to send a column from two of his posts,

Cape Girardeau and Bird's Point, to assist Union forces in driving the rebel commander M. Jeff Thompson into Arkansas. On his own, Grant ordered C. F. Smith to move all the troops he could spare from Paducah and Smithland downriver toward Columbus.

On the morning of November 6, Grant himself set out from Cairo by steamship with 3,000 men and dropped down the river to within approximately six miles of Columbus. There, he landed a handful of men on the Kentucky side and established pickets to connect with Smith's troops making their way to Columbus from Paducah.

He admitted in his memoirs that he had no orders contemplating an attack by Union troops, "nor did I intend anything of the kind when I started out from Cairo." He said he changed his mind after receiving a message about 2:00 A.M. on November 7 reporting that "the enemy was crossing troops from Columbus to the west bank to be dispatched against Oglesby." Colonel Richard J. Oglesby was one of Grant's commanders, and his column was one of those that had been assigned to chase the rebel Thompson back into Arkansas. "I knew there was a small camp of Confederates at Belmont, immediately opposite Columbus, and I speedily resolved to push down the river, land on the Missouri side, capture Belmont, break up the camp and return," Grant said in his memoirs.

Grant didn't mention the 2:00 A.M. message in his first report on the Belmont campaign. It was only in a second report, written at the end of the war, that the mysterious message first popped up. No one has ever found a copy of the message. In all probability, it never existed. For reasons that still puzzle historians, Grant chose to write any number of accounts of his performance at Belmont. One historian calculates that there were eleven of them altogether.

The likeliest explanation is that he was trying to justify actions that he knew in his heart had been questionable (and he might also have been a little embarrassed about his own post-battle claim of a "great victory"). He couldn't really say that he intended all along to attack the rebels (he had no orders permitting that), so he had to say something else. But making the attack almost certainly was on his mind from the moment he arrived in Cairo. He gave a hint of his real reasoning in his memoirs by saying "that the officers and men were elated at the prospect of at last having the opportunity of doing what they had volunteered to do—fight the enemies of their country. I did not see how I could maintain the discipline, or retain the confidence of my command, if we should return to Cairo without an effort to do something."

Substitute Grant himself for "officers and men," and you have it. No one was more keen to attack the rebels than Ulysses Grant.

Grant's little expedition consisted of five infantry regiments (the 22d, 27th, 30th, and 31st Illinois and the 7th Iowa), two companies of cavalry and a six-gun battery (four six-pounders and two 12-pound howitzers), all of them loaded aboard four steamships. They were accompanied by two of the slab-sided gunboats, *Tyler* and *Lexington*, led by one of Foote's captains, Henry Walke.

The ships tied up at a small steamboat landing at Hunter's Farm, three miles above Columbus, and Grant's soldiers began disembarking about 8:00 A.M. Corporal William H. Onstot of the 27th Illinois said it was one of the most beautiful mornings he had ever seen.

When he heard about the enemy landing, Polk ordered Pillow to take four regiments across the river to reinforce the one regiment of Arkansas infantry (with a battery of six guns and two troops of cavalry) who were already camped there. (This regiment served under Colonel James Tappan, a gentlemanly graduate of both Exeter and Yale.) One of the reasons Grant had risked landing at Belmont was his conviction that Gideon Pillow was a fool. Pillow now managed to prove him entirely correct in that belief. He pulled Tappan's troops back from their position at the edge of the woods and plunked them down in the middle of a corn field, sitting ducks for Yankee gunners and riflemen.

Because his "lumberclads" were so vulnerable to heavy artillery fire, Walke was reluctant to interrupt the passage of the boats ferrying the rebels from one side of the river to the other. Even so, he did take his two gunboats into range of the big rebel guns three times. The third time, a shell ripped through the *Tyler* and killed one sailor and wounded two others. Walke withdrew his gunboats from the deadly line of fire, figuring he had done the best he could.

Polk, in command at Columbus, was confused. He "had been deterred from sending in the first instance a larger force to meet Grant's attack by the reports which his scouts made of the movements of the transports upon the river, and of the position and numbers of the [Union] columns from Fort Holt and Paducah, — all tending to show that the landing upon the opposite shore was a mere feint, while the real design was an attack upon Columbus," his son, Captain William M. Polk, said. Even so, Captain Polk pointed out, his father had sent a force equal to Grant's to Belmont.

Grant's force was divided into two brigades, one commanded by Brigadier General McClernand, the ambitious Illinois congressman who had given a pep talk to the 21st Illinois, and the other by Colonel Henry Dougherty. (John Logan, the Illinois congressman who had given the second pep talk that day, was also on the battlefield, commanding the 31st Illinois.) Grant ordered five companies—400 or 500 men in all—from Dougherty's brigade to stay behind to guard the transports. This move was the closest he came to establishing a "reserve" for the battle that was now to take place.

They moved out on the main road to Belmont a little after 8:30, the cavalry in the lead, followed by two Illinois regiments, some artillery, the 7th Iowa, more artillery, and the two remaining Illinois regiments. As they spread out in line of battle, the regiment on Grant's right, Colonel Napoleon B. Buford's 27th Illinois, ran into what was described as a "slough," a pond, and he took a circuitous route to get around it, so circuitous that he and his regiment simply disappeared.

The skirmish lines from both armies, working their way through thick woods, made contact about 10:30. At that point, Grant wrote, "the *ball* may be said to have fairly opened." By 11:00, the fighting was general. Logan's boys found themselves in a sharp firefight with Tappan's 13th Arkansas. Logan's horse was shot from under him, and he escaped serious injury when a bullet glanced off his revolver. Not much later, Grant's horse was also shot from under him, "but I got another from one of my staff and kept well up with the advance until the river was reached."

Two of Pillow's regiments, the 21st and 22d Tennessee, were still hunkered down in the middle of that open cornfield. Pillow rode up behind Colonel Thomas J. Freeman's 22d and asked a company commander "if we could not charge and drive the rascals out." The captain replied he thought so, but Colonel Freeman said nothing. Pillow then directed the question to Freeman. He replied that he would charge if he were ordered to do so. Pillow gave the order, and the boys from Tennessee fixed bayonets—those who had them—and charged across the cornfield directly into a withering fire from Colonel Phil Foulke's 30th Illinois and Colonel Jacob G. Lauman's 7th Iowa. When it was over, and the charge was broken, an angry Freeman said "the charge was ill-judged and almost impossible to have been executed with success." Pillow was living up to all of Grant's expectations.

What happened next might have been worse. The two regiments fell back to their position in the center of the cornfield. There, they came under concentrated fire from Union artillery. The two regiments, forming the center of the rebel line, broke and began a retreat toward the river.

In the midst of all this, Colonel Buford and the 27th Illinois, not exactly sure just where they were, emerged from the woods to find themselves, serendipitously, on a plateau just behind what there was of the village of Belmont. In the middle of the plateau was the rebel camp, Camp Johnston, all of its tents neatly aligned. Opposing Buford were eighty men from Company A, 13th Tennessee. Buford waved his cap and told his men to charge.

By midday, Pillow's line had collapsed. The rebel retreat to Camp Johnston fell apart as the soldiers panicked.

William L. Trask, skipper of the little steamer the *Charm,* which had been ferrying Confederate supplies across the river from Columbus to Belmont, said the landing on the Belmont side was "obstructed by our disorganized forces, who endeavored to board and take possession of our boat, and at the same time crying: 'Don't land!' 'Don't land!' 'We are whipped!' 'Go back!' etc. We, however, succeeded in landing six companies of Colonel [Samuel F.] Marks' regiment [the 11th Louisiana], when the disorganized troops previously spoken of made a rush on our boat and forced me to give the order to take the boat from the landing." The rebel troops were now huddled against the banks of the Mississippi.

Grant's soldiers dashed into the rebel camp and began celebrating. McClernand led them in, giving "three cheers for the Union." The "brave men around me," he said, "responded with the most enthusiastic applause." But what they were really cheering about was the chance to loot the rebel camp. One historian wrote that "Grant woefully failed to remember from his Mexican War experience the weakness of the American soldier, amounting almost to a passion for souvenirs, especially battle souvenirs."

"The moment the camp was reached," Grant said in his memoirs, "our men laid down their arms and commenced rummaging the tents to pick up trophies. Some of the higher officers were little better than privates. They galloped about from one cluster of men to another and at every halt delivered a short eulogy upon the Union cause and the achievements of the command. All this time the troops we had been engaged with for four hours lay crouched under cover of the river bank, ready to come up and surrender if summoned to do so."

With the Union soldiers gleefully tearing their way through the rebel tents, grabbing pistols, canteens, letters, and anything else they could get their hands on, an immediate pursuit of the defeated and broken rebels was out of the question. It was at this point that Grant should have brought his rested and disciplined reserves forward, to run the rebels down and force their surrender. He would later claim that the 500 or so soldiers he had left to guard his transports constituted his reserve, but he must have known better. They weren't the kind of reserve he needed; anyway, all 500 of them had taken refuge aboard the steamers several miles away.

Grant ordered the rebel camp set on fire; it was the only way he could think of to stop the looting. Some of the wounded rebels, it was charged after the battle, died in the flames.

Polk, from his vantage point across the river, could see what was happening. When he thought he could safely open fire on the Union troops without killing his own, he ordered the big guns into action. "Lady Polk," the giant Whitworth, threw a 128-pound projectile at the Union lines that whistled overhead like "a lamp post." It crashed into the camp ground and threw up a prodigious amount of dirt. It was fired a second time before it jammed. It wouldn't be fired again until four days later, presumably a test run, when it blew up, killing several of its crew and stunning General Polk so severely that he turned over his command to Pillow.

By 2:00 or so, Polk had finally come around to believe that Belmont was not a feint but a real attack and that no other Union troops were lurking nearby preparing to attack Columbus. That allowed him to commit his reserves—eight regiments by the end of the day—to the action across the river.

Grant was never very good at predicting what the enemy might do to him; he was always much more interested in what he was going to do to them. At Belmont, he should have given a little more thought to what would happen when thousands of fresh rebel troops came pouring across the river.

One of Grant's surgeons spotted the rebel steamships ferrying reinforcements to Belmont and rode up to Grant to tell him about it. They could see the smokestacks of the steamers, and they both were forced to agree they weren't the smokestacks of Captain Walke's gunboats. As they came closer, Grant could see the rebels clearly, soldiers cramming the ships from top to bottom and from end to end. Grant ordered his regiments to move out quickly and to make their way to the steamship landing at Hunter's Farm.

In his memoirs, Grant said that his column met resistance on its way to the landing, but that it was "feeble."

Feeble it wasn't. The reinforced rebels counterattacked vigorously, and for a while it was touch and go whether Grant's column would survive. One of the Union officers, Lieutenant Pat White, said the whole column was demoralized. "Officers would call to their men to fall in but the men would pay no attention. Every man was trying to save himself, some would throw down their arms and part of a regiment would take one rout[e] and the other part start another way."

It might have been worse if it hadn't been for Captain Ezra Taylor and his Chicago Light Battery. Black Jack Logan ordered Taylor and his guns (two of them captured from the rebels) to occupy the crest of a hill. They opened fire with double shot on top of canister, blowing great holes in the lines of the advancing Confederates. Logan then ordered his own regiment, the 31st Illinois, to charge through the opening, clearing the way for the others. "I took my flag," he said, "and told Capt. McCook to carry it at the head of the column, and die with it in his hands."

The 7th Iowa brought up the rear and paid dearly for it. Major Elliott W. Rice, taking command of the regiment after his senior officers were wounded, rallied what was left of it and led the Iowa boys through the woods to safety. Rice's horse was "pierced with 20 bullets, his sword scabbard shot in two and his sword belt shot away." Of the 512 men in the regiment, thirty-one were killed, seventy-seven wounded, and 114 missing in action, most of them rebel prisoners.

Napoleon Buford's 27th Illinois took no part in the fighting because, once again, it had managed to disappear. This time, it had taken a circuitous route to the landing that avoided the deadly guns of the resurgent rebels. Buford and his men finally found their way to the river some three miles north of the steamship landing, and Captain Walke sent steamers to pick them up. Grant's chief of staff, John Rawlins, said Buford had disobeyed orders. Had he obeyed them, Rawlins insisted, "he would have helped defeat the enemy in the fight coming out of Belmont [and] saved the lives of many gallant men."

The scene at the steamship landing was chaotic, as Union officers struggled to get the men, the horses, and the cannon safely aboard the four big steamships. One of the captains kept backing and filling, making it difficult to load anything on his steamer. Logan figured the man was a traitor and threatened to shoot him if he didn't hold still. The backing and filling stopped immediately.

Grant himself was one of the last to board the *Belle Memphis*. "The captain," he said, "...recognized me and ordered the engineer not to start the engine; he then had a plank run out for me. My horse seemed to take in the situation." He put his "fore feet over the bank without hesitation or urging, and, with his hind feet well under him, slid down the bank and trotted aboard the boat, twelve or fifteen feet away, over a single gang plank."

In trying to back away from the landing, the *Belle Memphis* became tangled, and the captain had to back and fill to get free. While that was going on, the rebels reached the landing and opened fire. Grant, resting on a sofa, heard the shots from shore and got up to investigate. "I had scarcely left," he said, "when a musket ball entered the room, struck the head of the sofa, passed through it and lodged in the foot."

Walke brought the *Lexington* and the *Tyler* in toward the landing. "We opened fire with our grape, cannister, and 5 second shells," he reported, "and completely routed them with great slaughter." Captain Taylor, on board the steamer *Chancellor*, wheeled his field guns into position on deck and opened fire too; he reported he caused considerable damage. The fact is, when the firing began, the rebels took cover. As far as anyone can tell, nobody was injured.

"We were soon out of range," Grant said in his memoirs, "and went peacefully on our way to Cairo, every man feeling that Belmont was a great victory and that he had contributed his share to it."

It is hard to believe that Grant, at the time or twenty years later, when he wrote his memoirs, really believed he had won a "great victory." Belmont always nagged at his conscience. It partly explains why he wrote so many accounts of it.

In his official report, Polk said Belmont was a great *rebel* victory. "The enemy were thoroughly routed. We pursued them to their boats seven miles, then drove their boats before us. The road was strewn with their dead and wounded, guns, ammunition, and equipments. Our loss considerable; theirs heavy." Union losses in the battle were ninety-five killed, 229 wounded, and 205 missing. The rebels counted 121 dead, 434 wounded, and 130 missing.

Patriotic Southerners rejoiced when they heard about Belmont. Songs were composed and a new dance, "The Belmont Quick Step," enjoyed a brief popularity.

Northerners didn't know quite what to think. They had never heard very much about Ulysses Grant and so might not have been prepared to take his report at face value. A few newspapers, led by the *Chicago Tribune*, pointedly questioned why Grant had made the attack at all.

Grant had taken unnecessary risks, hard to justify in a strictly tactical sense, but at Belmont he learned that he could lead an army—a small one, to be sure—into battle and that he could give as good as he received. Those whispering doubts about himself drifted away in the smoke of his first battle, and he and his men felt much better about themselves. With Belmont, Grant and the Union had seized the initiative in the Mississippi Valley, and they never again relinquished it.

Grant had barely begun to fight.

Chapter 3

FORTS HENRY AND DONELSON

ON JANUARY 28, 1862, Grant wired his commanding general, Major General Henry W. "Old Brains" Halleck, at his headquarters in St. Louis, respectfully suggesting "the propriety of subduing Fort Henry, near the Ky. and Tennessee line and holding the position."

Halleck responded by telegram two days later. "Make your preparations to take & hold Fort Henry," he said. "I will send you written instructions by mail."

Grant and his staff, still headquartered at Cairo, might have hoped Halleck, a bit of an old fusspot, would give them the go-ahead in time, but they were stunned by the promptness of his reply. They threw their hats into the air and kicked them with glee as they fell to the floor, one historian said. John Rawlins, who would be at Grant's side through the war and in the White House, knocked over several chairs and pounded his fist against the wall. Grant was amused, cautioning his staff to keep the noise down lest they awaken General Polk at Columbus.

The Confederacy had chosen to protect its navigable western waterways with forts, not gunboats. Fort Henry was built to block Union forces from invading the Confederate heartland—Tennessee and northern parts of Alabama, Georgia, and Mississippi—by way of the Tennessee River. "With Fort Henry in our hands," Grant wrote, "we had a navigable stream open to us up to Muscle Shoals, in Alabama." Twelve miles west of Fort Henry, the rebels had built Fort Donelson to block Union ships from invading the heartland by way of the Cumberland River. The Cumberland was especially significant, for it was a water highway that led directly to Nashville, a prosperous industrial city and railroad hub that was churning out cannon, rifles, pistols, swords, and other war matériel for the Confederate army. "Fort Donelson was the gate to Nashville—a place of great political and military importance," Grant said.

For years after the campaign, generals and armchair generals argued over who originated the idea of moving up the two rivers and seizing the two rebel forts. Confederate Colonel William P. Johnston, General Joe Johnston's son, answered that question best: "Grant *made* it and it made Grant."

The capture of Forts Henry and Donelson, and the surrender of thousands of Confederates at Donelson, was a sensation. Grant, the leather-store clerk from Galena, emerged from those two battles as a national hero. He deserved every bit of the adulation, for at Fort Donelson he demonstrated for the first time his qualities as a great fighting general. It was here at Fort Donelson as well that Grant made his connection with popular sentiment in the North, and all the successes that followed did nothing to change the glowing reputation he had won in his first great triumph. It was Fort Donelson that set him on his way to the White House.

Grant told General Smith, still commanding at Paducah and Smithland but now a part of Grant's new Department of Cairo, that he expected to start his advance upon Fort Henry on February 3 and that he wanted a brigade from Smith's command at Paducah and most of the troops at Smithland to take a part. "These troops," he said, "will take with them all their baggage but no baggage train, that being left to take up afterwards." He told Smith that his troops and civilians in the local communities should be kept in the dark, but "I am well aware this caution is entirely unnecessary to you." Grant trusted Smith; the old whiskered regular would in a few short weeks demonstrate just how much he deserved that trust.

Foote, the third member of the team, was now the navy's version of a major general, a "flag officer." (It wasn't until later in the war that the navy got around to creating admirals.) Flag Officer Foote was ready to do his part. He still had his three timberclads, and they were just as useful as ever, but now, at last, he had three of Eads's big ironclad gunboats—the *Cincinnati*, the flagship, and the *Carondelet* and the *St. Louis*, plus the *Essex* (formerly the *New Era*), a converted river steamboat only partly protected by iron plates. He told Grant he would take Fort Henry before the soldiers got there.

The South's western commander was Albert Sidney Johnston, thought by many at the time to be the best general in the rebel army, and he was having a terrible time convincing anyone in Richmond that he was in grave danger. He didn't have enough men, and those he did have were stretched perilously thin. He was promised more, but all he got was General Pierre G. T. Beauregard, the prickly Creole who had made his mark at First Bull Run. If the North had a problem with its generals in the East (until Grant, Sherman, and Sheridan arrived), the South *always* had a problem with its generals in the West. Johnston had to deal with the likes of Lloyd Tilghman, Gideon Pillow, and John B. Floyd, something no commander deserved.

Tilghman, the commanding officer at Fort Henry, was a West Pointer, and a whiner. He whined about almost everything and any-thing—he didn't like the elevating screws for one of his guns; another gun jumped its carriage every time it was fired. He didn't take orders very well either. He had been instructed to build fortifications across the river on a nicely positioned hill at a place grandly

called Fort Heiman, but he hadn't even surveyed the position. That
seemed to be a pattern among rebel officers in the west—General
Johnston had never bothered to visit either Fort Henry or Fort
Donelson.

Fort Henry itself was a disaster. Although it was strategically
placed at a bend in the river, it was too low to the water, and with
the heavy rainfall, the river had been rising rapidly. By the time
Foote and his flotilla set out, six of the fort's seventeen guns were
under water. The water was up so high that one officer arriving
from Fort Donelson rowed his way into the fort. In addition, most
of the "torpedoes"—underwater mines, in fact—had been swept
away by rapid currents and had drifted downstream out of harm's
way. Tilghman complained that "the history of military engineering records no parallel to this case."

The Civil War's most mischievous correspondent, Franc Bangs
Wilkie of *The New York Times*, accompanied Foote's flotilla as it set
out from Paducah, at the mouth of the Tennessee River, on February 4. He was not exactly sanguine. "It was nearly midnight before
the boats made their departure," he wrote, "and prior to that hour
everything seemed ominous of evil. The sky was hung with gloom
like a hearse. Not a single kindly star witnessed our departure. . . .
External indications were all against us."

Grant wrote one of his informative, down-to-earth letters to
Julia on Tuesday, February 4:

> I went up this morning on one of the gun boats [the *Essex*] to
> reconnoiter the fort. A few shots were exchanged with what
> effect upon the enemy it is impossible to say. Some of our shells
> went into the fort while one of the enemies passed through the
> Cabin of the boat I was on. Done no harm however. All the
> troops will be up by noon tomorrow, and Friday morning, if we
> are not attacked before, the fight will commence. The enemy are
> well fortified and have a strong force. I do not want to boast but
> I have a confidant feeling of success. . . . My anxiety will be great

tonight being at Paducah whilst my forces are almost within canon range of the enemy, and that too in inferior numbers.

He issued Field Orders No. 1 the next day. Brigadier General McClernand, the Illinois politician who had been with him at Belmont, was ordered to move his First Division at 11:00 the following morning and "under the guidance of Lieutenant Colonel [James B.] McPherson, . . . take a position on the roads from Fort Henry to Fort Donelson and Dover." McClernand, in other words, was to close off the garrison's escape route. McClernand said he would comply with Grant's orders but said he hoped Grant, by mentioning McPherson, wasn't intending "to interfere with my authority as commander." McPherson was an engineering officer; that was his role. McClernand surely understood that, but he was a very difficult man. John Keegan says he personified "in an extreme form the type of ambitious political general . . . who infested the Union army throughout the war." Grant's imperturbability was never so severely tested as it was in his dealings with McClernand.

Grant wrote Julia again on Wednesday, February 5. "We returned to-day [to a camp near Fort Henry] with most of the remainder of our troops. The sight of our camp fires on either side of the river is beautiful and no doubt inspires the enemy, who is in full view of them, with the idea that we have full 4,000 men." (He meant to say 40,000 men. He had, in fact, 15,000.) "To-morrow will come the tug of war. Our side or the other must to-morrow night rest in quiet possession of Fort Henry. What the strength of Fort Henry is I do not know accurately, probably 10,000 men [closer to 2,800]. . . . I am well and in good spirits yet feeling confidance in the success of our enterprise." He signed the letter, "Kiss the children for me. Kisses for yourself. Ulys."

Grant and his two leading generals, McClernand and Smith, met Foote in the flag officer's cabin aboard the *Cincinnati* on Wednesday afternoon. A young seaman aboard the gunboat reported that the *Conestoga* came alongside during the meeting with one of the torpedoes that had broken loose from its mooring. Sailors brought it aboard. It was 5 feet long and 18 inches wide, with a long rod attached at one end to hold it to the river bottom and another attached at the other end with prongs that when touched by a boat passing overhead would set off a seventy-pound bag of explosives. One of the sailors loosened a nut on the torpedo and it began making a hissing sound. The sailor, Eliot Callender, described the reaction:

> Believing that the hour for evening prayer had arrived, two of the army officers threw themselves face downward upon the deck. Admiral Foote, with the agility of a cat, sprang up the ship's ladder, followed with commendable enthusiasm by General Grant. Reaching the top, and realizing that the danger, if any, had passed, the Admiral turned around to General Grant, who was displaying more energy than grace in his first efforts on a ship's ladder, and said with his quiet smile, "General, why this haste?" "That the Navy may not get ahead of us," as quietly responded the General as he turned away to come down.

Grant had received news that rebel reinforcements were on the way. Haste, then, did seem important. He ordered the attack on Fort Henry to begin at about 11:00 A.M. on Thursday. He was wrong about reinforcements; they weren't on the way. In fact, Tilghman, who was under no illusions about the defensive capabilities of his position, had ordered most of his infantrymen to make their way cross-country to the more powerful Fort Donelson. He stayed behind with his gunners and a few officers.

Foote's sailors were told to clear for action about 10:20 A.M. They were steaming up the river a half-hour later. The column was led by the *Carondelet* and the *DeKalb*, lashed together on the left to make it easier for them to navigate through a narrow channel. They were followed by the *Cincinnati* (the flagship) and the *Essex* on the right. The timberclads *Tyler*, *Lexington*, and *Conestoga* brought up the rear, about a mile back.

Although much of the fort was under water, Tilghman still had about a dozen large guns on dry ground, including a huge 10-inch Columbiad that fired 128-pound shells. They were all positioned behind earthworks and sandbags.

Foote, unaware of Grant's whereabouts (he and his infantrymen were having trouble with the mud), ordered his flagship to open fire at 12:30 P.M. He despaired as the shells fell short. A parsimonious man, he had warned his gunners against waste, noting that each shell cost the Union government eight dollars. "I ran up rapidly to the distance of 700 yards," Foote wrote his wife after the battle. "It was a fearful struggle." He said his gunboat was hit thirty times. "I had the breath, for several seconds, knocked out of me, as a shot struck opposite my chest, in the iron clad pilot house on the deck."

It was almost 1:00, with the tide of the battle turning in favor of the gunboats, when a shot from the huge rebel Columbiad found an unprotected place on the port side of the *Essex* near a port hole, killing Acting Master's Mate Samuel B. "Boy" Brittan Jr. (His death later became the centerpiece of a popular Civil War poem, "Boy Brittan.") Another shot, probably from the Columbiad as well, also penetrated the *Essex*'s inadequately armored flank and blew up one of the boilers. The forward gunroom was filled with scalding steam, causing terrible havoc. "Those who could rushed aft, others leaped into the river through the ports, while Commander [William D.] Porter himself barely escaped with his life through a port on the starboard side, and was rescued by a seaman named John Walker," the naval historian Edgar Stanton Maclay writes. "Twenty-eight men were scalded, and many of them died. [That one terrible shell killed ten men, wounded twenty-three, and left another five missing.] The shellman of Gun No. 2, James Coffey, was found on his knees in the act of taking a shell from the box. While he was in this position the scalding steam had struck him full in the face, killing him instantly." The two civilian pilots were both killed, one of them still gripping the signal-bell rope. The *Essex* drifted downstream, out of control and out of the fight.

But the rebels inside the fort were having troubles too, some of it self-inflicted. First, a big, recently rebored rifle burst, killing its entire crew. Then, in an even bigger disaster, a careless gunner stuck a priming wire into the vent of the Columbiad and broke it, inadvertently spiking the gun. Devastating fire from the three remaining gunboats, the more securely protected Eads boats, knocked out more rebel guns. Their guns blew great holes in the fortifications.

With only four guns still firing, and surrounded by dead and wounded men, Tilghman decided he had had enough. He lowered the fort's flag a little before 2:00 P.M. Much to Foote's disgust, his sailors went wild with the news of the fort's surrender. His captains weren't much better; they raced for shore to accept the rebel commander's sword.

In an indication of things to come, Foote demanded an "unconditional surrender," but he did allow the Confederate officers to keep their side arms. With some of the fort's defenders slipping away, Foote bagged only seventy-eight rebels; sixteen more turned up in a small hospital boat. The rest of the garrison—2,500 men or so—was making its way to Donelson.

Correspondent Wilkie, the only reporter attached to the gunboats, said the sailors had a field day rounding up souvenirs. One naval officer managed to liberate Tilghman's shotgun; another captured the rebel general's bowie knife "of fearful size." Wilkie said he had managed to seize a weapon "nameless in the nomenclature of things offensive and defensive." He said it was "heavy and broad enough for a butcher's cleaver, jagged enough for a handsaw, with a handle like a claymore, but whether it was for shooting, stabbing, chopping sausage ... or scalping Yankees I cannot tell." Whatever it was, he was glad to have it.

While Wilkie and the sailors were having a grand time collecting souvenirs, Grant on the Fort Henry side and Smith across the river on the Fort Heiman side were still slogging through mud and clammy water, sometimes waist deep, trying to reach their destinations. Grant didn't arrive at Fort Henry, already flying the Stars and Stripes, until 3:00 P.M. Foote had won the challenge—the navy had beaten the army. Some generals might have been angry and frustrated. Not Grant; he was generous in crediting the victory to Foote and the navy. Foote, on the other hand, was diplomatic in saying that the army had faced difficult problems in making its way to the rebel positions.

It was an important victory, but it was Foote's day, not Grant's, and everybody knew it. Not very many hours after the battle ended, the reporter Albert D. Richardson of the *New York Tribune* stopped by Grant's tent to say good-bye, for he was leaving for New York in the morning.

"You had better wait a day or two," Grant said.

"Why?"

"Because I am going over to capture Fort Donelson tomorrow."

"How strong is it?"

"We have not been able to ascertain exactly, but I think we can take it. At all events, we will try."

In his brief report to Halleck in St. Louis, Grant confirmed the gist of the conversation. "I shall take and destroy Fort Donelson on the 8th [wishful thinking, as things turned out] and return to Fort Henry," he said. What extraordinary confidence; it borders on bravado. Nothing had been said up until this very moment about attacking Donelson, but Grant seemed to be taking the whole business as a sort of twelve-mile walk in the sun.

While Grant was pushing ahead, his commanding general, Halleck, was doing his best to replace him. Halleck distrusted Grant; he had gone out of his way to congratulate Foote on his success at Fort Henry without mentioning his own general. Now, on the excuse that he had too many brigadier generals with commissions dating from the same day, he urged the appointment of an older man with an older commission, Brigadier General Ethan Allen Hitchcock, to succeed Grant, but Hitchcock, an honorable fellow, declined the offer. McClellan, the supreme commander, wasn't much of a Grant fan either; he urged Halleck and the other major player in the west, Don Carlos Buell, to take the field themselves. Nothing came of that either.

Grant had no idea of the conniving going on behind his back. In a letter to his sister Mary on February 9, he said, airily, "G. J. Pillow commands at Fort Donelson. I hope to give him a gig before you receive this." Pillow's presence at Donelson gave him all the inspiration he needed.

On Friday, February 7, the day after the fall of Fort Henry, Grant took his staff and some cavalry "and made a reconnaissance to within about a mile of the outer line of works at Donelson," Grant wrote in his memoirs. "I had known General Pillow in Mexico, and judged that with any force, no matter how small, I could march up to within gunshot of any entrenchments he was given to hold. I said this to the officers of my staff. I knew that [John B.] Floyd was in command, but he was no soldier, and I judged that he would yield to Pillow's pretensions."

Floyd didn't actually take command at Donelson until February 13—Grant was wrong about that—but he was right about the man himself. Floyd had been governor of Virginia and then secretary of war in President James Buchanan's administration; he was best remembered in that job for being indicted for malfeasance in office. Union sympathizers were convinced that he had stocked southern arsenals with weapons and spread the regular army far and wide on the eve of war to give the secessionists an advantage.

The third general at Donelson was Simon Bolivar Buckner, a West Pointer and an old friend of Grant's. When Grant had left the army in 1854, it was Buckner who had lent him money to get home.

Grant said the fort, just a little downriver from a small village called Dover, embraced about 100 acres, fronted on the east by the Cumberland River, on the north by Hickman's creek, on the south by a ravine, with open country to the west, in the direction of Fort Henry. A circular line of rifle pits defended the western approaches.

The fort was built on a bluff rising 120 feet above the river (no submerged guns this time). The lower battery contained nine 32-pounders and another of those big 10-inch Columbiads; a mid-level battery was armed with another Columbiad, this one rifled as a 32-pounder, along with a number of smaller field guns. Several more big guns were mounted on the top of the ridge.

The fort was defended by 18,000 men, most of them attached to twenty-eight infantry regiments. The cavalry included a regiment from Tennessee led by a little-known, hard-driving colonel, Nathan Bedford Forrest. Johnston could have sent more troops to defend Donelson, but he was torn by indecision. William J. Hardee had 14,000 men at Bowling Green; Polk had another 17,000 at Columbus, and thousands more were scattered here and there. This battle was shaping up as the decisive one for the Southern heartland. That being patently so, he should have rushed troops to Fort Donelson. It was already becoming clear that Johnston was not the ablest general in the Confederate army.

Grant commanded about 20,000 men, including thirty regiments of infantry. It was hardly the kind of overwhelming superiority in manpower that the manuals said was needed to attack a well-defended position.

One of his generals was Lew Wallace, the Hoosier politician who would win greater fame as the author of *Ben Hur*. What struck Wallace most about Grant, at this early stage of the war, was his demeanor. "From the first," he said, "his silence was remarkable. He knew how to keep his temper. In battle, as in camp, he went about quietly, speaking in a conversational tone, yet he appeared to see everything that went on, and was always intent on business. . . . In dress he was plain, even negligent; in partial amendment of that his horse was always a good one and well kept. At the council—calling it such by grace—he smoked, but never said a word. In all probability he was framing the orders of march which were issued that night."

Wallace commanded Grant's Third Division. The other division commanders were the Belmont veterans McClernand (the First) and Smith (the Second).

Grant set out for Fort Donelson on the morning of February 12. It was a clear and sunny Wednesday, unseasonably warm, and the men soon began shedding their overcoats and blankets. The bands played, and Grant seemed almost mischievous as he danced ahead of the column on his powerful horse.

As they approached the enemy's pickets, John W. Birge's Missouri sharpshooters began to spread out. "Theirs was a peculiar service," Lew Wallace said. "Each was a preferred marksman, and carried a long-range Henry rifle, with sights delicately arranged as for target practice. In action each was perfectly independent." Their only order was to "hunt your holes, boys." Sometimes they dug holes; sometimes they climbed into trees. "Once in a good location," Wallace said, "they stayed there the day."

The Union troops were more or less in position on Thursday morning, with Grant set up in his headquarters—the kitchen of the Widow Crisp's humble farmhouse. The only serious fighting that took place that day was a three-regiment attack led by McClernand (without orders from Grant) on a rebel artillery position. "The battery was in the main line of the enemy," Grant wrote, "which was defended by the whole army present. Of course the assault was a failure, and of course the loss on our side was great for the number of men engaged." McClernand truly was insufferable. He would get into even deeper trouble later, for he had failed to post his troops all the way to his right to the river itself.

Grant didn't seem to be feeling very much stress. He had allowed his son Fred, his and Julia's oldest child, to visit and be entertained. He sent the boy home just a day or two before he began his march on Fort Donelson. In a letter to Julia on Thursday, he noted, "I am still well and outside the fort. We have a large force to contend against but I expect to accomplish their subjugation." He was a little less certain in his letter to Julia the next day. "The taking of Fort Donelson," he said, "bids fair to be a long job ... but I feel confident of ultimate success."

That night, temperatures rapidly dropped, and snow and sleet began falling on soldiers who had earlier abandoned their blankets and overcoats and who had no tents in which to take refuge. Because they were so close to the enemy lines, they weren't allowed to build fires. Some of the men, simply to survive, stood under arms all night. The next morning most of them went without breakfast because the commissary wagons hadn't caught up.

Flag Officer Foote arrived with the main part of his flotilla at a landing place north of Fort Donelson about 11:30 P.M. Thursday. His flotilla was led this time by four of the Eads gunboats—his flagship, the *St. Louis*, and the *Carondelet*, the *Louisville*, and the *Pittsburg*. Two of the timberclads, the *Tyler* and the *Conestoga*, were on hand too.

The Carondelet had preceded him up the Cumberland and had dropped a few shells into the fort on Wednesday without receiving any return fire. It was back Thursday, and this time the rebels cut loose with everything they had. At about 11:30, a 128-pound cannon ball burst through the side of the gunboat and caromed around "like a wild beast pursuing its prey." A dozen men were injured, seven of them seriously. Commander Walke, the gunboat's skipper (he had been in command at Belmont), said he saved the huge cannon ball as a war souvenir. The *Carondelet* withdrew for an hour or so, repaired the damage, and returned to the attack at 12:15 P.M.

Fort Henry had been so low to the water that the gunboats had no worries about plunging artillery fire. Donelson, with its guns fixed in positions high above the river, was a different—and far more dangerous—matter. Foote, privately, doubted the wisdom of the attack, suspecting his gunboats were more vulnerable than most people imagined. He and his captains did what they could; the decks of the gunboats were covered with chains, lumber, and bags of coal, anything to resist the force of the plunging shot and shell.

Acting under Grant's orders, Foote's gunboats began their attack on the fort at about 3:00 P.M. on Friday. Just as Foote had feared, it was a disaster, the Union Navy's worst day in the entire war.

One of the problems was that Foote took the boats so close to the fort that the inexperienced rebel gunners could hardly miss. Walke, commanding the *Carondelet*, wrote:

> We heard the deafening crack of the bursting shells, the crash of the solid shot, and the whizzing of fragments of shell and wood as they sped through the vessel. Soon a 128-pounder struck our anchor, smashed it into flying bolts, and bounded over the vessel, taking away a part of our smoke-stack; then another cut away the iron boat-davits as if they were pipe stems, whereupon the boat dropped into the water. Another ripped up the iron plating and lodged in the heavy casemate; another struck the pilothouse, knocking the plating into pieces, and sent fragments of iron and splinters into the [civilian] pilots, one of whom fell mortally wounded.... Still they came, harder and faster, taking flag-staffs and smoke-stacks, and tearing off the side armor as lightning tears the bark from a tree.

One of the guns blew up, stunning Walke. Fires began to break out. In the midst of it all, two shots entered the bow ports, killed four men, and wounded three others. "They were borne past me, three with their heads cut off. The sight almost sickened me, and I turned my head away," Walke recalled.

The other ships were having a bad time too. Foote's flagship, the *St. Louis*, was struck fifty-nine times. One of the shells entered the pilothouse, killing the pilot and wounding Foote in—where else?—the foot. Badly mauled, their steering gear destroyed, all four gunboats drifted out of the battle.

The Confederates were elated. The first round in the battle had been won, and won decisively, by their gunners. That night, the rebel generals—Floyd, Pillow, Buckner, and Bushrod Johnson—held a council of war, in which they decided to attack the Union lines the next morning. The target would be McClernand's exposed position, his right flank, unsupported by reserves and "hanging in the air."

Noisy preparations for the attack went on all night, but nobody on the Union side heard a thing. "The character of the night must be remembered," Lew Wallace said. It was cold and windy. "The pickets of the Federals were struggling for life against the blast, and probably did not keep good watch."

Grant's reluctance to consider the possibility that an enemy might be preparing to attack him—first noted at Belmont—cropped up again at Donelson. When the rebels launched their attack on Saturday—it was led by Grant's *bête noire*, Pillow—he was on board the *St. Louis*, talking to Foote. "When I left the National line to visit Flag-Officer Foote," he admitted in his memoirs, "I had no idea that there would be any engagement on land unless I brought it on myself."

The attack, accompanied by rebel yells, began about 6:00 A.M. More than 6,000 Confederates, led by Bushrod Johnson, fell on Colonel Richard Oglesby's brigade, made up mostly of troops from Illinois. "A rapid exchange of volleys ensued," Wallace wrote. "The distance intervening between the [rebel] works on one side and the [Union] bivouac on the other was so short that the action began before Pillow could effect a deployment." By 7:00 A.M., the Confederates had managed to bring their troops into some sort of line and were threatening McClernand's position, from one end to the other. At the same time, Forrest's cavalry was making its way around the Union's exposed right flank.

"The tenor of the fighting became well-established over the next two hours," Benjamin Franklin Cooling said in his campaign history. "There were sharp fights between individual regiments and brigades, slashing thrusts by Confederate infantry and cavalry in combined assaults, and stubborn resistance from determined Federals."

The Confederate attack moved laterally so that it came up

against the brigade commanded by W. H. L. Wallace (no relation to Lew Wallace). "It was now 10 o'clock," Lew Wallace said, "and over on the right Oglesby was beginning to fare badly. The pressure on his front grew stronger.... To add to his doubts, officers were riding to him with a sickening story that their commands were getting out of ammunition, and asking where they could go for a supply." At about the same time, Buckner opened a feeble attack against the Union lines, so slow in forming that McClernand had time to rally some of his troops to oppose it.

The real problem was on the right, where Pillow and Johnson finally had the Union troops on the run. McClernand, fearing that he was being outflanked, ordered a retreat. For these brief moments, victory was in the rebels' hands. All they had to do was press on, break through the Union lines, and march off to a safe haven, maybe Nashville. Pillow sent a telegram to Albert Sidney Johnston. "On the honor of a soldier," he said, "the day is ours."

And so it should have been. But Floyd was in charge, and he failed to give the order to press the attack. "The road was his," said Wallace.

Grant was still missing. McClernand had sent two members of his staff to Mrs. Crisp's little farmhouse to tell the commanding general what was happening. But, of course, he wasn't there; he was with Foote on the flagship. Messengers were sent to him there to alert him to the danger, but all that took time.

Lew Wallace saved the day. Acting on his own, he had sent one of his brigades—Colonel Charles Cruft's—to help McClernand early in the day, probably sometime around 9:00 A.M. Cruft and his four regiments—boys from Kentucky and Illinois—managed to lose their way. When they finally turned up, McClernand put them in reserve, for reasons never adequately explained. An hour later, McClernand was calling on Wallace for more help. This time, again acting without orders, he committed his own and John Thayer's brigade, made up of soldiers from Illinois and Nebraska. It was about all he had left.

Wallace said he was standing in a road talking with Grant's chief of staff, John Rawlins, when McClernand's troops, routed by the rebels, began stumbling past. At about the same time, the other Wallace—W. H. L.—"dropped into the road with such of his command as staid by their colors."

"Are they pursuing you?" Lew Wallace asked.

"Yes," W. H. L. Wallace replied.

"How far are they behind?"

The colonel thought about it for a minute and then replied, "You will have about time to form a line of battle right here."

Lieutenant Peter Wood's six-gun Battery A of the First (Chicago) Light Artillery was brought forward at full speed. Thayer then brought his brigade forward at the double-quick—the 1st Nebraska and 58th Illinois on the right, and the 58th Ohio on the left. Hardly had the battery unlimbered, Lew Wallace wrote, "before the enemy appeared, and firing began. For ten minutes or thereabouts the scenes of the morning were reenacted. The Confederates struggled hard to perfect their deployments. The woods rang with musketry and artillery.... Colonel Thayer and his regiments behaved with great gallantry, and the assailants fell back in confusion."

W. H. L. Wallace and Oglesby reformed their broken commands, resupplied themselves with ammunition, "and stood at rest waiting for orders. There was then a lull in the battle. Even the cannonading ceased, and everybody was asking, What next?"

Just then, said Wallace, "Grant rode up to where General McClernand and I were in conversation. He was almost unattended.... Wholly unexcited, he saluted and received the salutations of his subordinates."

It was a key moment—a key moment for the Union army and a key moment for Grant himself. What next?

Grant's first thought was to order the troops to fall back on a ridge and to reposition themselves. Then he changed his mind. No, he said, "the position on the right must be retaken," and galloped away, leaving McClernand and Wallace to figure out how to get the job done.

In those brief few minutes, Grant had figured out that Floyd and Pillow had put everything they had into this attack in an attempt to escape. "Some of our men are pretty badly demoralized," he said he told one of his aides, Colonel J. D. Webster, "but the enemy must be more so, for he has attempted to force his way out, but has fallen back; the one who attacks first now will be victorious and the enemy will have to be in a hurry if he gets ahead of me."

He wrote those words twenty years after the battle, and it's doubtful that's exactly what he said. But, surely, it represented his thinking. He *knew* what he wanted to do. He wanted McClernand and Wallace to counterattack on his right. Then, and more important, he wanted to throw the rest of his army, now heavily reinforced, into a shattering, decisive attack on his left.

> I determined to make the assault at once on our left. It was clear to my mind that the enemy had started to march out with his entire force, except a few pickets, and if our attack could be made on the left before the enemy could redistribute his forces along the line, we would find but little opposition except from the intervening abatis. I directed Colonel Webster to ride with me and call out to the men as we passed: "Fill your cartridge boxes quick, and get into line; the enemy is trying to escape and he must not be permitted to do so." This acted like a charm. The men only wanted someone to give them a command.

Grant and Webster rode rapidly to C. H. Smith's headquarters, "where I explained the situation to him and directed him to charge the enemy's works in his front with his whole division [thirteen infantry regiments and four artillery batteries], saying at the same time that he would find nothing but a very thin line to contend with."

"General Smith," Grant told the tough old regular, "all has failed on our right, you must take Fort Donelson."

"I will do it," he replied.

Smith rode over to his favorite regiment, the 2d Iowa, and ordered them to remove the percussion caps from their muskets; this attack, he said, would be made by bayonet alone. Lew Wallace had doubted Smith's loyalty (he was a Virginian) and had connived to have him replaced. But Smith's performance at Fort Donelson on February 15, 1862, erased all those doubts.

"General Smith, on his horse, took position in the front and center of the line," Wallace wrote. "Occasionally he turned in the saddle to see how the alignment was kept. For the most part, however, he held his face steadily toward the enemy. He was, of course, a conspicuous target for the sharpshooters in the rifle pits. The air around him twittered with minié balls. Erect as if on review, he rode on, timing the gait of his horse with the movement of his colors." At the abatis—a defensive line composed of felled trees and sharpened stakes—"the fire seemed to get trebly hot" and some of the men began to hesitate. "General Smith put his cap on the point of his sword, held it aloft, and called out, 'No flinching now, my lads. Here—this is the way! Come on!' He picked a path through the jagged limbs of the trees, holding his cap all the time in sight; and the effect was magical. The men swarmed in after him, and got through in the best order they could.... At the last moment the keepers of the rifle pits clambered out and fled." Smith and his boys from Iowa (plus some others from Indiana) had broken the rebel lines without firing a shot.

The rebels retreated to a second ridge, where they were joined by most of Buckner's division. The new position was a stronger one, manned by more men, and Smith's attack bogged down. At the other end of the line, on the right, McClernand and Wallace made their own attack, and they too forced the rebels back. The day ended with both sides pretty much in the same place they had been when the day began.

That night, the three rebel commanders—Floyd, Pillow, and Buckner—held a council of war in the army's headquarters at the

Rice house in Dover. They decided to ship the wounded out, and they were packed aboard steamers and sent upriver to Clarksville and Nashville around midnight. The steamers, of course, could have been used to help physically fit soldiers make their escape.

By most accounts, the soldiers themselves were in fairly good spirits, fully expecting to make another effort to break out the following morning. Floyd, at first, seemed to favor making the attack. He said the quartermasters should burn their stores, the artillery commanders should spike their guns, and everybody should be ready at 4:00 A.M. to get underway. But he was a worried man. He was convinced that Grant now had some eighty regiments circling Fort Donelson, even though in reality it was less than half that number. More than anything, though, he was petrified of being captured; capture would mean he might be taken to Washington and put on trial for all those nasty things he had done as Secretary of War in the final days of the Buchanan administration.

Forrest joined the meeting and said his patrols showed that there were still ways in which most of the army could escape. Pillow said he was in favor of trying. But Buckner was morose. "I cannot hold my position half an hour after an attack," he said, and he may have been the first to suggest surrender. Buckner was the professional, the only West Pointer, and his views carried weight. "The scene rapidly approached bittersweet comedy," Cooling, the campaign historian, said. "Floyd and Buckner rationalized that the army had fulfilled its mission to buy time for Johnston," without going into what Johnston was supposed to be doing with that time. Pillow, never a strong advocate for continuing the fight, capitulated, making the decision to surrender unanimous. Of course, he added, he couldn't surrender himself, for he was on the Union Army's most-wanted list. He said he planned to slip away. Floyd said he couldn't surrender either, for he might end up on trial. So he said he would be forced to slip away too. Floyd turned to Pillow and said, "I turn the command over, sir."

Pillow replied, "I pass it."

Buckner said, "I assume it."

Forrest, the only real soldier in the room, was disgusted, and he told the three generals what he thought of them. He stormed out of the house, called his troopers together, and led his 500 men, plus 200 infantrymen who tagged along, to safety (and to a subsequent career as the most daring and successful of all cavalry commanders in the war). It was just as easy as he had said it would be.

Pillow escaped across the river in a small skiff and eventually made his way to Clarksville. Floyd commandeered a steamer that had just arrived at the landing with 400 reinforcements. He pushed everyone else aside and boarded the boat with part of his brigade. He supposedly shouted to his men, "Come on, my brave Virginia boys!" The boat steamed away half empty as the brave Virginia boys broke open one or two barrels of whiskey.

Buckner raised white flags over the fort's outer works on Sunday morning, February 16, and sent a delegation under Major Nathaniel F. Cheairs to parley with the Union commanders. The rebels first approached General Smith, who told them, curtly, that his terms were "unconditional and immediate surrender." Smith then took the rebels to the Crisp house to see Grant.

There, they delivered Buckner's note to the Union commander. "In consideration of all the circumstances governing the present situation of affairs at this station," the note said, pompously, "I propose to the commanding officers of the Federal forces the appointment of commissioners to agree upon terms of capitulation of the forces and post under my command, and in that view suggest an armistice until 12 o'clock today."

While Cheairs and the other rebels cooled their heels outside, Smith and Grant read the note, and Grant drafted a reply. It said:

Yours of this date proposing Armistice and appointment of Commissioners to settle terms of Capitulation is just received. No terms except unconditional and immediate surrender can be accepted. I propose to move immediately upon your works.

Buckner didn't like the tone of Grant's note—after all, this was his old friend, the man he had bailed out of tough times with a timely loan—and he thought the note was ungenerous. But he had no choice; he accepted it. The two commanders met later in the morning at a little hotel in Dover. Pillow's absence was noted. Grant said that was all right; if he had captured him, he would have turned him loose, for "I would rather have him in command of you fellows than as a prisoner."

Just how many men were left in the fort at the time of surrender remains a mystery: thousands of them, surely, maybe as many as 12,000. In a letter to Julia the next day, Grant said he had achieved "the greatest victory of the season. Some 12 or 15 thousand prisoners have fallen into our possession to say nothing of 5 to 7 thousand that escaped in the darkness of the night last night. This is the largest capture I believe ever made on the continent."

"The great victory is a crusher," Colonel Rutherford B. Hayes of the 23d Ohio Volunteers wrote his uncle. And so it was. The whole rebel line collapsed. Columbus, the Gibraltar of the Mississippi, was abandoned without a shot being fired. Johnston retreated from Bowling Green and then had to withdraw—a terrible blow to the Confederacy—from Nashville. But what resonated then, and what still resonates today, was Grant's note to Buckner.

The note, Bruce Catton says, "caught men's imagination. It had an exultant, Star-Spangled, Yankee Doodle ring to it—put up or shut up, fight or quit, this thing is not going to stop until one or the other of us cannot get off the floor.... People who had hardly heard of U.S. Grant before now began to discover with delight that his very initials stood for the words of triumph—Unconditional Surrender." With that note, said Silas W. Burt, the New York state historian at the time of the Civil War, "there was a thrill of exultation and pride in the heart of every patriotic citizen and thenceforth the name of 'Ulysses S. Grant' was a household word beneath every loyal roof-tree." Lincoln felt his own thrill of exultation—he sent just one name to the Senate for promotion to major general: Grant's.

Foote and C. H. Smith wouldn't live to see it (Foote died from illness and complications from his wound in 1863, and Smith didn't survive Shiloh), but Grant, in the great American tradition of Washington and Jackson and Taylor, was on his way to the White House, and there was almost nothing he or anyone else could do to stop it.

Chapter 4

THE BIG SANDY VALLEY

KENTUCKY, everyone said, was important. Except, perhaps, the remote southeastern corner, down in the Cumberland mountains, the place called the Big Sandy Valley, a four-county area so impoverished it had no banks, no railroads, only one newspaper, hardly any roads, no bridges for the few roads that did exist, and very few people who knew much about the outside world. This place was the hillbilly country that would generate all those stories and ballads about the Hatfields and the McCoys. The Big Sandy Valley in 1861 was not the kind of place you would choose to visit.

But it was to this god-awful corner of the war that James A. Garfield and the boys of the 42d Ohio were headed. In that valley, they would fight a campaign so obscure that no mention of it—not even a lonely footnote—turns up in either Shelby Foote's or Bruce Catton's immensely detailed accounts of the fighting. And yet Garfield's victory in the Big Sandy over that magnificent Falstaffian figure, the 300-pound Confederate general Humphrey Marshall, was at the time fairly well celebrated all across the North (it made page one in the *New York Times*). Back home in Ohio, it did wonders for Garfield's reputation, paving the way for his political successes, just as Grant's truly impressive victories not so far away in Tennessee had put him on the march to the White House.

Of all these future presidents, only two commanded armies in the field. Grant, of course, was one of them. The other was Garfield; he led his own little army in the Big Sandy Valley with confidence—overconfidence, some might say—and a surprising amount of cunning and skill. Garfield served in the army for a little more than two years, but in that short time he demonstrated that he had the nerve and the intelligence to become a successful field commander on a grander scale. He proved that in the Big Sandy Valley.

Garfield received his marching orders on Saturday, December 14, 1861, in a telegram from Major General Don Carlos Buell, commanding officer of the Department of the Ohio. (Buell had succeeded William Tecumseh Sherman, who was working his way through one of his blackest moods.) He and the boys of the 42d broke camp at 9:00 A.M. the next morning and marched to the train depot in Columbus.

"Upon reaching Columbus," Private Owen Johnston Hopkins of Company K remembered, "we found the streets lined with people assembled to witness our march through the city. Flags both great and small waved from window, terrace, and balcony, and the streets were boisterous with busy life.... Marching to the Cincinnati & Columbus R.R. depot, the Regiment was formed in a hollow square and received from Governor Dennison a magnificent stand of colors, which the Governor said he hoped we would never trail in the dust—or words to that effect. Our Colonel, James A. Garfield, in a short but appropriate speech, assured him that no enemy of our country should wrest that beautiful standard from us.... Giving the Governor 'three times three,' we embarked on the [railroad] cars and were whirled on toward Cincinnati."

In a letter to his wife, Crete, Garfield said he received another message from Buell as soon as he stepped off the cars, "telling me to send the regiment on towards its destination [Catlettsburg, Kentucky], and report myself at his Head Quarters [in Louisville] for orders." For the rest of the night, though, working steadily until 2:00 A.M., Garfield supervised loading the regiment on two steamers at the foot of Vine Street.

Sergeant Charles E. Henry, attached to Company A, recalled that it was a miserable night. The troop ships, the *Lady Jackson* and the *Izetta*, were "wretched little steamboats. Officers filled the berths, and the men lay down on deck and cabin floors to a cold and sleepless night, amidst the hubbub of braying mules, whistling steamboats, and the clangor of loading." The regimental historian, Private F. S. Mason, also of Company A, agreed; he said the boats were "marvels of dreariness and discomfort."

Garfield told Crete that along with 1,000 men, they loaded 150 mules, twenty-five army wagons, and six ambulances for the sick and, in time, the wounded, aboard the two little steamers. "The boys were very much crowded, and I fear they will not be comfortable," he told Crete. It was an omen of things to come. The two steamers set off up the Ohio about 8:00 A.M. Monday. Garfield, bidding them farewell, rushed off to Louisville and met Buell there at 9:00 that evening.

In a letter to his friend Harry Rhodes, Garfield reported that he had spent three-quarters of an hour with the general. Buell, he said, "is a direct, martial-spirited man [another West Pointer] and has an air of decision and business which I like. He told me at once that he knew of me and that knowledge had led him to put me in command of the expedition to drive back the rebels from Eastern Kentucky."

Buell hoped to pull his ragtag army—one day to become the mighty Army of the Cumberland—into shape and to cross into Tennessee. But before he could do that, he had to deal with two Confederate armies moving through mountain passes into southeastern Kentucky and threatening his left flank. One of them, the larger and the more dangerous of the two, was making its way from Tennessee through the Cumberland Gap. It was commanded by Brigadier General Felix Kirk Zollicoffer, a Tennessee newspaper editor and politician. Buell dispatched his best general, George H. Thomas, to deal with him. The other army, Humphrey Marshall's, was moving into Kentucky from Virginia through Pound Gap. No one in Buell's headquarters really knew very much about Marshall's intentions or the size of his army.

Marshall, however, was a well-known figure, North and South. He was graduated from West Point in 1832 (forty-second in a class of forty-five), taking part in the Black Hawk war against the Sac and Fox Indians that year and resigning his commission the next year. He studied law, married (and eventually had nine children), and prospered in Louisville. He returned to the army during the War with Mexico in command of the First Kentucky Cavalry and led a charge at the battle of Buena Vista. He was a Whig member of Congress from 1849 to 1852, after which he left Washington to become President Millard Fillmore's consul in China. He came home two years later and returned to Congress as a member of the American Party, the xenophobic "Know-Nothings," serving from 1855 to 1859. By November 1861, when he took the field as a Confederate brigadier general, he was fifty years old and uncomfortably fat.

Almost from the start, he believed Confederate strategists were neglecting possibilities in the western theater, and—Marshall being a prolific and bombastic letter writer—he let them know about it. He came to be a part of the "Western concentration bloc," a faction led by Generals Joseph E. Johnston, Wade Hampton, James Longstreet, and others, that challenged Robert E. Lee and what they thought was his fixation upon Virginia. In 1861, though, he was completely committed to the simpler idea that the Big Sandy Valley was the best route that masses of rebel troops could take to pierce Union lines and flood into "bluegrass Kentucky," in the populous central part of the state. There, thousands of sympathetic young men would rally to Marshall's colors.

It is hard not to sympathize with Marshall; he was a good-hearted fellow, and his Kentucky troops idolized him. "Humphrey Marshall, he's our boss," they chanted, "big as hell, brave as a hoss." He endeared himself to his soldiers by giving up his tent to the sick and the wounded and sleeping beneath his wagon. But he wasn't much of a soldier. One of his officers conceded that he was ill suited to mountain warfare, "owing to his great size." Nor, he said, was Marshall well suited to command volunteers, "being the most democratic of men. His heart was tender as a woman's. For these reasons he could not enforce the rigorous discipline of an army. So well known was his leniency that an officer of his staff made a standing offer to eat the first man the general should shoot for any crime."

He was no strategist either. Pound Gap, at an elevation of more than 2,000 feet, wasn't much of a gap at all. It was tough, mountainous terrain, and hauling supplies through it to feed and equip an army in the field would prove to be a daunting task. The Union commanders had a much easier supply line. They could use steamboats to bring men and supplies as far south as Catlettsburg, where the Big Sandy (it flows north) meets the Ohio. When the water was high, smaller steamers could travel the Big Sandy as far south (and upriver) as Louisa.

The valley, backwater though it was, had already seen some fighting. A Union commander, a former Navy lieutenant named William "Bull" Nelson, another 300-pounder—why, one wonders, did the parched Big Sandy Valley attract men of such extraordinary girth?—had defeated a rebel colonel, John S. Williams, commanding the 5th Kentucky, the South's "Ragamuffin Regiment," on November 8 and 9 at Piketon. Williams withdrew to Pound Gap, where he was succeeded in command by Marshall. Nelson was transferred elsewhere, leading to the opening that Garfield was now being asked to fill. In the absence of troops from either side in the field, all semblance of law and order had broken down in the valley. "Anarchy reigned everywhere and people prayed for occupation once again, it mattered not by which side," one Kentucky historian wrote. "Neighbors remembered old insults and grudges,

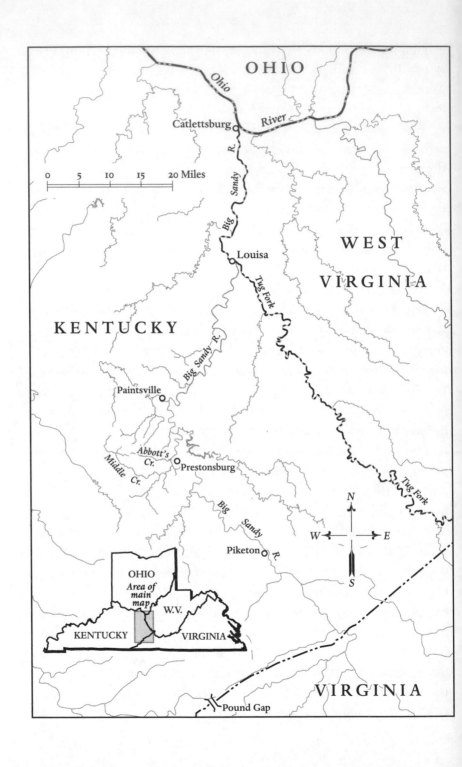

stalked the object of their enmity in the night. Many to feel secure, joined with strong bands around some prominent farmer. There were few nights red flames of burning houses did not increase the terror and the thirst for vengeance."

Bushwhacking took place in most contested states, but it was especially bloody in isolated mountain regions, Kentucky among them. The situation in Kentucky was compounded by the fact that sentiment was so narrowly divided between North and South. Both the Union and Confederate armies contained Kentucky regiments.

Garfield knew nothing of this. In his letter to Harry Rhodes, he had said that Buell told him that Williams and Marshall "have returned [to the valley] with a force variously estimated at from 2,000 to 6,000 men including cavalry and artillery. The General [Buell] says the information is so vague and his own knowledge of the country in that section so limited that he must trust the management of the expedition to my discretion.... The work will be positively enormous, for a large share of the Kentucky forces are as yet unarmed and undisciplined. It is a horrible country.... He said (and I fully agree with him) that he would have much preferred to have me with him in the grand column, but yet he said I would have a much greater chance for distinction. I must go to study geography. The General told me to make memoranda of such a plan and such questions as I might think important, and call on him this morning."

Garfield returned to his hotel—it was now past 10:00 P.M.—and with the help of "Collins's large atlas" put together his battle plan for defeating Humphrey Marshall. Having had almost no sleep, he returned to Buell's headquarters at 9:00 A.M. Tuesday morning and explained what he planned to do. Basically, he said, he was prepared to move up the Big Sandy by steamboat to Catlettsburg with his own regiment, the 42d, and then to march up the valley to join forces with two undermanned Kentucky regiments at Louisa. The three regiments would then continue up the valley until they encountered the rebel army under Marshall. At the same time, another column would set off from Paris, Kentucky, and try to cut off Marshall by sneaking in behind him at Prestonburg.

At no time did Garfield question seriously his ability to take on such extraordinary responsibility. It is this sort of self-confidence that separates him from the other amateur soldier-presidents. He was absolutely certain that he could lead an army just as well as any West Pointer. West Pointers, he believed, were slow-moving, slow-witted, and probably unpatriotic. He told Crete that he was "pleased with the prospect of work."

Garfield told Buell what he wanted to do and then asked some questions and made some demands. What, he asked, was the extent of his authority in reference to command, discipline, court martial? What was the condition of the troops to be placed under his command, and how many of them were there? What should he do about captured slaves? Would his regimental commanders be reporting to him or to Buell's headquarters? And then—what gall—he demanded more tents, more overcoats, more blankets, more money, more mechanics and muleteers, and a battery of artillery. He was satisfied on most of his questions and got most of what he demanded—except the artillery. Buell said he wouldn't need the guns in the mountains but Garfield, aware that Marshall had artillery, never ceased pestering headquarters for some of his own.

Buell took it all in, or at least he seemed to, and issued orders—officially Special Order No. 35—creating the 18th Brigade, with Garfield in command, and consisting of his own 42d Ohio, now commanded by Lieutenant Colonel Lionel A. Sheldon, Colonel Jonathan Cranor's 40th Ohio, two Kentucky regiments, or what there was of them anyway—the 14th under Colonel Laban T. Moore, most of its soldiers recruited in the Big Sandy Valley, and the 22d under Colonel George W. Monroe—two companies of Ohio cavalry under Major William McLaughlin, and six companies from the First Kentucky Cavalry under Colonel John W. Letcher, about 3,000 men in all. He then pretty much instructed Garfield to get on with it. At no time did he point out to Garfield that it might be inadvisable to proceed with two columns—his and Cranor's—separated by 100 miles of mountains in the face of an enemy that might actually outnumber him.

Garfield's boys in the 42d Ohio and their rickety steamboats reached Catlettsburg on Thursday, December 19, not without incident. Private Mason, the regimental historian, said that the *Lady Jackson* sprang a leak just before reaching its destination. "All hands were ordered below to tumble the ammunition and beans out of the hold." The captain, "with a recklessness which would have chilled the marrow of a seafaring man, turned his prow to the shore and beached her, head on high and dry, in the oozy sand.... This then was the end of our voyage—Catlettsburg at the mouth of the Big Sandy, the dividing line between Kentucky and [West] Virginia. But wherefore? Why had we come there? Where was the enemy?"

Private Hopkins of Company K said they were greeted in Catlettsburg by the entire 14th Kentucky Volunteers, all lined up on the river bank in their new sky blue uniforms. "They made the welkin ring with cheers and shouts of welcome." That's not the way Private Mason remembered it. He said the only soldiers from the 14th Kentucky he saw were a slovenly group, maybe six or seven in all, "who straggled out of a tavern and made a faint effort at three cheers." They proved to be "the farthest-frightened ragged fringe of the stragglers who had fled down the Valley before the victorious advance of Humphrey Marshall. They had come on foot, some had lost their muskets, all were frightened, and the blood-curdling accounts which they gave were sufficient to perceptibly check the hilarity of the 42d for that day."

The boys from Ohio had never seen anything quite like this corner of Kentucky. "We had not supposed that within so short a distance of home there was any such wilderness as this," Private Mason said. "How little we, even then, knew or imagined of the primeval barbarism that lay before us in Eastern Kentucky."

And then there were the mules, all 150 of them, few of whom "had ever felt the restraint of a halter or a bridle." Would any veteran of the 42d "ever forget that afternoon with the mules?" Mason asked. "How utterly the volunteers of that early day failed to comprehend the moral obliquity of the mule."

The 900 men from the 42d Ohio and the 500 men from the 14th Kentucky set off on foot—they left the 22d Kentucky behind because many, maybe most, of its soldiers still had no weapons—the next morning for Louisa, a village twenty miles to the south, located at the junction of the Big Sandy and Tug Fork. They were joined there by Colonel Garfield, who was no doubt a little tired and grumpy from his long trip and didn't like what he was seeing and hearing. The camp was alive to the sound of "squalling hens and other noises [that] denoted the reign of terror amongst the feathered tribe," Private Hopkins said. "I succeeded in unearthing two large cabbage heads and a wheel of corn pone, and my comrade had secured a brace of chickens, all of which we were preparing to make hash of, when the long roll beat and the Regiment flew to arms."

Garfield sat on his horse, silently, for a minute or so before addressing his own Ohio boys, in very much the same way he had lectured his students at the Eclectic.

> Men of the 42d, I thought when I left our old Buckeye State at the head of this fine-looking body of soldiers that I was the proud commander of a Regiment of gentlemen, but your actions this evening, were I not better acquainted with each and all of you, would bitterly dispel that illusion. Soldiers, we came to Kentucky to help her sons free her sacred soil from the feet of the rebel horde now lying just behind that mountain range. Tonight, we go to dislodge him. Show these Kentuckians, who are your comrades under one flag, that you did not come to rob and steal, but came to indicate the true character of the American soldier.

Private Hopkins said he and the rest of the Buckeyes, their "illgotten gains" hanging from their shoulders, were contrite. "Before the colonel had half-done speaking, every man had deposited his chicken, cabbage-head, ham, or sack of corn meal, on the ground." Such feelings of guilt, Hopkins said, didn't last very long. "As time moved on, and our faces became bronzed, . . . we totally forgot the moral teachings of Colonel Garfield." So, for that matter, did Garfield himself.

Louisa did not impress the boys from Ohio. It was "at best a straggling, unpainted hamlet but the hostilities of six months had greatly increased its thriftless, untidy aspect," Private Mason wrote. "The men were nearly all in the army on one side or the other; the court house had been used as a barrack by the half barbarous volunteers of the mountain region, and a shabby brick tavern with its kitchen dismantled and its windows broken, still struggled against extinction as a public house by keeping a red nosed ex-hosteler and a jug of new applejack behind the bar."

Private Mason said he doubted "whether any regiment was seasoned to the hard work and discomfort of campaigning more abruptly than the Forty-second. In five days they had come from the comfort of barrack life to the hardships of a Winter campaign in a wilderness."

One of Garfield's major challenges was his lack of intelligence about the enemy or, for that matter, about Colonel Cranor's column, marching toward Prestonburg. Garfield had a flair for secret intelligence, and it surfaced for the first time here in these early days in the valley. His primary agent was John Jordan, one of the soldiers in the 14th Kentucky, "a tall, gaunt, sallow man of about thirty, with small, gray eyes, a fine falsetto voice, pitched in the minor key, and his speech was the rude dialect of the mountains," an early Garfield biographer wrote. Jordan was a typical product of the Big Sandy Valley. "Born among the hills, where the crops are stones, and sheep's noses are sharpened before they can nibble the thin grass between them, his life has been one of hardest toil and privation."

Garfield wrote a note on tissue paper to Colonel Cranor, commander of his other column, fast becoming a sort of lost patrol, urging him to make haste for Prestonburg to take part in the decisive battle he reckoned would be fought in a matter of days. The note was folded into a ball and then coated with warm lead so it resembled a bullet. Jordan rode most of the day, stopping for the night at the home of a woman he knew to be sympathetic to the Union cause (even though her husband was serving with Humphrey Marshall). But rebel spies were on to his game, and mounted horsemen—partisans who were terrorizing the valley—had set out in pursuit. They caught up with Jordan at the loyal woman's cottage. Jordan gave the disguised letter to the lady, urged her to make sure it got safely to Colonel Cranor, jumped on his horse, and made a dash for the woods. Two of the rebel horsemen set off in pursuit; Jordan killed them both with well-aimed shots from his two revolvers. He eventually made it safely back to camp, and the loyal woman caught up with Colonel Cranor and delivered Garfield's message.

In a letter to Crete, dated New Year's Day 1862, Garfield said he had just about given up on his scout, fearing he might have been captured. But, "15 minutes ago," he wrote, Jordan—he called him "Kit Carson"—had ridden into camp. "He had been shot at, twice surrounded by enemies, once escaped by stratagem, and, once, when aided by a party of Union men, fought and captured several prisoners."

Garfield told Crete he was organizing a system of spies and scouts, "which is giving me full and satisfactory information of the doings of the enemy. He is now entrenched on a hill three miles back of Paintsville on the Prestonburg road and is fortifying still more."

Garfield's confidence, never shaken, was now surging. "I dare hardly hope that I shall capture a whole army," he said, "and I always feel very reluctant to say I think I shall do a thing when I may fail of succeeding. But I do think I am getting into a position from which I have good ground to hope that I shall capture them. I cannot tell you how deeply alive to the scheme in hand are all the impulses and energies of my nature. I begin to see the obstacles melt away before me and the old feeling of succeeding in what I undertake gradually taking quiet possession of me."

Garfield, in fact, was now clearly touched with fire. Marshall, on the other hand, was not.

Marshall had set out on his campaign to save Kentucky for the Confederacy with high hopes. Kentucky, he said, "was a region inhabited by my friends, who know my name, and where the people will flock around my banner as the Italians did to that of Garibaldi. I am not mistaken—I know, because they have sent me word, and they have been looking for me, as for their deliverance from accursed bondage."

But, late in December, he was holed up at Paintsville, thirty miles south of Louisa, with no more than 2,000 men fit for duty and no sign of any volunteers flocking to his banner. "The people hereabouts are perfectly terrified or apparently apathetic," he wrote. "I imagine most of them are Unionists, but so ignorant they do not understand the question at issue."

His army was ragged and undisciplined. Residents of a small Shaker community remembered that his soldiers looked more like "bipeds of pandemonium than beings of this earth" when they came marching through. "They surrounded our wells like the locusts of Egypt . . . and they thronged our kitchen doors, begging for bread like hungry wolves."

Missing from Marshall's ranks was Colonel William D. Stuart's 56th Virginia Regiment, ordered to report to him as early as November 21 but still malingering at Abingdon, the general's base camp in Virginia. Stuart hadn't budged a month later (nor, in fact, would he ever budge). "I send express to you to move your regiment without delay," Marshall commanded Stuart on December 21. "I am before a force so much superior to me in number, according to the report of reliable scouts, that I can scarcely hope to avoid a collision—it may be disastrous to us—until you arrive. . . . I shall struggle to keep off the evil day as long as possible for you to arrive."

Missing as well were Colonel A. C. Moore and the 300 men he had recruited to form the 29th Virginia Infantry. Marshall was so furious about Moore's absence that he told his commanding general, Albert Sidney Johnston, that he had been compelled to arrest him, although an actual physical arrest was somewhat out of the question because he had no idea where Moore was. On January 3, however, Moore and 320 men showed up, joining Marshall at Paintsville. Marshall said he quickly "pretermitted" the order of arrest.

Marshall was also outraged by Richmond's apparent determination to place him under the command of Brigadier General George B. Crittenden, son of John J. Crittenden, former governor and senator from Kentucky and a supporter of the Union. Marshall distrusted General Crittenden and viewed him as a political rival. He preferred what he thought was the original arrangement—that he would report directly to General Johnston at Bowling Green. He wrote Vice President Alexander Stephens that he would rather resign his commission than take orders from George Crittenden.

Marshall surely had ample reason to be discouraged. His little army was in terrible shape, some of his soldiers barefoot, and many of them carrying shotguns or squirrel rifles. He pleaded with Richmond for help, and at one point they did send him what his aide Edward O. Guerrant described as "one thousand suits of clothes, including hats and shoes." The suits caught up with Marshall at Whiteburg, on the Kentucky side of Pound Gap. "When the quartermaster distributed the clothing among the soldiers, it was noticed that they examined with suspicion the peculiar color and texture of the cloth. General Marshall discovered it was *cotton*, and fearing the result of such a discovery by his men, rose to the occasion with a stirring speech, in which he eulogized the courage, endurance, and patriotism of his men, and commended the Government for its thoughtful care of them, and relieved their fears as to the quality of the goods by assuring them that they were 'woven out of the best quality of southern wool, with which, doubtless, many of the Kentuckians were not acquainted.' The men took the general's word for it (with a grain of salt) and walked off to their quarters with their cottonade suits."

"May God forgive me [for lying to his foot soldiers]," Marshall wrote. He said his cavalrymen were in even worse shape. They have had "no other clothes through all the winter, and are now searching for clothes like Japhet in search of his father.... For what have I undergone all this exposure and hardship? For what am I at fifty years of age ... exiled from the haunts of cultivated man—and partaking of all the vicissitudes of a winter's campaign in the mountain peaks of this wild and inhospitable region?" He went on to say he was disappointed his old friends, President Jefferson Davis and Vice President Stephens, had not seen fit to enlarge his "sphere of action ... to give my intellect and my exertion full play with means at my command to do something worthy of the cause and worthy of myself."

On a more personal level, he was outraged that one of his sons, John, had been taken prisoner "in the streets of New Liberty [a popular retreat for Kentucky politicians] by scoundrels [who] beat my riding horse to death." John, he added almost as an after-thought, had been taken to a prison in Ohio.

Imagine, then, his despair when he was told that General Robert E. Lee was unable to furnish his men with modern rifles, but that he was prepared to send them *pikes*.

What Marshall did have—and what Garfield wanted more than anything else—was guns. The rebels had a battery, sixty men under Captain W. C. Jeffress, with one smooth-bore six-pounder and three smooth-bore twelve-pounders, all of them firing hollow, spherical shells. The six-pounder weighed 884 pounds, the twelve-pounders 1,227 pounds. Marshall reported that he was moving as best he could through cold rain and deep, sticky mud, dragging the cannon and the heavily loaded ammunition wagons. "I found the roads nearly impassable," Marshall complained. "With great labor my battery was moved six miles [in a day], but some of my wagons could not move four miles."

The units in Marshall's little army included the 5th Kentucky, the "ragamuffins," under Colonel Williams (600 men); a battalion of mounted Kentucky troops under Colonel W. F. Simms (360); the 54th Virginia, under Colonel John H. Trigg (580); and the newly arrived 29th Virginia, under Colonel Moore (320), plus the artillerymen and one or two depleted cavalry companies.

They were established at what Marshall called Camp Hagar, three miles from Paintsville. His scouts had given him a pretty good idea of the force that was moving against him, now only eighteen miles away. "They have Garfield's Ohio regiment ...," he said, "which is 1,000 strong," plus two Kentucky regiments and some Ohio cavalry, "and what artillery I cannot learn." He also knew that Colonel Cranor and the 40th Ohio were advancing toward him from the west. He said he hoped he could come to terms with Garfield before Cranor made his appearance.

Garfield really was in no position to attack Marshall. All he had fit for duty were the 900 men in his own green but well-disciplined regiment, the 42d, plus 500 men in Colonel Moore's 14th Kentucky. The 14th, Garfield believed, was "composed of excellent material, but is in a wretched state of discipline.... It can be considered little better than a well-disposed, Union-loving mob, which ... may be converted into a very serviceable regiment." His other Kentucky regiment, the even more undisciplined 22d, was still waiting for its muskets. The prudent thing would have been to order Cranor and the 40th Ohio to join him in the valley and then to advance together against Marshall. Even that, given the odds, was a little chancy. Instead, he again sent word to Cranor to circle behind Marshall and cut off his retreat at Prestonburg, ten miles south of Marshall's position at Paintsville.

"It was a very rash and imprudent affair on my part," Garfield admitted years later. It certainly was.

With his favorite scout, John Jordan, in the lead, Garfield and the boys from the 42d Ohio and the 14th Kentucky set out from Louisa about noon on December 23 to attack Marshall and his rebels, holed up waiting for them in Paintsville, thirty miles upstream. That first day, they traveled only ten miles on icy roads that were little more than bridle paths, fording one stream twenty-six times. When they reached the point where George's Creek meets the Big Sandy, the sun came out, and the little army settled down to enjoy it and get ready for the final assault. They would wait there for nearly two weeks.

By January 3, it was sleeting again, and Private Hopkins found himself and Private Dick Bailey on picket guard duty on a mountain top about two miles from the George's Creek camp. "We watched through the night in a heavy storm of sleet and snow," Hopkins wrote. The next morning, the fog and the pine trees were so thick and impenetrable they couldn't see more than 50 feet down the mountain side. It was then, Hopkins said, that "we saw the absurdity of watching [from] such a position." Noontime arrived, with no relief, now long overdue, in sight. They built a rude shelter from sticks and branches and ate the last of their rations. Still no relief. They stuck to their frigid post through the next night as well, waking up to the sound of "rumbling wagons moving over a distant mountain road." Hopkins said he roused Bailey and "informed him of my belief that our little army was on the move. Cold and stiff, we decided, 'in council assembled,' to move also from our position.—which we soon after did."

They overtook the brigade that evening, after a long and difficult march, and registered a complaint, first to their captain and then to Colonel Garfield himself, that they had been forgotten and left behind. Garfield issued an order on the spot, "reducing to the ranks the sergeant of the guard who had neglected to relieve us."

Garfield was delighted when 300 troopers under Colonel William M. Bolles, from the 2d (West) Virginia Cavalry, came riding into camp on January 4. They had been loaned to Garfield by his old roommate in Columbus and fellow state senator, Jacob Dolson Cox, now a major general and commanding his own army in nearby West Virginia. Civil War infantry usually disparaged their comrades in the cavalry, but the boys from Ohio were impressed with Bolles's unit. "They were armed with sabers and a curious sort of horse-pistol, rigged with an adjustable butt or stock, so as to serve as a carbine," Mason said. "They were, besides, well-mounted, had seen service and learned to obey orders without wondering what the ultimate purpose was or feeling any individual responsibility in the result."

Three roads led into Paintsville. The road on Garfield's left followed Muddy Branch to the Big Sandy and then ran along that creek to the point where it met Paint Creek, a mile from town. The road on the right meandered up and down several hills to a ford over Jenny's Creek, also about a mile from town. The third road, the roughest of the lot, ran smack down the middle from Garfield's position into town.

Garfield really had a flair for military operations. The wiliest of all these soldier-presidents, he now decided to confuse Marshall by attacking on all three roads. He made his move the morning of January 5.

"By dividing his cavalry, moving it rapidly and supporting it with small detachments of infantry, he managed to strike the three [rebel] pickets, one after the other in such a way as to entirely mask his own intentions and give Marshall the impression that a mighty army was bearing down upon him from all directions," Mason wrote.

Marshall didn't need any convincing. He had already convinced himself, ignoring his previous calculations, that Garfield was advancing on him with 4,000 men—"five full regiments of infantry, 200 cavalry, and two batteries of artillery." He had captured a letter from Garfield to Cranor, and he was convinced that Cranor was still acting independently, moving against him with an additional 1,300 men. Although he was campaigning in what should have been friendly territory, with its inhabitants eager to provide him with reliable intelligence, his source for this wildly inaccurate estimate of the enemy's strength was a copy of the *Cincinnati Enquirer*.

Garfield's strategy worked perfectly. As his first detachment advanced, Marshall dispatched men and artillery to meet it. No sooner had he done that than another Union detachment began attacking at a different point. Marshall ordered his troops and guns to meet that threat. Still without a clue that Garfield was playing games with him, he rushed his weary troops and artillerymen to meet a *third* attack.

"The [rebel] regiment and battery were hurried frantically from one road to another, as the point of attack seemed to be changed," Mason said, "and in the midst of the panic the straggling troops in the town retreated across the river." Marshall, confused and convinced he was facing overwhelming numbers, simply skeddadled. Garfield and his boys occupied Paintsville without firing a shot.

"I planned and conducted a little series of maneuvers intended to mislead the enemy in regard to my own intentions," Garfield wrote Crete. "I believe I was entirely successful."

Clever it may have been, but surely this move was the most reckless of all Garfield's maneuvers. He had advanced against Marshall's main force without Cranor's 40th Ohio, without the 22d Kentucky, which was still waiting for its rifles, and without Bolles's cavalrymen, the most experienced soldiers in his army. He had sent them off to Jenny's Creek, about thirteen miles away, to track down Marshall's cavalry, believed to be camped there. If Marshall had had any fire in that enormous belly, he would have attacked Garfield at Paintsville, when the numbers were overwhelmingly in his favor. But that was not his style.

In Paintsville the hastily abandoned rebel camp fires were still smoldering, and Garfield had barely sat down at what had been Marshall's desk when Bolles sent word that his scouts had located the enemy cavalry, waiting in ambush. Garfield, his own fires burning brightly, sent back word to Bolles to "get as near the ambush as possible without making the attack, and I [will] march across the hills and attack the rebels in the rear." It was a pincers strategy, something Garfield had picked up from those military manuals he had studied.

Private Hopkins was part of that expedition, and he always remembered it as the hardest marching he endured in the entire war. "The expedition was a severe one," he wrote, "owing to a heavy fall of snow and the desperate condition of the road. Wading streams of floating ice, climbing rocky steeps, and struggling through the half-frozen mud, made the march extremely tiresome, and many of the men fell exhausted and straggled back to camp, or were picked up by the guerrillas."

Jenny's Creek, cold and swollen, had to be crossed twice. Garfield himself, his jacket removed and his sleeves rolled up, waded into the water to help build one of the log bridges. It was almost midnight when the 400-man detachment stumbled upon the rebel camp. It was deserted, with cooking fires still burning. What Garfield and his men didn't know was that Bolles had attacked the rebel troopers in disregard of Garfield's orders. The rebels had been completely routed with the loss of six killed and several wounded. Bolles's cavalrymen lost two killed and one wounded.

Private Mason was amazed at the rebel camp, known, he found out later, as "Fort Marshall." It was "crazy and absurd," he said, "built to guard a road which could easily have been dispensed with by taking the parallel one three miles to the right.... It was built upon ground so high that an attacking force ... would have been protected by the impossibility of depressing the guns of the redoubt so as to bring them to bear."

Garfield and his weary men rested for an hour or so and then began the slow march back to Paintsville. They soon came upon the body of one of the rebel cavalrymen, killed by Bolles's troopers earlier. "He was the commonest kind of a backwoods bushwhacker," Mason wrote, "clad in the coarse, dirty gray of the mountaineer, but to us he was the first dead Rebel of the war, and the picture of his pallid face as he lay in the flickering torchlight; his frowzy, yellow hair, and his whitened hands raised by his stiffened arms as if in appeal to the cavalrymen who had gone galloping over him, left an impression on our minds that not all the carnage of the succeeding two years could efface."

The march back, with nothing in the way of excitement to look forward to, was tougher than the march out. "Once or twice," said Hopkins, "I was tempted to give up, but feared that I might fall asleep and freeze to death." It was easier for the officers, he said, "mounted on good horses." They "seemed to forget that they had a troop of tired and sleepy soldiers plodding on behind them."

"It was the hardest march I ever made," Garfield admitted. "But it had a fine influence on the regiment. It schooled them to danger, for there was not a half hour of that gloomy night in which we did not have reasonable apprehensions of an attack." In fact, he said, they came under fire for the first time in the war as they approached Paintsville the morning of January 8. The fire came from two companies of his own brigade, from the 14th Kentucky. "They mistook us for an enemy and fired on us." Fortunately, no one was hurt.

When Garfield and his expedition finally straggled into camp, they discovered they had company. Cranor's 40th Ohio, accompanied by Colonel Letcher's cavalrymen, had come to join the brigade. Their arrival, Private Hopkins said, "was not greeted with any great display of enthusiasm on either hand." The two regiments had trained together at Camp Chase and had developed a competitive antipathy to one another. Garfield, however, was delighted to see his missing column. Cranor's 40th, he knew, was a well-disciplined unit, just as competent as his own 42d. He was not so pleased with Colonel Letcher's cavalry. Letcher, Garfield said, "is an admirable gentleman, but a more demoralized, discouraged body of men I have never seen."

Cranor explained that he had decided against moving to cut off Marshall at Prestonburg when he discovered the whole rebel army was advancing in his direction. What they were doing, of course, was retreating after the fiasco at Paintsville. Garfield got more good news that evening when three companies (about 200 men) from the 22d Kentucky, finally equipped with rifles, came bustling into camp. The others, he was told, were not far behind. For the first time since General Buell had created it, the 18th Brigade was complete.

Complete, but pretty well worn out, and short of provisions. Still, Garfield said, he was "unwilling [Marshall] should get away without a trial of our strength." Garfield, amateur that he was, had the right instincts—engage the enemy—that were so conspicuously lacking in a number of other Union generals early in the war. Garfield was Lincoln's kind of soldier.

Bolles's men had been called back to West Virginia, so Garfield had to send Letcher's wretched troopers along with the better-trained veterans from Major McLaughlin's Ohio squadron up Jenny's Creek to "harass the enemy's rear if still retreating." Then, with 1,100 of the best men he could find in his four infantry regiments, on Thursday, January 9, he set out himself at about noon up the Big Sandy toward Prestonburg. The foot soldiers carried three days' rations—crackers, for the most part—in their knapsacks; it was all that Garfield could scrape together. He left the rest of his brigade behind to await more supplies expected sometime soon by small steamer or push boat.

"I fear we shall not be able to catch the enemy in a stern chase," Garfield said, "but we will give it a try."

But a chase really wasn't necessary because Marshall wasn't running. He had set up camp three miles upriver from Paintsville and had fortified the position. On January 3, Marshall reported he had 2,240 men under arms (almost twice as many as Garfield had in his column), but only 1,967 were fit for duty. "Measles and mumps," he said, "have played sad work among the men."

Worst of all, some of his Virginia officers were prepared to call it a day. In a round-robin letter dated January 9, all ten captains in the 54th Virginia regiment urged Marshall to retreat to some point in Virginia or Tennessee, "contiguous to a line of railroad," and hunker down for the rest of the winter.

The people among whom we have come have not appreciated our cause to the extent of quitting their homes to unite with us, and we are now in mid-winter, in a country poorly provided with the means of subsistence, exposed to an enemy more than double or treble our number, with roads which, if not now entirely impassable, must shortly become blocked up with snow and ice.... We do therefore most earnestly and respectfully solicit you to order our regiment to such point that we can go into winter quarters without the apprehension of being harassed by our enemies.

But it was too late. By 8:00 Thursday night, Garfield and his 1,200-man column had reached the mouth of Abbott's Creek, one mile below Prestonburg. Garfield's scouts had reported that the enemy was three miles upstream, waiting for his attack. But the scouts were wrong about this. The only rebels on Abbott's Creek were foragers sent there by Marshall to grind some wheat at an old mill. Marshall's main force was a mile away on Middle Creek, running parallel to Abbott's Creek. Garfield, harking back again to his old military manuals, conceived another pincers movement. He would move up Middle Creek and then cut across and fall on what he thought was Marshall's rear on Abbott's Creek. He expected his cavalry, which had been instructed to follow Marshall's column, to be in position to join in an attack on the rebel position on Abbott's Creek. They would then combine to close the vice and crush Marshall. The problem, of course, was that Marshall and his main force were in camp, in a fortified position, on Middle Creek. Hard to believe, but both of Garfield's columns were pursuing the enemy up the wrong valleys. Colonel Letcher and the cavalry were moving up Abbott's Creek to attack an enemy camp that wasn't there; Garfield and the infantrymen were advancing up a supposedly undefended Middle Creek to circle behind the enemy he believed to be on Abbott's Creek.

Garfield and his men settled down on a hilltop for the night.

Concerned that enemy scouts might be nearby, he issued orders forbidding the lighting of comforting fires. He also sent back word to Paintsville ordering Colonel Sheldon to bring up the reserves as quickly as possible, along with food and ammunition that had just arrived by steamboat. "At half-past 12 o'clock," he wrote, "I ... rolled myself up in the blanket, while the cold, drizzling rain poured down upon us during the whole night. At three in the morning I turned out and called up the boys to take their crackers and prepare for the march. I assure you that it was a very dreary prospect. The deepest, worst mud I ever saw was under foot, and a dense cold fog hung around us as the boys filed slowly down the hillside."

He was still in the dark about Marshall's location. "Supposing the enemy to be encamped on Abbott's Creek," he wrote in his official report on the engagement, "it was my intention to advance up Middle Creek and cut off his retreat, while the cavalry should attack his rear."

What a surprise, then, when Garfield and his column were sharply engaged by rebel cavalry at the mouth of Middle Creek. Skirmishing continued as Garfield pushed up two miles more. It was only then that the truth began to dawn—Marshall was there waiting for him on Middle Creek, his four guns in position and aimed straight at the advancing Union column.

Garfield and his army passed around a steep hill and found a level plain stretching before them. More than 200 rebel cavalrymen dashed at him, fired a few shots, and then fell back "behind a ridge which ran near half way across the valley," he later wrote to Crete.

Private Henry remembered that when the Confederate cavalry first appeared, "some fool officer yelled, 'Rebel cavalry coming, form hollow square against cavalry.' The men broke for the steep hillside nearby, the sensible thing to do."

The Confederate cavalry "seemed to be posted behind the ridge in force and their officers rode up on its point and looked at us through their glasses," Garfield told Crete. He saw that the ridge on his right commanded the rebel position, and he ordered two companies to take it. Meanwhile, in a wonderful demonstration of Garfield's flair for unconventional battlefield tactics, "I ordered a battalion drill, and we formed squares and wheeled from column into line, while the long line of our rear was trailing round the hill into the plain. I was willing the rebel officers should see the drill and should see the troops file on." The whole idea—Garfield's little column going around and around—was a form of psychological warfare to convince Marshall and the rest of the rebel commanders that they were facing a very large and imposing force. Marshall firmly believed that, so Garfield's demonstration merely served to reinforce what the rebel commander already knew to be true.

That wasn't all Garfield had in his bag of tricks. By now, he had a general idea about the location of the Confederate positions. To make sure, he told Crete, "I took my cavalry escort of ten, added a few mounted citizens who were armed and who were following with us, and ordered them to charge across the plain so as to draw the enemy's fire and thus induce him to reveal his position." It was all the horsemen he had because his main cavalry force was still looking for Marshall in the wrong valley.

"The ruse was boldly performed and was completely successful," Private Mason said. "As the little group of horsemen galloped up the creek and round the curve in the road, the battery fired harmlessly over their heads, and the whole infantry force, with the trepidation of new troops, opened fire at long range, and completely unmasked their position. They occupied the wooded hill from its base half way to its summit. It was now time for real work."

Garfield scurried up to the crest that had already been secured by two companies of infantry and established his command post. He learned later the crest was called, somewhat ominously, Graveyard Point, the burial ground for a number of local pioneer families. Even so, it was an "isolated crag which gave me a splendid prospect of the plain and all the hills."

Garfield launched his attack on Marshall's force, dug in on the

western side of Middle Creek, from Graveyard Point, on the eastern side, at about 3:00 P.M. That meant that all the attacking parties
had to wade waist-deep through the frigid waters of the creek,
keeping their long, cumbersome Belgian rifles and their cartridge
boxes high and dry.

First to go were two companies from the 42d Ohio under Captain Frederick A. Williams. This moment was the one for which
Marshall had waited for so long. It was time to bring his four guns
into play, and here was his first target—the boys from Ohio. With
them was Private Hopkins from K Company. "Marshall had one
small howitzer [in fact, he had four], which throughout the fight
sent its harmless, screeching shots high above our heads, doing
more damage among the limbs of lofty trees than to any other living thing."

The rebel gunners also took aim at Garfield and his reserves on
Graveyard Point. "Boom went a cannon," Garfield wrote to Crete,
"followed by another throwing a 12-pound shell which struck ...
within two feet of Adjutant [William W.] Olds, who was leading a
company of scouts. The shell tore up the earth in the midst of the
company, but did not explode. Had it done so, it would almost have
annihilated the company."

For poor Humphrey Marshall, this was the biggest disappoint-
ment of all. He and his soldiers had dragged those heavy guns over
mountain peaks and through freezing creeks and rivers, and now,
when they were finally needed most, they didn't work. Virtually
every shell the rebel gunners fired was a dud. The shells were
twenty years old, maybe even older, stored all that time in a militia
arsenal near Richmond. The gunpowder inside the shells was probably moldy and too damp to ignite. It was a lucky, lifesaving break
for Garfield and the men of the 18th Brigade.

For the boys from Ohio, leading the attack, it was still rough
going. "The mountain side was almost perpendicular," Private
Hopkins said, "and climbing this by the aid of branches and trees
and under heavy fire from the well-protected rebels' entire line was

extremely difficult, but the enthusiasm of the men was a motive power not easily baffled. Reaching a point near the summit, our line was formed, and a charge or two and heavy doses of minnie [minié] balls soon dislodged the Rebs, who were now sent flying down the opposite side, leaving the dead and wounded on the field."

It wasn't really quite as simple as Hopkins described it. Garfield watched the whole affair from his craggy command post on Grave-yard Point, and he didn't like what he was seeing. "It was one of the most terrific fights which has been recorded in this war," he told Crete (though, of course, it was no such thing). He was so concerned by the "terrible fire" being directed at Captain Williams and the Ohio boys that he sent two companies from the 14th Kentucky and about ninety men from the 42d Ohio's reserves, all of them under the command of Major Don A. Pardee, across the creek to help out. They came under heavy fire too, but Pardee "pushed on, fighting his way till he joined Captain Williams and both charged forward on the enemy, who were now so near that the combatants shouted and talked to each other while they fought," Garfield told Crete.

The hill being attacked by Williams and Pardee was defended by Colonel John H. Trigg's 54th Virginia Infantry. He and his men did indeed lay down a "terrible fire" on the Yankees working their way up the hill. "But," said Private Mason, who was there, "the Rebels fired unaccountably wild. They were fighting down a steep hill and, as usual with raw troops, they overshot their mark and their bullets for the most part merely barked and scarred the trees over their enemies heads." Additionally, a significant number of them were armed with "smooth-bore muskets and squirrel rifles of small caliber, and fought like a mob, without a plan or unity of action."

Garfield sent the 40th Ohio, under Colonel Cranor, to assist Williams and Pardee and then committed the 22d Kentucky, under Colonel George W. Monroe, to a battle that was rapidly becoming a mob scene. It was a "a regular bushwhackers action," one participant said. Monroe was ordered to attack another hill position, to the left of Triggs, that was held by Colonel John S. Williams's 5th Kentucky Infantry. This moment, then, was one of those tragic and dramatic moments that was repeated over and over again in the Civil War—boys from the same state and sometimes the same town fighting each other.

One of the reasons Garfield committed Monroe's Kentuckians to the attack was that his own position on Graveyard Point suddenly had come under fire, probably from the rebel Kentuckians. "They turned their whole fire upon me," Garfield wrote. "I have no doubt but that a thousand rifle balls came within a foot of me. They cut the twigs, splintered the rock, and cut a canteen which hung beside me. . . . Such terrific volleys I had never seen," he said, perhaps forgetting this was, after all, his first battle. "The hill trembled under the recoil."

Garfield had now committed just about everyone he had to the contest. "My reserve was . . . reduced to a mere handful," he told Crete, "and the agony of the moment was terrible; the whole hill was enshrouded in such a volume of smoke as rolls from the mouth of a volcanoe, thousands of gun flashes leaped like lightning from the cloud. In my agony of anxiety I prayed to God for the reinforcement to appear. I had sent back word to Colonel Sheldon to display the banner"—the one given to the regiment by its friends in Hiram—"as his column came in sight. I was just ordering my whole reserve into line and was going to lead them up the hill myself, when I looked behind us and saw the Hiram banner sweep round the hill. I shouted to our boys to look. They saw, and such a shout of joy never reached my ears. The reinforcement on double-quick returned the wild shout, and the fighters on the hill heard, saw and returned an answering shout."

For all of Garfield's hyperbole, it was a moment to savor.

The fiercest fighting probably took place in the fratricidal engagement between the two Kentucky regiments. Monroe's Kentuckians, the ones fighting for the North, finally dislodged

Williams's Kentuckians, fighting for the South, with a bayonet charge. It was done in "gallant style," Garfield said, and it brought the day's fighting to an end.

It was now 4:30 in the afternoon, and both sides were exhausted. In his overblown letter to Crete, Garfield said he saw a rebel colonel on horseback on one of the hills shouting to his men to retreat. "Seven Ohio boys leveled their rifles at him and fired. Horse and rider tumbled back over the hill." And yet the records show that no rebel colonel, or lieutenant colonel for that matter, was killed or wounded in the engagement. It can be concluded, then, that the Ohio boys missed. Most soldiers in the Battle of Middle Creek, on both sides, missed.

The enemy, Garfield said, "were driven [from the field] in dire confusion. Night closed in upon us. I did not dare to pursue in the night, lest we should fire upon each other. We brought off our dead and wounded, built our camp fires, and lay down on the field, while the rain and the darkness covered us. Scarcely had the last gun been fired when a glare of fire lighted up the hill where the enemy's camp had been. He was burning his baggage and fleeing."

In his official report on the battle, Marshall said his troops "acted firmly and enthusiastically during the whole fight, and though the enemy numbered some 5,000 to our 1,500, they were certainly well whipped." He said he had lost eleven killed and fifteen wounded. He estimated Garfield's losses to be more than 250 killed and 300 wounded.

Marshall's numbers, however, were wishful conjecture. Garfield had clearly won the Battle of Middle Creek. He had been foolish, he had been lucky, but he also had been combative and imaginative. He had come to grips with Kentucky's own Humphrey Marshall in appalling winter conditions, and he had sent him flying back to Virginia. The Big Sandy Valley had been cleared of the enemy, precisely what General Buell had wanted Garfield to do in the first place. And Garfield had done it all with the loss of only three killed and twenty wounded. It was an extraordinary achievement, fully justifying Garfield's belief that West Pointers weren't the only ones who could command successful armies.

Because no newspaper reporters had accompanied Garfield's column into action, it took news of his success a few days to capture the public's attention. But when word did reach the offices of newspapers big and small, it caused a stir.

The page one headline in *The New York Times* looked like this:

Important from Kentucky
Full Confirmation of the
Reported Rout of Humphrey
Marshall's Rebels
Col. Garfield in Possession of Prestonburgh
Marshall's Whole Army Flying in Utter Confusion
Official Dispatches from Colonel Garfield

The editorial writers had a field day.

"The braggart, Humph. Marshall, and his murderous minions, have ingloriously fled before the intrepid command of Colonel Garfield," the *Cincinnati Daily Gazette* reported.

"The fat Knight of Kentucky has met the enemy, and they are not his," the *Cincinnati Commercial* said.

"Humphrey Marshall, the rotund rebel of Kentucky, has come to grief," *The New York Times* noted.

Middle Creek may not have been Fort Donelson. But, for Garfield, it was just as crucial to his future expectations.

Chapter 5

POLITICAL ADVANCEMENT

HUMPHREY MARSHALL had seen enough. Declaring he had "developed a personal hatred for the country," he took himself and his bedraggled little army back into Virginia, leaving just a small outpost behind at Pound Gap. "I am an exile from the graves of my kindred and the home of my nativity," he complained in one of the dozens of wordy letters he wrote to friends and associates.

After the battle, Garfield retired to Paintsville to be closer to his supplies. There, on January 16, he issued a proclamation to the citizens of the Big Sandy Valley. "I have come among you to restore the honor of the Union," he said, "and to bring back the old banner which you all once loved, but which by the machinations of evil men and by mutual misunderstandings have been dishonored among you." He promised full protection of the government to those who declined to give aid and comfort to the enemy. To those who refused to cooperate, "I offer only the alternative of battle or unconditional surrender."

Late in January, the rain began falling, steadily, day after day.

The current in the Big Sandy was moving so swiftly that steamboat captains were refusing to bring supplies upriver from Catlettsburg. "Indeed," said Garfield in a letter to Crete dated January 26, "it was a fearful sight. The river raised nearly 50 feet. We were getting short of provisions. I went down to Catlettsburg last Sunday and ordered our boats to go up at once. The captains of boats said it was impossible to go up and the attempt would be dangerous in the extreme. They utterly refused to try."

And so, he said, he commandeered a small steamer—the *Sandy Valley*, owned by a local judge—and at 3:00 P.M. the next day set off upriver with a full load of supplies. "I found that my old canal experience was then very valuable to me," he told Crete. "I took the helm and stood at it night and day, with the exception of six hours, till Wednesday near noon, when we reached this place [Paintsville] with a load of provisions just as the last was being eaten. There were a few times in the night, in the midst of the fearful current and the drift of fallen trees sweeping down, when we came very near sinking.... The boys on board implored me to stop, but I thought that our boys might be starving ... and I pushed on. So you see I have turned sailor at last."

Never mind that Garfield had worked with a canal boat for only six weeks and had spent most of that time on dry land, trudging along with the tow horses and mules. He knew it was a good story, and he squeezed it dry. He expected Crete to pass the letter around—he had instructed her to make his letters available to friends and supporters—and pass it around she did.

His friends and biographers liked the story so much they added a few touches of their own. In his 1880 presidential campaign biography, Charles Carleton Coffin told it this way:

> In rounding an abrupt bend in the river, the boat was caught by the current and swung around, hard and heavy, on a bar of quicksand. Every effort to back and spar her off failed. Tools were brought and excavations dug around the embedded bow, but in vain.

"Get a line to the opposite shore," ordered Garfield.

The boatman protested, and swore that it could not be done. The Colonel himself leaped into the yawl and steered it across. The current swept them down, but finally they reached the shore, made fast a line, twisted it with a grail until the strain drew the steamer from her bed, and once more she headed upriver.

The picture of the brave Garfield, steady hand at the helm, making the terrible passage up the Big Sandy to feed his hungry boys, would one day appeal to voters.

On February 22, Garfield moved his troops to Piketon and a position closer to Pound Gap, Marshall's last remaining outpost. The rain kept coming down, in torrents. "I have never seen the fearfulness of water before," Garfield wrote to Crete the next day. "In one hour the water rose twelve feet. It surrounded the camp of the 40th [Ohio] and they barely had time to get their guns and ammunition and save themselves. This morning discloses a fearful scene. The house where I am staying, which is sixty feet above the usual level of the river, is now surrounded. A wild river roars around it on all sides.... Two large steamboats are up in the principal street of the village. Houses, stacks of wheat and hay, gigantic trees, saw-logs, fences, and all things that float are careening by with fearful velocity. The terrified people of the village have fled to the hills.... I hope the flood has reached its height. Three inches more and it will wash through the room in which I am sitting." Later that day, though, the sun peeped through, and the worst flood in the Big Sandy Valley in 100 years began to recede.

Garfield had now dealt with a rebel army and a terrible flood. "It seems to be my fortune to have a constant round of strange adventures," he told Crete. His next assignment was to pacify the valley, in which he and his soldiers represented the only functioning civil authority. The problem was bushwhackers—riding through the night, burning and pillaging.

Private Hopkins volunteered to be a part of a small expedition, ten men under the command of Major William Jones of the 40th Ohio, to track down a company of bushwhackers said to be operating a number of miles upriver. In his account, it was a gruesome assignment:

> We were piloted over the hills by a specimen of the Southern "poor trash"—a woman who rode without a saddle astride a very lean specimen of the genus horse, whose swaying bow legs betokened a slim allowance of oats, and bad use....
>
> On the evening of the first day out, we came suddenly upon the corpse of a man suspended over a creek by the neck, who, our guide informed us, had been hung the night before by the guerrillas.... We cut the rope, took down the body, and carried it about a fourth of a mile up the valley to his house, which was a rude hut built of logs. On entering, we discovered on a cot in one corner an old man with a minnie ball in his side. The same party of guerrillas had shot him at the same time they had compelled his son to go with them, and whom they afterwards hung. [He] had been accused of being a Union man.

Private Mason called the incident "a page from a chapter in the history of the war which the northern people, to this day, very imperfectly understand—the desperate, malignant struggle between the poor Union men of the mountains and their Confederate neighbors and foes."

The little patrol caught up with the bushwhackers the next day and engaged in a spirited running fight that lasted several hours. It came to an inglorious conclusion when Major Jones was shot in the head. "The expedition abandoned all other purposes but the one of bringing the wounded officer back to camp," Mason said. Most of Garfield's patrols ended on a happier note, and, slowly and steadily, he brought something approaching law and order to "these bloodthirsty Kentuckians" in the Big Sandy.

All the marching up and down the valley, the excitement of the battle itself, and the aftereffects of the flood began to take their toll. Garfield himself was sickly. Ever since joining the army, he had complained to Crete about his bouts with diarrhea, but now, he said, they were worse than ever. He also had been weakened by his reaction to a smallpox vaccination. All in all, he said, he had lost twenty pounds. He was more worried about his men; 400 of them were in the hospital, where as many as fifty had died, twenty-two of them from his own 42d Ohio. "A noble young man from Medina County died a few days ago," he said. "I enlisted him, but not till I had spent two hours in answering the objections of his father who urged he was too young to stand the exposure. He was the only child.... I declare to you there are mothers and fathers in Ohio that I hardly know how I can ever endure to meet."

Garfield, too, had had enough of the Big Sandy. But, before leaving, he had one more job to do—attack Pound Gap and destroy Marshall's camp there. It was from that camp, Garfield believed, that the bushwhackers were getting their supplies and their orders.

On March 15, he set out upriver with a force of 600 infantry and 100 cavalry, all picked (and fit-for-duty) men. To make things easier, the column was divided into two detachments, part of the infantry and all the cavalry under Major McLaughlin following the river, the rest of the infantry under Garfield taking what amounted to a rough bridle path over some of the meanest terrain in all of Kentucky. "It is the worst country to get around in I ever saw," Garfield wrote his mother, Eliza.

Garfield's plan of attack was once again—what else?—his favorite pincers movement. McLaughlin's cavalry was to proceed along the river road to the foot of the Gap, "then march boldly up and make a show of an attack in front, keeping at sufficient distance to avoid serious losses, but pressing the attack with enough vigor to keep the enemy busy and interested," Private Mason said. Meanwhile, Garfield and the bulk of the infantrymen were to climb to the mountain crest—miserable, hard work—and then to descend on the enemy's flank and rear, cutting off their retreat. Unfortu-

nately, McLaughlin's column began its part of the show at a time
when Garfield and the main column were still a mile or more of
rugged ground from their destination, delayed by a heavy snowfall.
The Gap's 300 defenders were alerted by McLaughlin's premature
demonstration, and when pickets came running into camp with the
news that more Yankees were making their way down the mountain side, they all began to scamper. "A sharp fire was immediately
opened upon them," Mason recalled, "but it was like shooting birds
on the wing. Three of the enemy were killed, four wounded, and
four or five captured; the rest escaped." Garfield himself took up
arms. "I fired one shot among them and the boys say I felled one,
but I think and hope not." The "hope not" is interesting. Garfield at
this stage of the war was belligerent, but his attitude against the
South still hadn't hardened completely.

Garfield's men were surprised by the enemy's cozy quarters.
"Sixty permanent and comfortable log huts, including a quartermaster's and commissary department, magazine and hospital, were
abandoned in a few minutes," Mason said. "Food was left cooking
before the fires, dinner left unfinished, and guns, clothing and other
property abandoned in terrified haste and confusion." The Yankees
took what they could carry, ate the rebels' dinner, and then burned
everything in sight.

When Marshall, still recuperating at his headquarters at Abingdon, heard about the raid, he called out the militia to meet what he
said was an invasion of Virginia by an army of 7,500 men. Garfield
and his 700-man patrol returned to their base in Piketon, their
work in the Big Sandy Valley finished.

Back home in Ohio, Garfield's friends, armed with stories about
his military prowess, had been busily promoting his career. On February 3, all the members of the Ohio state senate (with the exception of two who were at home sick) signed a letter to President
Lincoln urging the commissioning of Colonel Garfield as a
brigadier general. The senators said Garfield's "ability and skill" had
been amply manifested in "meeting and vanquishing" Humphrey

Marshall. His sycophantic friend Harry Rhodes said that some Buckeyes were even expressing the belief that Garfield should succeed General McClellan. His chief Washington lobbyist was no less a power broker than Salmon P. Chase, the treasury secretary and the former governor of Ohio.

Who would dare say no? Garfield received his promotion on March 19, backdated to January 10 to mark his victory at Middle Creek.

On March 24, General Garfield and the boys of the 42d began moving downriver, out of the terrible Big Sandy Valley and on to Louisville and the big war. Colonel Cranor was left behind with his own regiment, the 40th Ohio, and the 14th Kentucky to maintain order in the valley. Private Mason said the regimental band played a familiar gospel hymn, "Oh, ain't I glad to get out of the wilderness," as the steamers pulled away. The regiment arrived in Louisville on March 29 and went into camp in "civilized surroundings," where, Mason said, it "gave itself up to the work of preparing pay-rolls, and restoring its clothing and equipage to the proper order."

Garfield received orders on April 3 to report to Buell's head-quarters for a new assignment. His regiment received orders at the same time to join the 7th Division, commanded by General George W. Morgan and operating near the Cumberland Gap. The boys of the 42d boarded the railroad cars on April 13, feeling instinctively, Mason said, "that the beloved commander who had created the Forty-second and led it to its first victory, was lost to it, and that as a Regiment it would see him no more."

Parting was bittersweet for Garfield too, made all the more grievous by the news that his favorite officer, Major Williams, one of the heroes at Middle Creek, had died of typhoid fever. Garfield left his old command without making a formal farewell. "I dare not let the 42d Regiment know I am going," he told Crete. "It might make a scene. I know it would nearly break me down."

His new assignment was command of the 20th Brigade, made up of the 64th and 65th Ohio, the 13th Michigan, and the 51st Indiana regiments. The first night, the bands from the two Ohio regiments appeared in front of his tent and gave him a nice welcoming serenade. "But no matter what other regiments may be to me," he said, "I mourn like a bereaved lover for my dear old 42d."

Garfield's victory in Kentucky was part of a string of Union successes in the winter of 1861–1862 that included Thomas's victory at Mill Springs over Zolicoffer and Grant's dramatic capture of both Forts Henry and Donelson. The road was now clear for Grant, with his 42,000-man Army of the Tennessee, and Buell, with his 20,000-man Army of the Ohio, acting together to clear all of central Tennessee and to secure the entire Mississippi Valley.

Grant engaged the Confederate general Albert Sidney Johnston and his 45,000 rebels at Pittsburg Landing, or Shiloh, on April 6 and April 7 in a decisive battle so bloody and so desperate it stunned the entire nation, North and South. Bruce Catton, the grandest of all Civil War historians, says Shiloh "underlined one of the basic facts about the war—that it was being fought by men of enormous innate pugnacity: tenacious men who would quit a fight once begun only when someone was *beaten.*"

Buell's Army of the Ohio arrived on the battlefield the second day, greeted by cries of joy from Grant's exhausted soldiers, who had come so close to losing the battle. Garfield's brigade brought up Buell's rear, the last to cross the river, and as a result saw very little of the action. But Garfield for the first time witnessed the detritus of a terrible battle. "The horrible sights I have witnessed on this field I can never describe," he told Crete. "No blaze of glory that flashes around the magnificent triumphs of war can ever atone for the unwritten and unutterable horrors of the scene of carnage."

A few days after the battle, he met two of the war's finest correspondents, Whitelaw Reid of the *Cincinnati Gazette* (whose 12,000-word story about the battle was a stunning achievement) and his future biographer, Charles Carleton Coffin of the *Boston Morning Journal.* "I saw the commander of a brigade exercising it upon the double-quick," Coffin wrote years later in his campaign biography of Garfield. "The troops were marching in column, moving with precision at the word of command, charging bayonets, wheeling to the right and left, in admirable order.

"'It is Colonel Garfield, who won the Battle of Middle Creek,' said my fellow-correspondent, Whitelaw Reid. . . . Courteous and hearty our reception."

Garfield was impressed; these were important men to a soldier with political aspirations. Reid had aspirations too; he would become a celebrated New York editor and Benjamin Harrison's running mate in his losing bid for reelection in 1892. No wonder Garfield was courteous and hearty. In a letter to Crete the next day, he urged her and their friends to read Reid's dispatch, for "it is, in the main, very correct and is one of the best battle sketches I have seen."

The question of slavery didn't arise in the Big Sandy Valley for the simple reason the white farmers there were too poor to own slaves. Confederate officers, though, traveled with personal slaves and one of them, known simply as Jim, "fully armed and equipped and dressed in rebel uniform, braving the fire of both parties, climbed down the hillside and came to our men and said he wanted to see the commander," Garfield told Crete. "I kept him in camp a few weeks and found him to be very intelligent and thoroughly honest and faithful." Jim eventually made his way to Hiram and went to work for the Garfields.

In Tennessee, Garfield was forced to deal with slavery in a much more challenging way. One day an escaped slave, badly bruised, arrived in Garfield's camp and pleaded for sanctuary. Two or three days later, a horseman rode into camp demanding that Garfield deliver the escaped slave so that he could return him to his master. One of Garfield's early biographers, John Clark Ridpath, said the "human bloodhound" ordered Garfield to hunt the escaped slave down. Garfield refused, in an act requiring a certain amount of courage at this early stage of the war. "My soldiers are here for other purposes than hunting and returning fugitive slaves," he said.

"My people on the Western Reserve of Ohio did not send my boys and myself down here to that kind of business, and they will back me up in my action."

In a revealing letter to Harry Rhodes from his camp in the field nine miles from the Shiloh battlefield, Garfield expounded on his increasingly radical views:

> A command in the army is a sort of tyranny and in a narrow and ignoble mind engenders a despotic spirit, which makes him [the commander] sympathize with slavery and slaveholders. There is at the same time in the position of a soldier in the ranks which makes him feel the abridgment of liberty and the power of tyranny.... When as at Nashville our soldiers were obliged to stand ground at the gates of wealthy rebel nabobs and be insulted and abused by the very men and women whose homes they were protecting, they cannot but be taught the lesson that slavery and its ministers hate the man who walks in any humble path of duty....
>
> There is something amounting almost to a conspiracy among leading officers, especially those of the regular army, to taboo the whole question of anti-slavery and throw as much discredit on it as upon treason. This purpose is seen in both their words and acts. I have been made deeply indignant at many things which I hope some day to tell you. So far from these things influencing me, I find myself coming nearer and nearer to downright abolitionism.

The professional officers reluctant to condemn slavery were, for the most part, Democrats, and increasingly Garfield came to equate those opinions with treason. His opinion of West Pointers was hardly improved by the bumbling performance of General Halleck, generalissimo of all Union forces in the West, as he slowly inched his way toward the Confederate stronghold at Corinth, Mississippi. The whole campaign—hardly a shot was fired in anger—ended in fiasco when the rebels abandoned the position and quietly slipped away. "It makes me indignant to see the attempts made by General Halleck to show that 'the enemy were furiously cannonaded and forced to make a hurried and disastrous retreat.' There could be no greater falsehood. Our cannonading was wholly a work of outposts. We threw shells into the bushes with light artillery but not one shot was fired from any of the hundred heavy siege guns that for ten days could have filled Corinth with shells." The whole business was a "disgrace," Garfield fumed.

Perhaps his friends back home sensed his frustration. At any rate, they began working behind the scenes to make him a member of the House of Representatives in the 1862 elections. "I dare not think of Congress now," Garfield wrote Crete, while giving it very serious thought indeed, "though I should be pleased to take part in the legislation of the next few years." In another letter to his wife, Garfield said he remembered promising his friend and fellow teacher at the Eclectic, Almeda Booth, that he would not use his military success "as a stepping stone to political preferment, and I shall make no effort. But if the people want me, they can say so even if I should not be out of the army by December."

"I cannot for a moment think of taking any course which may even by inference throw a shadow of suspicion upon those motives as being for political and demagogical purposes," he told Harry Rhodes.

His friends knew their man. They concluded—for all his hand-wringing—that, when the time came, he would be eager to move on to a new challenge in the House of Representatives. Crete, alone, seemed doubtful. "I don't know," she said, presciently, "but *politics* is to be the death of you yet."

His health continued to be a nagging problem—this time, he said, he lost forty-three pounds—and he finally managed to return home to Hiram on a well-deserved sick leave in August. He was still at home recuperating when the Republicans held their nominating convention for the open seat in the 19th District in Garrettsville on September 2. It was a spirited contest—even without

Garfield in the hall—and he didn't vanquish his opponent, John Hutchins, until the eighth ballot. In the general election in October, he easily carried the district by 7,000 votes. But since the 38th Congress would not convene until December 1863, there was no immediate need for him to resign his commission.

It was while he was still at home, in mid-September, that he received a telegram from Secretary of War Edwin Stanton ordering him to report to the nation's capital for reassignment. He hadn't been in town very long before he was occupying a comfortable room in Secretary Chase's home and being entertained by the secretary's lively daughter, Kate, the belle of Washington society. Crete got wind of this and was not pleased. "From your letters to others I learn that you and Miss Kate are taking dinners out, visiting camps, etc., and I have a good deal of woman's curiosity to hear about some of these doings; and is Miss Kate a very charming, interesting young lady? I may be *jealous* if she is, since you have such a fashion of being enamoured with brilliant young ladies."

Garfield's reply was probably not exactly what Crete wanted to hear. "She is a woman of good sense and pretty good culture," he said, "has a good form but not a pretty face, its beauty being marred by a nose slightly inclined to pug. She has probably more social influence and makes a better impression generally than any other cabinet lady."

Two days later, on October 14, Garfield told Crete he was planning to travel to Lewisboro, New York, to visit his old flame when he was at Williams College, Rebecca Selleck, who had almost succeeded in breaking up their engagement. Of all the women in the world Crete distrusted the most, Rebecca topped the list. On October 19, in a postscript, Garfield told Crete, "Rebecca sends love to you and Trot."

That same day, Crete wrote this remarkable letter to "my own Jamie."

I suppose you are with Rebecca today.... I have been passing through a great struggle since I received your letter last night, and whether I should write anything to you of it has been a serious question. Before you came home last summer, I had settled down on this conviction that the threads of our lives had become so entangled with others that it was only useless to try and unravel them, and the best we could do was to gather them up as they came and finish out the rest of our life as best we could. But during your visit [on sick leave] you know how unintentionally and almost unconsciously we turned back together and looked through the tangled past and with what surprise and great joy we found the links we called broken only hidden.... In the new light and life and love which sprang up around and before us, I then resolved—cost what it might—no concealment of anything in my heart should ever again be allowed. You should know all the love and tenderness it felt, and if the darkness of doubt or distrust fell upon it you should know that too. Now, darling, don't begin to tremble lest something terrible is to come. When I read your purpose to visit Rebecca, the old pain came back to my heart, and I seemed to be going all back into that cold darkness, and in all that you had said to me. I began to fear there was only inconsistency which showed nothing but a desire to deceive me. Now, Jamie, I have confessed all.... I have asked myself why I should tell you of it at all, and it is not so much that you should know it as to school my own heart to a perfect freedom with you.

Garfield answered this moving letter by telling Crete that he prayed she would be ready "to bear with me if at any future moment my heart should for a time go down again into the deeps." Crete replied that if he should go down in the deeps again he shouldn't think of trying to conceal it from her. "Your eye never deceives me," she said. All of this was going on at a confusing time when Crete and little Trot were trying to settle down in the family's first real home in Hiram.

Garfield could be a trial. Crete was distressed and irritated again when Harry Rhodes showed her a letter Garfield had written to him in which he whined about how poor he had once been, "overgrown, uncombed, unwashed," and how much his early struggles still troubled him. Crete, in her own gentle way, told Garfield to pull his socks up and get on with his life. "I do not believe," she said, "you would have been as good and noble and not half as great had not your career been one of struggle. Jamie, how it would break your little mother's heart to read that letter [to Harry Rhodes], and I beg of you do not indulge in any more such *wicked*—yes, I do feel they were wicked—reprovings."

She wrote again on December 21, after being told her husband wouldn't be coming home for Christmas. By now, it would appear, even Crete's overflowing good nature was being severely tested. "Jamie," she said, "I should not blame my heart if it lost all faith in you, but I hope it may not. I am not going to let it; but I shall not be forever *telling* you how much I love you when there is evidently no more desire on your part for it than present manifestations indicate."

That letter really stung. "I want you to look at your words again," Garfield said in a passage marked *Personal and Confidential,* "and ask yourself whether you ought to have written them to me. A husband should not only be a faithful husband but should also be a noble manly friend and a wife should be a noble womanly friend. Now Crete, if a mere friend should write such a sentence to me, I should consider it an imputation upon my honesty." He begged Crete never to write to him in that way again.

At the very end of the letter, he told Crete his heart "longs to clasp you to it and answer all your doubts by the warmth of its presence and love. Write to me and forgive me if I have wronged you. Ever and forever. Your James." Crete had made her point, and from then on the relationship took a turn for the better.

It probably helped that Garfield was put to work in Washington, serving as a judge in the war's most controversial court-martial, the trial of Brigadier General Fitz John Porter (West Point, Class of

1845) for disobeying orders and misbehaving in the face of the enemy at the Second Battle of Bull Run on August 29 and 30, 1862.

Porter, in fact, had not distinguished himself in the battle, but then, hardly anyone else had either, least of all the bumbling Union commander Major General John Pope, outfought and outgeneraled by Robert E. Lee and Thomas "Stonewall" Jackson. Porter's particular problem was his politics; he was a Democrat and a McClellan disciple, and McClellan was the man the Radical Republicans really wanted to destroy. The Radical Republicans, led by Benjamin Wade, Thaddeus Stevens, and Charles Sumner and supported by Treasury Secretary Chase, favored emancipation, the sooner the better, and believed a vigorous prosecution of the war, leading to unconditional victory, was the only way to destroy slavery. They firmly believed that West Point itself was unacceptably aristocratic and suspected that most West Pointers opposed emancipation and favored a negotiated end to the war.

Lincoln laid down a serious challenge to his opponents when he delivered the preliminary version of his Emancipation Proclamation on September 22, less than a month after Pope's terrible defeat at Bull Run but just a few days following McClellan's finest hour, his standoff with Lee and Jackson at Antietam.

Lincoln and his supporters worried what the army might do, and the army they had in mind was McClellan's army, the Army of the Potomac. It was the only army high command that had openly and even passionately aligned itself with the administration's opponents.

General Porter expressed his opposition to the emancipation proclamation in letters to the *New York World,* an outspoken Democratic newspaper. He said "the proclamation was resented in the army . . . amounting, I have heard, to insubordination." Fighting men, he said, "are tired of the war and wish to see it ended honorably by a restoration of the union—not merely a suppression of the rebellion." He said the proclamation was "absurd" and that the man who had issued it, his commander in chief, was a "political coward."

Surely it is true that Porter was court-martialed as a kind of substitute for McClellan and that the case against him was not very convincing (one historian called it, hyperbolically, "an American Dreyfus affair"), but it is hard to work up much sympathy for him.

Secretary of War Stanton named the judges for the court-martial—three major generals and seven brigadiers. Secretary Chase undoubtedly put forward Garfield's name, knowing he shared almost all of the views of the Radical Republicans. "Great things are expected from you on the court," Chase is said to have told Garfield.

Garfield didn't need prompting. Porter must have seemed to him the personification of everything he disliked about the army—the arrogance of the West Pointers, the failure of so many generals to act boldly when facing the enemy, the treasonable behavior of Democrats in general and Democratic generals in particular. (He and Chase were convinced that McClellan was a part of a scheme to overthrow the government. Fortunately Lincoln, a calmer, wiser man, didn't share their views.) Garfield said after the war that no public act with which he had ever been associated seemed so right to him as the unanimous verdict against Porter.

Porter was "cashiered" from the army on January 10, 1863. For years thereafter, his supporters labored to repair his reputation, and Garfield fought them every step of the way. It wasn't until 1886, five years after Garfield's death, that Porter was placed once again on the army's active roll by a special act of Congress signed by President Grover Cleveland, a Democrat who had avoided military service by paying a man to take his place in the Union army.

Chapter 6

CHICKAMAUGA

OFFICIALS AT THE War Department knew they had something of a tartar on their hands in the person of James Garfield—a congressman-elect, a close confidant of Secretary Chase, and an increasingly noisy supporter of the Radical Republicans' agenda. Garfield himself, still seeking glory on the battlefield, wanted some kind of independent command to demonstrate to the West Pointers how to win battles. Opportunities were dangled in front of him and then just as quickly pulled away—an expedition to Florida, a campaign to capture Charleston, a command in East Tennessee. To while the time away, he began (but never finished) writing a biography of Frederick the Great.

His patience was running short when he was offered a job with Major General William S. "Old Rosy" Rosecrans, who had started the war as colonel of Hayes's and McKinley's 23d Ohio. Rosecrans had moved on to succeed Buell as the commanding general of the Army of the Cumberland and had recently (December 31–January 2) defeated Braxton Bragg in a bloody encounter at Stones River, near

Murfreesboro, Tennessee. In that battle, Rosecrans's chief of staff, the much-admired Julius P. Garesche, had been killed when a rebel shell struck him square in the face. Rosecrans needed a new chief of staff. The thirty-one-year-old Garfield came riding into Rosecrans's camp on January 25, 1863, a prime candidate to fill that vacancy.

They talked for hours that night, and for many nights thereafter, probing deeply into the war and their own views of man and his relationship with God. Rosecrans, forty-three years old and a West Point graduate (Class of 1842), was a devout Roman Catholic—"a Jesuit of the highest style of Roman piety," Garfield noted, "a man of very decided and muscular thoughts and with a rare Friedrichian quality of having his mind made up on every important question." He is, said Garfield, "an effective, successful general."

Rosecrans was a clever and inventive character. In his early days in the army, he had designed barracks, forts, wharves, and a new Washington navy yard. He had invented much-improved dredging machinery and found a new way to lay concrete piers under water. After he resigned his commission, he had built refineries and invented what his biographer said was "the first kerosene lamp successfully to burn a round wick."

In his experiments with kerosene, he had burned himself badly and had been left with "distorting, livid scars [that] gave a permanent 'smirk' to his face." It was perhaps because of this disfigurement that he shied away from public speaking. One thing he may have liked about Garfield was his boisterous nature and his willingness to face public scrutiny. Garfield, he figured, could be his spokesman.

Rosecrans's main concern about Garfield was that he might be too political and that he had come to his army to spy for his friends in Washington. That first night's long bull session, with all of its deep probing into the meaning of God's will, may have relieved many of those doubts. Garfield, on the other hand, understood that his friends in Washington worried that Rosecrans was hard to handle and a chronic complainer. "By taking that position [as chief of staff]," he had written Harry Rhodes, "I should make a large investment in General Rosecrans, and will it be wise to risk so much stock in that market?" Garfield could talk a good Christian game about the meaning of life after death, but he was just as concerned about what was going to happen to him here on Earth.

It wasn't until February 13—after hours of talk—that Rosecrans offered Garfield the chief of staff job. "I am almost alone in regard to counsel and assistance in my plans," he told Garfield, "and I want a power concentrated here that can reach out through the entire army and give it unity and strength." Garfield caught the drift of what Rosecrans was trying to tell him—that he needed more than just a paper-shuffling chief of staff. What he really wanted "was an adviser, a kind of alter ego," a chief of staff in the European mold, "the most important and desirable position next to the Commanding General himself." Garfield saw possibilities in that role.

In a letter to Secretary Chase the next day, Garfield said he thought that he had seen the "interior of General Rosecrans' nature as fully as I ever did that of any man I ever knew and am glad to tell you that he is sound to the bone on the great questions of the war and the way it should be conducted." In other words, he was sound politically. Garfield shouldn't have been writing private appraisals of his commanding general to a powerful member of President Lincoln's cabinet; this time, though, it did no harm because the letter was so positive. In the future, Garfield's letters to his Washington patron would be critical, and controversial.

For week after week, Rosecrans's army dallied and dithered, never moving from its base camp at Murfreesboro. This inaction was precisely the sort of thing that drove Garfield mad; he hated delay of any kind. Besides, he only had so much time left to give to the war before taking his seat in Congress in December. But he put up with the delays, going along with Rosecrans's constant complaints that he needed more of this and more of that. Horses were a particular obsession; he could never get enough of them (and many of those he did get he had to send back because they weren't fit). Quartermaster Montgomery Meigs replied, with a heavy dose of sarcasm, that even "a herd of buffalo resting for four months on a prairie in one place would starve.... The rebels will never be conquered by sitting in their front."

Garfield craved action. He figured, quite sensibly, that if rebel raiders such as Nathan Bedford Forrest, John Hunt Morgan, and Joe Wheeler could raise such hell behind his lines, why couldn't he raise the same kind of hell behind theirs? It was his idea—he wrote the orders—to send a brigade commanded by Colonel John Coburn of the 33d Indiana to scout enemy dispositions in front of Rosecrans's lines and to do a little foraging. They set out from Franklin, Tennessee, on March 4 and were ambushed the very next day by rebel Major General Earl Van Dorn and 6,000 cavalrymen at Thompson's Station. Coburn lost forty-eight men killed, 247 wounded, and more than 1,150 captured. Garfield said he was mortified by the defeat. "The rebels drew our military fools into a regular cul-de-sac and then closed up on them and captured them," he told Crete.

But he wasn't so mortified he wouldn't keep trying. A month later, he urged the formation of a Union raiding party to destroy rebel trains, wagons, and supplies in Alabama, with himself in command. "I have set my heart on this expedition more than on any one thing since I have been here," he told Secretary Chase. Rosecrans gave the go-ahead to the raiding party but said Garfield was too important to him to be spared. Instead, the command of the expedition was given to Colonel Abel D. Streight of the 51st Indiana. "I have had the entire burden of getting up and fitting out the expedition," he told Crete.

The expedition set out from Eastport, Mississippi, on April 22; it probably was doomed from the start. Only half the men were mounted—on mules, the idea being they would capture enough mules en route to mount the rest. Many of the mules, though, suffered from distemper, and the ones who weren't sick were so lively that the infantrymen assigned to ride them kept falling off. They were joined by another column from Grant's command in Corinth, Mississippi, under Colonel Greenville Dodge, who was to be the decoy. Dodge was supposed to draw the rebel cavalry away from Streight as he made his way back to Grant's lines. Unfortunately, the rebel cavalry was commanded by Nathan Bedford Forrest himself, and he wasn't fooled. He pursued Streight for 125 miles until he finally cornered him, hungry and exhausted, between Gadsden, Alabama, and Rome, Georgia. Streight surrendered the whole party on May 3—1,446 men and whatever number of mules were still fit for service. Brigadier General David S. Stanley, who would be Garfield's severest critic, called the expedition a "fool's plan" that had ended in a "contemptible fizzle." It was, he said, all Garfield's fault, for the chief of staff was a man with "no military ability."

In fact, however, it wasn't as bad as all that. If Rosecrans had assigned cavalrymen riding healthy horses to undertake the raid, things might have worked out better. Mules were a mistake.

Garfield, amateur soldier that he was, had a better idea of what this war was about than some of the West Pointers. In a letter to Chase on May 5, two days after Streight surrendered to Forrest, he said:

I [have] been anxious to impress upon the general [Rosecrans] the truth that our true objective point of operations is the rebel army and not any particular position or territory. In Europe, if an army becomes master of London, Paris, Vienna, or Berlin, it has conquered England, France, Austria, or Prussia. Not so with the Confederacy. We may take Richmond, but they can put their government with all its archives on wheels and trundle it away into the interior in 48 hours. Nothing but hard blows that will break their armies, and pulverize them can destroy the Confederacy. I am, therefore, for striking, striking, and striking again till we do break them.

But striking and striking again didn't seem to be what Rosecrans had in mind. Lincoln and the War Department had been testy
about Rosecrans all along, and now they were positively irate. "I
would not push you to any rashness," a sarcastic Lincoln wired
Rosecrans, "but I am very anxious that you do your utmost, short
of rashness, to keep Bragg from getting off to help [Joe] Johnston
against Grant." Rosecrans's army was the only one that could do
something (Grant's Army of the Tennessee was tied down in front
of Vicksburg, and the Army of the Potomac seemed institutionally
incapable of making any movement at all), but Rosecrans wouldn't
budge. Washington wanted him to attack Bragg, now.

Everything was ready—except Rosecrans. On June 8, he tried
to pass the buck to his three corps and thirteen divisional commanders. He asked each of them to answer three key questions.
One: Do you think that Bragg's army has been so weakened by
sending detachments to other fronts that attacking him at this time
could reasonably lead to a great and successful battle? Two: Do you
think an advance by our army at this time would be likely to pre-
vent additional reinforcements being sent against Grant by Bragg?
Three: Do you think an immediate or early advance of our army
advisable?

They all met in Rosecrans's tent on June 9, with several newspaper reporters lurking outside, looking for news (of which, so far,
there had been precious little). All of the generals, including Phil
Sheridan and George Thomas, made the first two questions pretty
much moot by saying, in answer to the third, that they opposed an
early attack. Not one believed Rosecrans should advance "until
Vicksburg's fate is determined." That was an extraordinary thing
to say because the whole point of a move by Rosecrans's powerful
army was to engage rebels who might otherwise be used to lift the
siege and to destroy Grant.

One of the reporters, James R. Gilmore, had been sent by his
boss, Horace Greeley, the foolish and eccentric proprietor of the
New York Tribune, to sound out Rosecrans on the possibility of

challenging President Lincoln for the Republican nomination in 1864. Greeley, for whom being panic-stricken was almost a way of life, was convinced Lincoln was a failure. Nothing would come of the Rosecrans bubble.

Garfield couldn't vote in this conclave because he was a line officer, not a field commander, but he stepped into the discussion anyway and told the sixteen generals, West Pointers for the most part, that they were all wrong and then went on—in a long paper that marks a highlight of his military career—to tell them just why they were wrong. Garfield may have been wrong himself on one or two points; basically, though, he had it right. His report, said Whitelaw Reid, that paragon of war correspondents, was "the ablest military document known to have been submitted by a Chief of Staff to his superior during the war." Garfield, Reid said, "stood absolutely alone, every General commanding troops ... either openly opposed or failed to approve an advance. But his statements were so clear and his arguments so forcible that he carried conviction."

He made a number of salient points. Bragg's army, he said, was now weaker than it was at Stones River, Rosecrans's bloody victory in January. So, with superior strength, now was the time to move. Chances are good, he said, that a sudden and rapid movement would lead to a general engagement, "and the defeat of Bragg would be in the highest degree disastrous to the rebellion." Finally, Garfield, the loyal Republican, said a great victory would guarantee Lincoln's success at the polls in 1864.

Twelve days later, the army moved. An angry Major General Thomas L. Crittenden approached Garfield the morning the advance began. "It is understood, sir," he said, "by the general officers of the army, that this movement is your work. I wish you to understand that it is a rash and fatal move, for which you will be held responsible."

The army moved because Garfield, outnumbered sixteen to one by the professionals, carried the day. Garfield was smart, maybe even brilliant. His role in getting Rosecrans and all those generals to begin the advance against Bragg was an astonishing personal success.

We know that Garfield played a key role in getting the army moving. What we don't know for sure is just how big a role he played in designing the strategy for a brilliant campaign of maneuver that forced Bragg out of central Tennessee without firing very many shots.

Garfield himself never took credit for being the father of that strategy, although he came close in a letter to Crete dated June 29. "Our operations thus far have been successful beyond the expectations of every one outside headquarters," he said. "I have studied all these movements carefully beforehand, and I am delighted to see how fully my judgment has been vindicated."

The campaign looked curiously like Garfield's campaign in the Big Sandy Valley. It was bold and aggressive, and it made the most of good intelligence. It was filled with diversions—campfires with no soldiers, troops rushing here and there to confuse the enemy. These were all Garfield trademarks.

Rosecrans himself, when the campaign was successfully concluded, said he was indebted to Garfield, "ever active, prudent and sagacious. I feel much indebted to him for both counsel and assistance in the administration of this army. He possesses the energy and instincts of a great commander."

Bragg's army, based at Tullahoma, manned a defensive line on hilltops behind the Duck River, between Murfreesboro and the Tennessee River. The hilltops were broken by four gaps—Manchester, Liberty, Bellbuckle, and Guy's, each defended by cavalry and infantry. The Union Army moved against each of the passes in rapid succession, just as Garfield had moved on the three roads leading to Paintsville.

Rosecrans's first move was a feint to his west, toward Shelbyville, led by Gordon Granger and his corps, hoping by that move to pin down the rebel defender, William J. Hardee. Thomas Crittenden and his corps would lead a feint at the other end of the line,

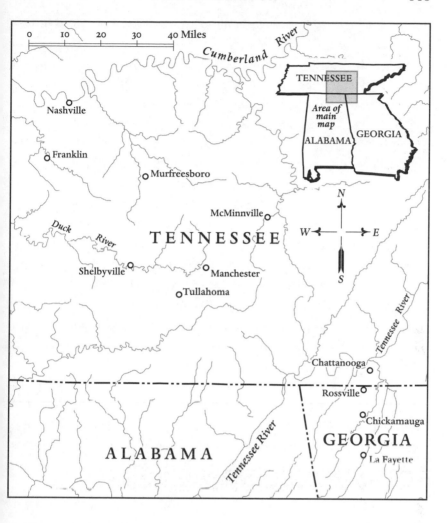

toward McMinnville. The main attack, led by Thomas and Alexander McCook, would come straight down the middle, pointed toward Manchester. It was wonderfully complex—a sure sign of Garfield's hand—involving feints within feints and campfires where there were no soldiers.

The dash through Manchester (or Hoover's) Gap was led by Colonel John T. Wilder's brigade of mounted infantrymen from Indiana and Illinois. Wilder's men were armed with five-shot

Spencer repeating carbines. Wilder himself had borrowed money from bankers back home in Greensburg, Indiana, to buy the weapons, and they were now being used for the first time in the western theater. They more than made up for the cavalry shortage Rosecrans had complained about—for so long and so frequently that the War Department had begun to grumble about the telegraph bills.

Wilder's 2,000 Yankees raced through the lightly defended three-mile gap (the feints were working) and overran a veteran rebel regiment, the 1st Kentucky, capturing its colors. Wilder then dug in and repelled a counterattack until Thomas's and McCook's infantrymen, slogging through a steady and unrelenting rainfall, arrived. The way was now open to advance on Manchester and cut off the retreat of both Hardee and Bishop Polk. It was the sort of maneuver Garfield had always dreamed about, and it almost worked. Just in the nick of time, Bragg, suffering from boils and feeling poorly, saw what Rosecrans (and Garfield) were up to and ordered a hasty retreat to Tullahoma, his main depot, eighteen miles away.

"Tullahoma had then only a small garrison," Garfield told Crete, "and we could have gotten in ahead of Bragg as our plan was, but for the extraordinary rains which rendered the roads almost impassable. I have never seen so much rain fall in the same length of time. It began the morning we started and it has rained every day since." The rain was something nobody could do anything about. But Rosecrans had another problem—one he had allowed to happen before—excess baggage. His officers and men had brought too many personal belongings with them, and they were filling the wagons and clogging the roads. Garfield, as chief of staff, was outraged. "Officers and soldiers who are ready to die," he said in a formal order, "do not hesitate to disgrace themselves and imperil the army by [bringing with them] luxuries unworthy of a soldier." Get rid of the stuff, he commanded.

With Wilder causing consternation in his rear and with the formidable Thomas threatening him with eight veteran divisions on his flank, Bragg reckoned once again that he had been outgeneraled. He ordered another retreat, and this one would take his army all the way to Chattanooga, down on the Georgia line, an immensely significant railroad depot the South simply couldn't afford to lose. And so, in a brilliant campaign of maneuver, Rosecrans and his chief of staff, exercising "the energy and instincts of a great commander," had forced the enemy to abandon all of fertile Middle Tennessee. "This is a great disaster," Bragg conceded.

But Garfield knew what might have been, if only the army had begun its campaign earlier, when the weather was so much better. "I shall never cease to regret," he said, "the sad delay which lost us so great an opportunity to inflict a mortal blow upon the centre of the Rebellion." Even so, the army's success proved Garfield had been right and those sixteen generals wrong when he had stood alone in calling for the campaign to begin.

He must have had mixed feelings when he heard the smashing news that George Gordon Meade had won a great victory over Lee at Gettysburg on July 3 and that Vicksburg and its 30,000 defenders had fallen to Grant on Independence Day. What a perfect trifecta it would have been if Rosecrans had also managed to destroy Bragg's army.

Garfield pleaded with Rosecrans to keep trying, to pursue Bragg and to force an engagement. "There are the strongest possible reasons for using every moment now before the rebels can recover from their late disaster," he said. Timing was even more important than he thought because for the first time in the war the Confederates were thinking about using some of Lee's troops to reinforce a western army, in this instance Bragg's Army of Tennessee. Jefferson Davis, a West Pointer himself, was worried; Ambrose Burnside's independent corps had taken Knoxville on September 3, and a junction of Burnside's and Rosecrans's armies seemed imminent. He summoned Lee to Richmond, and they discussed strategy in talks that ranged over two full weeks. At Davis's urging, Lee finally agreed to send James Longstreet and two divisions (12,000 men) to Chattanooga. Joe Johnston had already agreed to send two more divisions (another 12,000 men) to Chattanooga from his army in Mississippi. Eight thousand more rebel troops were called in from Simon Bolivar Buckner's army in East Tennessee. It was, in fact, the kind of joint exercise that the so-called western concentration bloc had been urging for months. Rosecrans and Garfield didn't know it, but Bragg would soon be a much tougher nut to crack.

To Garfield's disgust, Rosecrans crawled back in his shell and refused to come out. On July 27, three weeks following the successful Tullahoma campaign, Garfield wrote a dramatic letter to his patron Secretary Chase in Washington, severely criticizing his own commanding general. Rosecrans's worst fears about Garfield—that he would be a spy for his friends in Washington—were now realized (although he wouldn't know about the letter until years later).

Garfield told Secretary Chase that the railroad bridges had all been rebuilt by July 18 and that the trains "were in full communication from the Cumberland to the Tennessee [Rivers]. I have since then urged with all the earnestness I possess a rapid advance while Bragg's army was shattered and before Johnston and he could effect a junction." He continued:

> Thus far the General has been singularly disinclined to grasp the situation with a strong hand and make the advantage his own. I write this with more sorrow than I can tell you, for I love every bone in his body, and next to my desire to see the rebellion blasted is my anxiety to see him blessed. But even the breadth of my love is not sufficient to cover this almost fatal delay.
>
> My personal relations with General Rosecrans are all that I could desire. Officially I share his counsels and responsibilities even more than I desire, but I beg you to know that this delay is against my judgment and my every wish. Pleasant as are my relations here, I would rather command a battalion that would

follow and follow, and strike and strike, than to hang back while such golden moments are passing. But the General and myself believe that I can do more service in my present place than in command of a division, though I am aware that it is the position that promises better in the way of promotion or popular credit. But if this inaction continues long I shall ask to be relieved and sent elsewhere, where I can be part of a working army.

A number of things can be said about his ill-conceived letter. First, to give Garfield his due, he undoubtedly was upset and distressed by Rosecrans's failure to pursue Bragg and force a decisive battle. He was always a man of action, and so those feelings in the letter were quite genuine. But he knew what he was doing. He was Rosecrans's chief of staff, a position demanding discretion and, above all, loyalty, and he was being both indiscreet and disloyal. The letter is self-serving. Don't blame me, he is telling Chase (who, he knows, will tell others), I may love every bone in Rosecrans's body, but I'm not responsible for what's going on here. Furthermore, if things get worse, I'm going to abandon my general, join a "working army," and win "popular credit." On the other hand, if things get better, I will still be here, the chief of staff, in a position to win part of the credit.

West Pointers despised and distrusted political generals; they were convinced the politicians in uniform put their own careers ahead of the army. Garfield, at moments such as this, was what they had in mind.

What part Garfield's letter played in Rosecrans's downfall is still debated. Surely it set the stage for the ensuing drama.

Rosecrans finally set off over the rugged Cumberland Mountains for Chattanooga the morning of August 16. In a letter to Crete on September 1, Garfield boasted that "it is not vanity for me to say that no man in this army can fill my place during this movement. It would take him several months to learn the character and condition of affairs as I know them and to hold that influence with the Commanding General that I do."

The advance on Chattanooga was filled with the special effects that marked all of the campaigns in which Garfield had played a part. Wilder and his "lightning brigade" created a diversion, setting up once again a string of camp fires to warm and feed nonexistent soldiers and even tossing wooden scraps into the river to convince rebels downstream that he and his men were building pontoon bridges.

The ruse worked. By September 8, all three of the infantry corps had crossed the Tennessee River (even though the cavalry, to Rosecrans's dismay, seemed to be hanging back). The next day, Crittenden's corps entered an empty Chattanooga; Bragg had pulled out, and Rosecrans figured he had his enemy on the run, speculating he was headed for Rome, Georgia, more than fifty miles away.

But Bragg was a better soldier than that. He saw that Rosecrans's three corps were widely separated, too far from each other to come to one another's assistance in the event of an attack. With his reinforcements streaming in by railroad cars, his army was now bigger than his enemy's, the kind of advantage that rarely fell into a rebel general's lap. "They are better able to fight us now with some chance of success than they have been before for a long time," Garfield told Crete. He didn't say so—he hardly needed to—but by delaying his movement for so long, Rosecrans had allowed Bragg the chance to make a counterattack.

Of Rosecrans's three corps, Thomas's, advancing toward La Fayette, was the most exposed, and Bragg ordered two of his generals, Thomas C. Hindman and Daniel H. Hill, to make an attack that seemed to offer every chance of success. But things never worked out for Bragg, and both generals, unbelievably, refused to move. The next day, September 11, Bragg ordered another attack, this one by Hindman (again) and Buckner. They also refused. By this time, Thomas had caught on that he was exposed and in trouble and had begun a withdrawal. Bragg turned next to Polk and ordered him to attack Crittenden's corps, also exposed and isolated, on September 13. But—no surprise—Polk balked. Bragg by now had ordered four different generals to attack exposed Union positions, and all four had refused. It is hard to imagine that anything quite like this had ever happened to a Confederate army (or many other professional armies, for that matter). It allowed Rosecrans time to concentrate his army and avoid what could have been a humiliating piecemeal defeat.

"A battle is imminent," Garfield wrote Harry Rhodes on September 13. "I believe the enemy now intends to fight us. He has a large force and the advantage in position. Unless we can outmaneuver him we shall be in a perilous position. But we will try. Our strategic success has been most brilliant thus far."

Rosecrans's army was positioned at McLemore's Cove, a break in the mountains between Missionary Ridge and Pigeon Mountain. Bragg's army was positioned behind Pigeon Mountain. All that separated them was a valley, through which the Chickamauga Creek flowed. Bragg now came up with a plan that met the approval of his cranky generals—he would send troops up the valley, cross the creek, crack through to Rossville and the only road leading through Missionary Ridge to Chattanooga twelve miles away, and catch Rosecrans in a warren of dead-end alleys from which there would be no escape.

It would have worked on Friday, September 18, because there weren't enough Union soldiers standing in the way to stop it. By Saturday, though, "Old Pap" Thomas (he was only forty-seven; he just seemed much older) had filled the gap; he had marched all night, burning picket fences to light the way, to get in position in the woods just east of Snodgrass Hill. Bragg began his attack at dawn on Saturday, sending his troops against what he thought was Rosecrans's vulnerable left flank. The fighting quickly turned into a melee, "a soldier's battle," the ebb and flow of which was understood by no one. Colonel Wilder, commander of the lightning brigade, said years later that "the two armies came together like two wild beasts, and each fought as long as it could stand up in a knock-down and drag-out encounter."

Garfield and Rosecrans tried to direct the battle from their headquarters in the kitchen of the Widow Glenn's home south of Snodgrass Hill. Garfield spread out his maps and dispatches on the kitchen table, according to Allan Peskin, his biographer. The widow herself, "with frightened children clinging to her skirt, hovered nervously by. Every now and then, Garfield would look up from his work to give the children a reassuring pat on the head."

But there wasn't very much to direct, for neither Rosecrans nor Garfield had any notion of what was happening. The fighting raged all day, in woods and underbrush, concentrated more and more in front of Thomas's position. There wasn't much room for artillery or horses; one rebel general, never an admirer of cavalry, was astonished to find that Nathan Bedford Forrest's troopers had entered the battle as foot soldiers.

Both sides rested fitfully that night, knowing the battle would be decided the next day. Bragg reorganized his army into two divisions during the night, putting Polk in command on his right, with corps commanded by Hill and Robert J. Walker, plus Benjamin F. Cheatham's division and Forrest's cavalry. He put Longstreet, freshly arrived from the east, in command on his left, with John Bell Hood's and Simon Buckner's corps, Hindman's division, and Joe Wheeler's cavalry. Still hoping to crush Rosecrans's left, he ordered Polk to attack at daybreak. But in the great tradition of nothing ever going right for Bragg, Polk didn't make his move until 9:00 A.M. Sunday. Thomas, the best fighting man on the field, held his position against wave after wave of rebel attackers, bearing the brunt of the battle. He had no choice but to ask Rosecrans for help. In response to that appeal, Rosecrans ordered a division from his right, where there wasn't much going on, to go to Thomas's aid, but the division lost its way. When reinforcements failed to arrive, Thomas asked again for help, and Rosecrans, believing that Thomas must be in truly desperate circumstances, sent more reinforcements. By doing so, he gradually depleted the number of troops holding the front south of Snodgrass Hill.

At about 10:30, a messenger arrived at Rosecrans's headquarters to report that one of the Union divisions, John Brannan's, was out of position, leaving an inviting gap between divisions commanded by Thomas J. Wood and Joseph J. Reynolds. Rosecrans hastily dictated an order to Wood, who had a history of disregarding Rosecrans's orders (they had had a fight over an order just a few days earlier). "The general commanding directs that you close upon Reynolds as fast as possible and support him," it said. Garfield wrote all the orders at Chickamauga—except this one. This one—the fatal one—was taken down by Major Frank Bond. But Garfield was there, and when he saw a puzzled look on the messenger's face, he said the order simply charged Wood with closing the gap caused by Brannan's withdrawal from the front line.

The distance between Rosecrans's headquarters and General Wood's headquarters was only 600 yards, perhaps a one-minute gallop or a five-minute walk. Wood had the order in his hand minutes after it was written, and he was puzzled by what it seemed to be saying, and well he might have been. He knew, if Rosecrans did not, that Brannan hadn't pulled his division out of the line at all. He was right where he had always been, holding the ground between Wood's and Reynolds's divisions. Wood told the messenger that no gap in the lines existed, and the messenger rode back to Rosecrans's headquarters and explained that Brannan was still in position and that the confusion had been cleared up.

But Wood, still stewing over his altercation with his commanding general, took the order at face value—and, incredibly, pulled his division out of line and marched it around behind Brannan's division so he could "close upon Reynolds as fast as possible and support him." He never told Rosecrans what he was doing, even though he could have easily strolled over to his headquarters to make sure he was doing the right thing.

The timing couldn't have been worse. Just as the petulant Wood marched his division away, Longstreet with more than half of the rebel army came crashing through the position he had so recently abandoned. Charles A. Dana, the New York journalist who had become the assistant secretary of war, was visiting the Army of the Cumberland when the fighting began. He had been taking a quick nap when Longstreet's soldiers came charging into the Union lines, hollering triumphant rebel yells. Awakened, he said, "by the most infernal noise I ever heard," the first thing he remembered seeing was Rosecrans, the devout Roman Catholic, crossing himself. "Hello," he said, "if the general is crossing himself we are in a desperate situation."

Desperate it was. The whole right wing of Rosecrans's army had given way, terrified soldiers running pell-mell to the rear, carrying the commanding general, the assistant secretary of war, the chief of staff, and everything else with them.

Garfield and Rosecrans made their way on horseback to the Dry Valley Road, and down that road toward Rossville, at the opening of the gap that led to Chattanooga and safety. Garfield never wrote a full account of the day's terrible events, but he did talk to friends, and it is from those talks that we get his damaging testimony about Rosecrans's behavior. One of the friends he talked to was his old friend and state senate roommate, General Cox.

We sat alone in my room [in Cincinnati], face to face, at midnight, and Garfield described to me the scene on the 20th of September on the battlefield, when through the gap in the line made by the withdrawal of Wood's division the Confederates poured. He pictured the astonishment of all who witnessed it; the doubt as to the evidence of their own senses; the effort of Sheridan further to the right to change front and strike the enemy in flank; the hesitation of the men; the wavering and then the breaking of the right wing into a panic-stricken rout, each man running for life to the Dry Valley Road, thinking only how he might reach Chattanooga before the enemy should overtake him, officers and men swept along in that most helpless of mobs, a disorganized army. He described the efforts of Rosecrans and the staff to rally the fugitives....

The staff and orderlies gathered about Rosecrans and tried to make their way out of the press. With the conviction that nothing more could be done, mental and physical weakness seemed to overcome the general. He rode silently along, abstracted, as if he neither saw nor heard. Garfield went to him and suggested that he be allowed to try to make his way by Rossville to Thomas, the sound of whose battle seemed to indicate he was not yet broken. Rosecrans assented listlessly and mechanically. As Garfield told it to me, he leaned forward, bringing his excited face close to mine, and his hand came heavily down upon my knee as in whispered tones he described the collapse of nerve and of will that had befallen his chief. The words burned themselves into my memory.

Garfield, Cox wrote, called for volunteers to accompany him in his ride to join Thomas, to give him the bad news about the rest of the army and to see how Thomas was faring, but only two orderlies and his aide-de-camp followed him. They passed through a "gauntlet of the enemy's fire" as they passed Kelly's farm. In a letter to his mother, Garfield said he undertook the ride "with very little expectation of passing through unharmed and how I escaped death I do not know. I do not know the orderly who fell by my side. My horse Billy was not killed. He was slightly wounded but he is now well again, and I love him all the more for being hit."

The ride became a legend, the one event in Garfield's life that was remembered best by all his contemporaries (other than his death itself) and by all those who chose to vote for him in 1880. "Cannon shot plow the ground beneath his horse's feet," Coffin wrote in his campaign biography, "shells burst around him. He rides through a shower of leaden rain—runs a gauntlet of fire, and comes out upon a knoll where he can overlook the battlefield. . . . General Garfield beholds the scene. It is the one supreme moment of his life. The battle is not lost after all. 'Our flag is still there!'"

John Clark Ridpath, a more imaginative biographer, took it up another notch:

Then began the world-famous ride.... It was a race between the rebel column and the noble steed on which Garfield rode. Up and down along the stony valley road, sparks flying from the horse's heels, two of the party hatless, and all breathless, without delay or doubt on dashed the heroes.... At last they reached a cotton field. If the enemy was near, it was almost certain death. Suddenly a rifle-ball whizzed past Garfield's face. Turning in his saddle, he saw the fence on the right glittering with murderous rifles. A second later a shower of balls rattled around the little party. Garfield shouted, "Scatter gentlemen, scatter," and wheeled abruptly to the left. Along that side was a ridge. If it could be reached, they would be safe. The two orderlies never reached it. Captain Gano's horse was shot through the lungs, and his own leg broken by the fall. [Ridpath forgot to mention what happened to the second orderly.] Garfield was now the single target for the enemy.... In ten minutes Garfield was at his [Thomas's] side, hurriedly explaining the catastrophe at noon. They stood on a knoll overlooking the field of battle. The horse which had borne Garfield on his memorable ride dropped dead at his feet.

There was even a popular poem, called "Garfield's Ride at Chickamauga," by Heze Butterworth. Here's a sampling:

> *I see Longstreet's darkening host*
> *Sweep through our lines of flame,*
> *And here again, "The Right is lost!"*
> *Swart Rosecrans exclaim.*
> *"But not the left," young Garfield cries;*
> *"From that we must not sever,*
> *While Thomas holds the field that lies*
> *On Chickamauga River."*
>
> *Through tongues of flame, through*
> *Meadows brown,*

Dry valley roads concealed,
Ohio's hero dashes down
Upon the rebel field.
And swift, on reeling charger borne,
He threads the wooded plain.
By twice a hundred cannon mown,
And reddened with the slain.

O chief of staff, the nation's fate,
That red field crossed with thee....

During his lifetime, Rosecrans gave a number of versions of what happened at Chickamauga on September 20, 1863. In the first one—his official report about the battle—he said that when he heard "the enemy's advancing musketry and cheers, I became doubtful whether the left had held its ground, and started for Rossville. On consultation and further reflection, however, I determined to send General Garfield there, while I went to Chattanooga, to give orders for the security of the pontoon bridges at Battle Creek and Bridgeport, and to make preliminary dispositions either to forward ammunition and supplies, should we hold our ground, or to withdraw the troops into good position.... General Garfield dispatched me the [news of] the triumphant defense our troops there made against the assaults of the enemy."

But Garfield always insisted it was his idea to make the gallant ride to join Thomas, and that a beaten and dispirited Rosecrans agreed to let him go. Either way, Rosecrans made the wrong decision. He should have galloped to Thomas's side (he had done the same sort of thing with ringing success at Stones River), and Garfield should have gone to Chattanooga. It was a big mistake, and it was seen as such at the time. "It was the fatal mistake of his life," Whitelaw Reid reported. "I do not know that his friends make any defense for him on this point."

There wasn't much Garfield could do for Thomas except deliver the bad news that the rest of the army had been routed. "We have repulsed every attack so far," Thomas told Garfield, "and we can hold our ground if the enemy can be kept from our rear." Garfield was deeply impressed. It was "a glorious moment," he said, and he spent the rest of day in what his biographer called "a fever of exaltation." He must have known he was witnessing history— Thomas's rock-like defense against wave after wave of rebel attackers. Thomas, "the Rock of Chickamauga," became Garfield's greatest military hero.

Rosecrans and Dana knew little of this. Dana, who had been sending telegraphs back to the War Department for two days, reporting the ups and downs of the battle like one of those early dot-dash baseball broadcasters, reached a peroration with the one sent at 4:00 P.M. that stated, MY REPORT TODAY IS OF DEPLORABLE IMPORTANCE. CHICKAMAUGA IS AS FATAL A NAME IN OUR HISTORY AS BULL RUN.

In his wire to Halleck, the commanding general in Washington, Rosecrans was just as gloomy. WE HAVE MET WITH A SERIOUS DISASTER; EXTENT NOT YET ASCERTAINED. ENEMY OVERWHELMED US, DROVE OUR RIGHT, PIERCED OUR CENTER, AND SCATTERED TROOPS THERE. Thomas, he added, with seven divisions, "remained intact at last news." He learned more about his army's plight when he received a report from Garfield at about 5:00 P.M. "General Thomas has Brannan's, Baird's, Reynolds', Wood's, Palmer's and Johnson's divisions still intact after terrible fighting. [Gordon] Granger [and his reserves] is here, closed up with Thomas and is fighting terribly on the right. Sheridan is in with the bulk of his division, but in ragged shape, though plucky and fighting.... I hope General Thomas will be able to hold on here till night." Four hours later, he sent another report to Rosecrans, arguing that the rebels were played out and could be whipped by an attack in the morning. "Thank God," Rosecrans cried out, as he read the good news from Garfield. He sent a reply to Garfield, telling him he could spend the night with Thomas and adding, "I like your suggestions."

By 8:00 P.M., then, it was clear that the defeat wasn't as bad as everyone but Thomas thought. In two days of bloody fighting, Bragg had lost a third of his army, most of them piled in stacks in front of Thomas's position, seasoned troops he was unlikely ever to replace. And Rosecrans, battered and defeated as he may have been, still held Chattanooga, which, after all, had been the campaign's objective from the beginning.

Thomas, worried about being cut off, marched his weary troops back to Chattanooga that night, leaving the field to the rebels. By 8:00, even the gloomy Dana was able to say, in still another of his telegrams, I AM HAPPY TO SAY THAT MY DISPATCH OF 4:00 P.M. TODAY PROVES TO HAVE GIVEN TOO DARK A VIEW OF OUR DISASTER.

In a letter to Crete on September 23, Garfield said his memory of the two-day battle "fills me with grief and pride commingled.... We must save ourselves if saved at all. I expect the battle will be renewed this morning and with fury. If calamity befalls us you may be sure we will sell ourselves as dearly as possible."

On that same day, he sent an important telegram to his patron, Secretary Chase. WE CAN STAND HERE TEN DAYS, IF HELP WILL THEN ARRIVE. IF WE HOLD THIS POINT WE SHALL SAVE THE CAMPAIGN, EVEN IF WE LOSE THIS ARMY. Chase rushed over to the War Department, telegram in hand, and conferred with Secretary Stanton, who had already received a telegram from Dana making pretty much the same point. They were soon joined by President Lincoln, Secretary of State William H. Seward, and General Halleck. They agreed to rush reinforcements to Chattanooga by rail. Seven days later, 20,000 men, with all their equipment, poured into a depot near the beleaguered city on a train, divided into sections, that was six miles long. It was a vivid demonstration of the power of the railway steam engine.

Heading toward Chattanooga as well, by slower steam boat, were 17,000 veterans of Grant's Vicksburg campaign under William Tecumseh Sherman. The Union, then, was sending 37,000 men to reinforce Rosecrans; the Confederacy was sending just one—President Jefferson Davis. He arrived at Bragg's camp October 3 and found most of his generals in open rebellion against their commanding officer's leadership. They wanted a new man in charge, but Davis couldn't find anyone to fit the bill. He went home, and Bragg remained in command of an unhappy army.

Technically, Chickamauga was a Union defeat. But one of the rebel generals, Daniel Hill, wrote years later that "the élan of the Southern soldier was never seen after Chickamauga [in the Western theater].... He fought stoutly to the last, but, after Chickamauga, with the sullenness of despair and without the enthusiasm of hope." Rosecrans himself told Halleck that "we have taken the starch out of him."

Time was now running out for Congressman-elect Garfield. He was relieved as chief of staff on October 10 and sent on his way six days later with a ringing commendation from his chief. "His high intelligence, spotless integrity, business capacity, and thorough acquaintance with the wants of the army will render his services, if possible, more valuable to the country in Congress than with us," Rosecrans said. "Reluctantly yielding to this consideration, the General Commanding relieves him from duty as Chief of Staff. In doing so he returns his thanks to Gen. Garfield for the invaluable assistance he has rendered him by wise councils and assiduous labors, as well as for his gallantry, good judgment and efficiency at the Battle of Chickamauga." Garfield was specially urged to give a full and fair account of the army's condition to Secretary Stanton and General Halleck.

On his way to Louisville to meet Stanton, Garfield read in a newspaper that Rosecrans had been replaced as commanding general of the Army of the Cumberland by Thomas and that Grant had been placed in charge of all the armies in the west. In a letter to Rosecrans, he said, "The action of the War Dep't fell upon me like the sound of a fire bell. I am sure that it will be the verdict of the people that the War Dep't has made a great mistake and have done you a great wrong."

The letter was dishonest. Garfield hadn't been surprised by Rosecrans's downfall; he knew it was coming. He had, in fact, played his own small but significant role in making it happen. The *New York Herald*'s Henry Villard was in Chattanooga when Garfield was making his farewells and remembered Garfield telling him that his confidence in Rosecrans as a fighting man had been severely shaken and that he was not sorry to part company with him. Garfield repeated those same thoughts in his meeting with Stanton in Louisville.

The change in command undoubtedly was beneficial. Grant's army met Bragg at Chattanooga on November 23–25 and won one of the most lopsided victories in the entire war. Bragg's rebels were routed on Missionary Ridge by—and surely this was only justice— Pap Thomas and his Chickamauga veterans.

Garfield, promoted to major general by Lincoln in recognition of his services at Chickamauga, headed home to Hiram to meet his second child, Harry, and to renew his acquaintance with Crete and little Trot. He tarried there only briefly, hurrying on to Washington. Garfield had hardly unpacked his bags when Secretary Chase invited him to take part in an emancipation meeting in Baltimore and to address the crowd at Monument Square. By all accounts, Garfield's speech was a roaring success.

Everything was running in Garfield's direction—the war, politics, his own domestic life—until he was urged late in November to come home, for little Trot was gravely ill with "lung fever." In a letter to his friend Harmon Austin, dated December 1, he said, "Our darling Trot died at 7 o'clock this evening. We bury her day after tomorrow morning at 10 1/2 o'clock.... Only such as you can know how desolate our hearts are tonight." She was two-and-a-half years old.

He was back in Washington December 6, the day he resigned his army commission. He had served for a little over two years— from August 12, 1861, to December 6, 1863. He took his seat in the House of Representatives still dressed in his general's uniform.

Garfield's record in the army was a formidable one. He had led a small army, greatly outmatched, and won a striking victory in the Big Sandy Valley. He had played a major role in pushing a reluctant Rosecrans to move against Bragg, and he had been one of the principal framers, maybe *the* principal one, of the Tullahoma strategy that had chased Bragg completely out of central Tennessee. He had done the right thing in galloping to Thomas's side at Chickamauga. Rosecrans said he possessed the energy and instincts of a great commander, and quite possibly he did. All of these things are true, and yet they are forever marred by Garfield's own devious and self-serving nature. We can say in his defense that he genuinely believed in the Union cause; as a soldier, he was touched with fire. But what burned brightest was his passion for success as a politician.

Chapter 7

THE WEST VIRGINIA CAMPAIGN

PRIVATE WILLIAM McKINLEY said he first took note of Major Rutherford B. Hayes on July 23, 1861, the day the boys from the 23d Ohio Volunteer Regiment were issued rifles. They were clumsy old muskets, converted to percussion caps from flints. The men, McKinley said, were disappointed; they believed they were entitled to "the best arms then known to military science." They refused to accept them.

McKinley said the officers were particularly concerned because General John C. Fremont, the legendary pathfinder and Republican presidential candidate in 1856, was planning to stop by that day to review the troops. He was en route from Washington to St. Louis to take over the western command. The troops, McKinley said, were told the regiment would be disgraced if they didn't show up on the parade ground with their weapons. They seemed to agree with that and reluctantly accepted the old muskets, but only for the review. General Fremont, time running short, limited his inspection to the boys of the 23d. He "seemed a great man to me, a boy ...

whose mind had been thrilled with the story of his wonderful adventures in the west," McKinley recalled. "I remember he pounded my chest and looked square into my eyes, and finally pronounced me fit to be a soldier."

When they returned to their barracks following the parade, Hayes's friend, Lieutenant Colonel Stanley Matthews, told his troops that any man who refused to accept the old muskets would be shot, "depend upon it." Hayes, McKinley said, was more tactful. He went to their tents and cabins and reasoned with them. "He said that many of the most decisive battles of history had been won with the rudest weapons. At Lexington and Bunker Hill and many other engagements of the Revolution our forefathers had triumphed over the well-equipped English armies with the very poorest firearms—and that even pikes and scythes had done good work in that glorious conflict. Should we hesitate at the very start of another struggle for liberty and union, for the best and freest Government on earth, because we were not pleased with the pattern of our muskets, or with the caliber of our rifles?"

Anyway, Hayes said, most of the modern weapons had been stolen for the South, by the "mean craftiness" of President James Buchanan's last secretary of war, John B. Floyd. The old muskets being issued them—muzzle loaders, with smooth bores firing a round bullet and buckshot—were the best the government could find. They would get better weapons later, when they were available. The men thought briefly about what Hayes had said and nodded their heads in agreement. "Bully for Hayes!" one Irish private is supposed to have shouted. "Come boys, let's get our guns." They returned to the arsenal and collected their weapons.

It was only in this way—by the power of persuasion—that these Civil War volunteers could be led. Hayes understood that from the beginning. Hayes's manner, McKinley said, "was so generous and his relations with his men were so kind, and yet always dignified, that he won my heart almost from the start.... From that moment our confidence in our leader never wavered."

As the war progressed, Hayes, thirty-eight, and McKinley, eighteen, formed what was almost a father-son relationship.

At the start of the war, their regiment was commanded by Colonel Rosecrans, who would soon move on to bigger jobs. Matthews was the regiment's lieutenant colonel. Major Hayes was next down the chain of command.

"Ours is the best regiment, two companies from Cleveland, one from Sandusky, one from Bellefontaine, and one from Ashtabula [with five more still on the way]," Hayes told his wife, the redoubtable Lucy Webb. Colonel Rosecrans, he added, "is an energetic, educated West Pointer, very cheerful and sensible."

Hayes, determined, courageous, impetuous, would fight in a dozen battles and any number of smaller skirmishes and engagements. He would be wounded four times, once seriously. McKinley would see a fair share of action too, but never in the same dramatic way as Hayes.

"Hayes took desperate chances in battle," McKinley said, years after the Civil War ended. "He seemed like one inspired. His quiet nature at once changed. He permitted nothing to stand in his way, and he often recklessly exposed himself."

For four years he commanded the 23d Ohio Volunteers or the brigade to which the 23d was attached. Hayes, who always said he would rather be a good colonel than a poor general, was a very good colonel indeed, the apotheosis of the successful volunteer soldier. "Without these colonels, men like Hayes just out of civilian life but who were able to master the art of war, the armies could not have operated," the historian T. Harry Williams writes.

McKinley said Hayes "was the most beloved officer in the regiment from the beginning to the end of the war. He was ever looking after the care and well-being of the thousand young men who came from different parts of the state, strangers to him, with no military experience, and no experience in taking care of themselves." The regiment cherished Lucy too; she often came to camp, with one or more of the children, to visit her husband.

"There was no flaw in his character," McKinley said, with a certain amount of exaggeration. "He was not a brilliant man as we speak of brilliant men, but he was a wise man—always safe and always in touch with the best thought of the people. He was steady in thought and purpose."

Of all these future presidents, McKinley was the only one who entered the army as an enlisted man. In the first year of the war, most of the enlisted men were teenagers. They were all volunteers, eager and patriotic in ways that the young men who followed them (and had read about the horrors of war) never were. Bell Irvin Wiley, the great Civil War historian, examined the muster rolls of scores of Union companies and discovered more than 300 occupations and specialties. Artists and barkeepers, brokers and brakemen, chemists and contractors, dancing masters and ditchers, grocers and glass blowers, hairdressers and heelers, Indian lecturers and ironworkers, landlords and locksmiths. The list went on and on.

There were more farmers than anything else. Laborers, carpenters, shoemakers, clerks, blacksmiths, and house painters came next. The typical northern regiment had in it men who could do all kinds of things. Wiley said a colonel of a Michigan regiment asked during dress parade if there was anyone in the regiment with printing experience. Eight men stepped forward. Benjamin Harrison discovered the same thing when his 70th Indiana Volunteers, riding on railroad cars, found the rebels had destroyed a bridge over a ravine. Several of his men had worked on railroads, Harrison was told, and one of his officers had supervised the building of railroad lines. They rebuilt the bridge in three hours.

Most of the men—three-quarters or more—were American-born. That was true of the 23d Ohio; it was mostly native-born, with all the men speaking English. Other regiments, however, contained ordinary soldiers from many places—Germany most frequently, then Ireland. But there were also soldiers from England, Canada, Scandinavia, Switzerland, France, Mexico, and Poland. Some of those men spoke English haltingly or not at all.

Almost all of the native-born Americans could read and write—but not very well. Spelling was always a bit of a problem, even for the generals. McKinley, a very good speller, was more refined than most. He had been reared in a well-educated family, and he had spent a few weeks at college. It was inevitable that his commanding officers, sooner or later, would put his skills to work.

McKinley was deeply private, cautious, and very religious as a young man. He wrote a few entries in a diary he kept during his early days in the army and mailed a few gossipy letters to newspapers back home, but nothing after that. But he too, on a smaller scale, was a successful soldier—moving up the ranks from private to commissary sergeant to lieutenant, captain, and, by the end of the war, when he was twenty-two years old, major. The Civil War was McKinley's undergraduate education.

We know a lot about Hayes because he wrote a diary almost every day during his entire adult life. During the Civil War, he wrote hundreds of letters, most of them to Lucy or to his uncle and surrogate father, Sardis Birchard. They have all been preserved (including Lucy's "Dearest Ruddy" letters to him).

Rosecrans didn't linger long as commander of the 23d. He was promoted to brigadier general and transferred to western Virginia to command Union troops there. Another West Pointer, Eliakim P. Scammon of Maine, succeeded him as colonel of the regiment. Hayes's friend, Matthews, who had vowed to shoot those who wouldn't accept the weapons, didn't understand how to deal with volunteers. Colonel Scammon wasn't any better. "He is a gentleman of military education and experience," Hayes wrote in his diary. "Amiable and friendly with us [his officers]—an intelligent, agreeable gentleman, but not fitted for volunteer command, and I fear somewhat deficient in health and vigor of nerve."

Hayes was happier about the regiment's new surgeon, Dr. Joseph Webb, Lucy's talented, good-natured brother. Dr. Joe served an important role in the months and years that followed, for he was someone Hayes could turn to for advice and comfort.

One of the 23d's officers, Captain Russell Hastings, recalled in his memoirs that the men were still "a ragged lot" at the end of June:

> We made the civilian clothes last from day to day and week to week, until Falstaff's rag-a-muffins were by comparison well dressed. The first issue of [army] clothes was only undershirts and drawers, blouses and trousers not arriving until some days afterwards. At the evening parade on the first day of the first issue, the regiment appeared dressed only in these shirts and underdrawers. Imagine Colonel Scammon's horror when he appeared on our front to take command of the parade. Later he ordered all the officers to his headquarters and such a lecture we got! We were quite content with words only as we feared being placed "under arrest," whatever that might be.

Hastings said the officers were almost as ragged as the men. It was up to the officers, he pointed out, to supply their own uniforms, including one suit at least with cocked hat, epaulets, and sword. "We were out of money and did not expect to see a paymaster for months, if ever. What should we do? The matter was solved one day by the appearance of a Jew clothier who solicited orders. He would give us credit until a paymaster should appear; but, we said, 'no one knows where we then will be or who will have been killed.' 'Oh!' he said, 'but you are all gentlemen and I trust you. If some are killed I will put that down to the cause. I began to think a Jew was not such a bad fellow." The uniforms arrived a few days later. The blue cloth, Hastings complained, soon turned to "a dingy purple."

With his superiors away on business in Cincinnati, Hayes found himself in command of the camp and its 2,500 recruits—"an odd position for a novice, so ignorant of all military things. All matters of discretion, of common judgment, I get along with easily, but I was for an instant puzzled when a captain in the twenty-fourth [regiment], of West Point education, asked me formally, as I sat in my tent, for his orders of the day, he being officer of the day. Acting on my motto, 'When you don't know what to say, say nothing,' I merely remarked that I thought of nothing requiring special attention; that if anything was wanted out of the usual routine I would let him know."

Hayes, sickly as a boy, adapted quickly and easily to camp life. "The evenings and night are capital," he wrote in his diary. "The music and hum, the cool air in the tent, and open-air exercise during the day, make the sleeping superb.... Our men are fully equal to the famous Massachusetts men in a mechanical way. They build quarters, ditches, roads, traps; dig wells, catch fish, kill squirrels, etc., etc., and it is really a new sensation, the affection and pride one feels respecting such a body of men in the aggregate."

At the same time, Hayes felt a little guilty about leaving Lucy to rear the boys and to manage the family's finances. "I am sorry you are to be left with so much responsibility," he told his devoted and competent wife, but, "with your mother's advice, do what you both agree is best and it will perfectly satisfy me."

On July 16, Hayes told his wealthy bachelor uncle Sardis, "our men are uniformed and we are daily receiving our needful equipments. The indications are that we shall soon move. In what direction and under whose command, we do not know. We are not very particular. We prefer the mountainous region of Virginia or Tennessee." Hayes's regiment broke camp on July 25 and set off by train and steamboat for the mountainous region of western Virginia.

The forty-six counties of western Virginia—what officially became the state of West Virginia in 1863—were populated by rugged men and women, descendants of the early Scotch-Irish and German settlers. The terrain wasn't much different from what Garfield and his Ohio boys had found not so far away in eastern Kentucky. But the populace was a little more sophisticated, just a little more interested in the world around them. What distinguished them especially was their long-standing distaste for the slaveholding aristocrats from the other side of the Blue Ridge

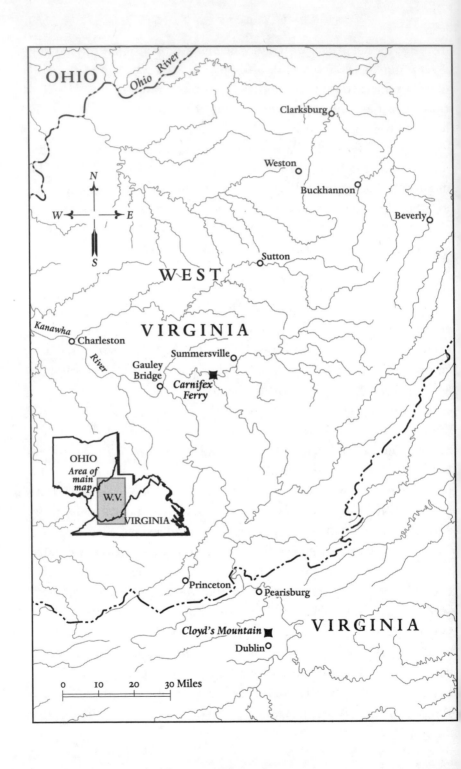

Mountains who had run their lives for decades. Most of the West Virginians wanted no part of secession. They began early on to separate themselves from the Confederacy.

Controlling western Virginia probably wasn't absolutely critical for either side, but it was widely seen to be important, for bragging rights if for no other reason. Confederate military leaders believed that by holding western Virginia they could threaten the Union's main lifeline to the west, the Baltimore & Ohio Railroad. Union leaders, on the other hand, believed their armies might be able to cut through western Virginia to Richmond or, failing that, to destroy the South's main lifeline to the west, the Virginia & Tennessee Railroad.

Fortunately for the Union, the South had more trouble organizing credible fighting armies in western Virginia than it had anywhere else. Fighting in western Virginia—let us call it West Virginia from now on—began in May 1861. Rebel forces were defeated at Philippi on June 3 and skedaddled from the battlefield with such alacrity that the engagement was celebrated in the North as the "Philippi Races." George B. McClellan commanded the Union troops and won such fame for his minor, inconsequential victories that Lincoln brought him east and put him in charge of the Army of the Potomac.

That left the war's two zaniest generals, the rebels Floyd and Henry A. Wise, in command in western Virginia. Floyd was the same fellow who surrendered Fort Donelson to Grant in February 1862. Wise was another former governor of Virginia, and he and Floyd, long-standing political rivals, hated each other with such a consuming passion that they had almost no time to think about what they should be doing to defeat their real enemies, the converging armies from the North.

Hayes and the 23d arrived in Clarksburg on July 26. "We were received everywhere with an enthusiasm I never saw anywhere before," he told Lucy. "Old men and women, boys and children— some fervently prayed for us, some laughed and some cried; all did

something which told the story. The secret of it is, the defeat at
Washington [Bull Run on July 21] and the departure of some thousands of three-month men of Ohio and Indiana led them to fear they
were left to the rebels of eastern Virginia. We were the first three-
years men filling the places of those who left. It was pleasant to see
we were not invading an enemy's country but defending the people
among whom we came. Our men enjoyed it beyond measure. Many
had never seen a mountain; none had ever seen such a reception."

General Rosecrans, Hayes noted in his letter to Lucy, "is with
us." The 23d's first colonel was, in fact, now the general in command of all Union troops in West Virginia.

Hayes and his boys had hardly settled down when Rosecrans
ordered them to pack up and move out to Weston, a village twenty-
three miles to the south. "Busy from 4 A.M. packing baggage,"
Hayes wrote in his diary. "Baggage enormous and extra; great
delays; great stew. Our new Irish quartermaster—a failure so far."
Because of all the confusion, the regiment didn't get underway
until almost noon. "Scenery fine," Hayes said. "Blackberries beyond
all experience line the road. . . . [We are] in the enemy's country,
although all we meet are Union men. Many [of the Union soldiers]
fancied threatening dangers in all novel sights. A broken limb in a
tree top was thought to be a spy looking down into the camp; fires
were seen; men riding by were scouts of the enemy, etc., etc."

Some of the soldiers, loaded down with fifty pounds of equipment, lightened their load and began to straggle. Scammon, the
West Pointer, was furious. "The march of yesterday," he said,
"should be enough to demonstrate to every officer and man of this
command the necessity of preserving discipline while on the
march. The march of a Battalion [the same thing as a regiment]
must not be allowed to become the straggling journey of a mob."
He continued to pick away in the days that followed, complaining
about foul smells in the camp and gambling among the troops.

Weston was an important strategic center, standing where the

Staunton and Parkersburg and the Weston and Gauley Bridge turnpikes crossed. From this location Union troops could defend the Baltimore & Ohio line to the north or move out in almost any direction to attack Confederate positions. At the same time, Weston stood in the way of rebel forces that might be tempted to move toward West Virginia's great valley, the Kanawha. Union troops under Jacob Dolson Cox, Garfield's old roommate in Columbus, had already occupied the valley.

Bushwhackers were always a problem in the mountain regions of the South, and they were active in West Virginia. These ubiquitous guerrillas knew the territory, all the lonely paths and trails. The terrain gave them a big advantage, for they could strike almost anywhere and retreat to sanctuaries buried inside the sparsely populated mountain valleys and ridges. There, rebel sympathizers would warn them of Union patrols, give them food and supplies, and protect them.

The very character of these mountaineers—"individualistic, undisciplined, slovenly, suspicious, and full of guile," according to one account—made bushwhacking a spontaneous or natural form of warfare. The disciplined Union troops, who had never seen such country as this or such people as these, feared and despised the mountain fighters.

In a diary entry, Hayes described the body of one of these mountain men brought in by a patrol from the 23d's sister regiment, the 10th Ohio. "He followed their regiment, shooting at them from the hills. They took him in the Bulltown region. He wore neither hat nor shoes, was of gigantic size—weighing two hundred and thirty pounds; had long hooked toes, fitted to climb—a very monster. They probably killed him after taking him prisoner—perhaps after a sort of trial. They say he was attempting to escape."

The Union troops did the best they could to track down these elusive "wild men of the mountains." "We are kept very busy," Hayes wrote Uncle Sardis, hunting up guerrillas, escorting trains, etc. Attacking parties are constantly met on the roads in the mountains, and small stations are surrounded and penned up.

We send daily parties of from ten to one hundred on these expeditions, distances of from ten to forty miles. Union men persecuted for opinion's sake are the informers. The Secessionists in this region are the wealthy and educated who do nothing openly, and the vagabonds, criminals, and ignorant barbarians of the country; while the Union men are the middle classes— the law-and-order, well-behaved folks. Persecutions are common, killings not rare, robberies an every-day occurrence.

Some bands of rebels are so strong that we are really in doubt whether they are guerrillas or parts of Wise's army coming in to drive us out. The Secessionists are boastful, telling of great forces which are coming. Altogether, it is stirring times just now.

Young McKinley said in a letter to his mother that he was on one of these bushwhacker patrols, "led by a certain lieutenant of our regiment. It would have done you good to have seen the above lieutenant prodding the thick bushes with his gilded sword, fancying to himself that he saw the hideous monster in the shape of a rebel. Ah—the ambitious officer was disappointed; instead of sticking a secesh [a secessionist], he without doubt stuck a skunk. We came to this conclusion from the fact that a strong smell, a venomous smell, instantly issued from the bushes."

McKinley recorded in his diary on August 16 that he was in camp in Glenville, "a town of about half dozen houses, and I should judge a similar number of inhabitants":

Tomorrow's sun will undoubtedly find me on the march. It may be I may never see the light of another day. Should this be my fate I fall in a good cause and hope to fall in the arms of my blessed redeemer. The record that I want left behind, that I not only fell as a soldier for my Country, but also a Soldier of Jesus. I may never be permitted to tread the pleasant soil of Ohio, or see and converse with my friends again. In this emergency let ... my parents, brothers and sisters, and friends have their anxiety removed by the thought that I am in the discharge of my duty, that I am doing nothing but [that which] my revolutionary fathers before me have done, and also let them be consoled with the solacing thought that if we never meet again on earth, we shall meet around God's throne in Heaven. Let my fate be what it may. I want to be ready and prepared.

The amusing skunk letter to his mother was the sort of thing you might expect from a lively teenaged soldier. The diary entry, on the other hand, is gloomy. The suspicion is that he may have been more spontaneous in his letters home, more pompous in the way of many teenagers in posting entries in his diary.

McKinley had good cause for concern. He wrote in his diary two days later that his patrol had been ambushed on the way from Glenville to Bulltown. "While on our road about three miles from Bulltown we were fired into by Rebels. Some five reports were made and only three taking effect, Corp. [Ferdinand] Becker, John Robinson, and Andy Tiady were wounded. In an instant after [the] firing, our Company pursued the enemy but returned without even discovering them. Arrived at Bulltown about 2 o'clock; stopped there until evening; thence moved forward about a quarter of a mile and stopped for the night. I slept upon the ground and never slept better."

Hayes reported the incident in a letter to Lucy on August 17. "This," he said, "is the first blood of our regiment shed in fight."

Scammon was not working out. "The men are disconcerted whenever the colonel approaches," Hayes wrote. "They expect to be pitched into about something. [He is] a good man, but impatient and fault-finding; in short, he is out of health, nervous system out of order.... He gives no instruction either in drill or other military duties but fritters his time away on little details which belong to clerks and inferior officers."

For all of the problems, Hayes was feeling tip-top. "I have not been in such robust health for a great while," he told his uncle. His horse, on the other hand, "is not tough enough for this service." Hayes's letters and diaries reveal a continuing struggle to find a horse up to the job. "The strongest horses seem to fail frequently," he said, "when rackabones stand it well."

The regiment moved out on August 19, marching sixteen miles in all, from Weston to Buckhannon. It was the beginning of the long trail for the 23d; those mountain marches none of them ever forgot. By the time the war was over, Hayes and the rest of the boys from the 23d could boast that not many regiments had marched so many miles, or through such difficult country, as they had.

From Buckhannon they moved on to Beverly, 40 miles to the southeast, in the Tygart Valley. Hayes led the column with his brother-in-law, Dr. Joe. The air, Hayes said, was "delicious," the mountain scenery "beautiful." "Dr. Joe and I," he said, "vote these two days the happiest of the war. Such air and scenery and streams and mountains and people glad to see us."

"I never enjoyed any business or mode of life as much as I do this," Hayes told Lucy, sentiments she may not have entirely welcomed. "I really feel badly when I think of several of my intimate friends who are compelled to stay at home. These marches and campaigns in the hills of western Virginia will always be among the pleasantest things I can remember. I know we are in frequent perils, that we may never return and all that, but the feeling that I am where I ought to be is a full compensation for all that is sinister, leaving me free to enjoy as if on a pleasure tour."

But, of course, Hayes and the boys of the 23d had still not fought a real battle. That would soon change.

The Confederates' peerless general, Robert E. Lee, had taken command of rebel troops in West Virginia on August 1 and had been doing his best to hammer some sense into his two feuding subordinates, Floyd and Wise. Rosecrans's idea was to join Cox in the Kanawha Valley with almost everything he had in West Virginia to confront Wise and Floyd before Lee or anyone else could do much about it. That meant a lot more marching.

The 23d, old hands at marching now, had to cross Cheat Mountain single file to make their way south to their rendezvous with the rest of Rosecrans's little army at Sutton, about thirty miles north of Summersville. "At the foot of the mountain," Hayes said, he put Captain Carlos A. Sperry, who was footsore, on his own tough little sorrel, Webby, "and pushed ahead afoot." Hayes seemed to think it was something of a lark. "We are having great times with forced marches over the hills," he wrote his mother, Sophia Hayes. "It agrees with me."

Rosecrans formed his army into three brigades—the first under Henry W. Benham, a West Pointer, with three Ohio regiments; the second, under Colonel Robert L. McCook, with three more Ohio regiments; and the third, under Colonel Scammon, with two Ohio regiments, including the 23d. With Scammon in charge of a brigade, leadership of the 23d fell to Hayes's friend, Lieutenant Colonel Matthews.

The Kanawha Valley runs almost 100 miles, from the junction of the Great Kanawha with the Ohio River in the north to Gauley Bridge, where the Kanawha joins the New and Gauley Rivers in the south. Charleston, now the state capital but not much more than a village in 1861, sits in the middle of the valley. Gauley Bridge was a natural stronghold and a key to the Kanawha Valley. General Cox, a surprisingly astute general, had seized the place and fortified it. That was a good move because it was against this position that the rebels were advancing.

Advancing they were, but not with very much skill. Lee was supposedly in command, but he was at Valley Mountain, far to the north, and out of touch. That meant that the two columns moving toward the Kanawha Valley were under the command of the feuding ex-governors, Wise and Floyd, each of them loud, angry, and totally irresponsible. The fact that Floyd outranked him—his commission was a few days older—drove Wise to paroxysms of fury. The result was predictable; Wise refused to obey Floyd's orders, even though Floyd was his commanding general.

Both Lee and Wise warned Floyd against crossing the Gauley River. It would be safer, they argued, to take up a position on the southern bank. But Floyd ignored both generals, crossed the river, and proceeded to fortify a plateau on the exposed northern bank of the river, on Henry Patterson's farm, near Carnifex Ferry. It was more of a camp than anything else—Floyd called it Camp Gauley—and log breastworks ran along the front for about 350 feet and down each flank. Floyd positioned his artillery and his troops, some of them raw militia, behind the breastworks and awaited the enemy attack. The position was relatively well prepared for an army that was convinced it outnumbered the enemy and was looking forward to a victory. The trouble was, if Floyd was routed, his men had no easy way to escape. The river was more than a mile behind them, and all that was available to get across it was a narrow pontoon bridge—not sturdy enough for heavy artillery—and two small flatboats.

On Tuesday, September 10, the 23d Ohio marched seventeen miles, drove the enemy pickets out of Summersville, and reached the Gauley River by midafternoon. "Enemy entrenched on a hill, high, steep, and hidden by bushes, three to six thousand strong," Hayes wrote in his diary. "We get ready to attack."

General Benham's First Brigade led the attack against the right-center of Floyd's lines. Rosecrans planned to follow that attack with a charge by Colonel McCook's Second Brigade against the center of the rebel position. But Rosecrans, seeing an unexpected opening on the right of the Confederate line, changed his mind. He pulled together bits and pieces from the First and Second Brigades and four companies from the Third, under Hayes, and sent them on their way.

Hayes said he and his troops marched over one or two hills and through a cornfield before they reached the brow of a hill overlooking the Gauley River. A staff officer who had accompanied the detachment told Hayes he should march to the sound of the guns, if and when he heard them. Other than that, he had no advice to give because he didn't know any more about the terrain than Hayes did.

Hayes moved forward, entered a deep woods, and stumbled down into a ravine. The enemy, he said, seemed to be positioned on the opposite hill. Drawing his sword, he and his men advanced up the hill until the head of his column came under enemy fire. Two of his men were wounded.

When darkness fell, and all firing ceased, Hayes withdrew his men to join the rest of the regiment in camp. The next morning, he said, there was great cheering; the enemy had skedaddled.

McKinley, part of Company E, took part in the action. What he remembered most, though, was the night following the fight. "With no blankets for a covering, no food to satisfy our almost starved bodies, we succeeded in procuring some straw which we laid upon," he wrote in his diary.

Carnifex Ferry wasn't much of a battle. Federal casualties amounted to seventeen killed and 141 wounded, some of them the result of friendly fire. None of the rebels was killed and only twenty were wounded, one of them Floyd himself. Floyd retreated to Big Sewall Mountain, where he was joined by his arch-rival, General Wise. In his official report, Floyd said, "I am very confident that I could have beaten the enemy and have marched directly to the valley of Kanawha if the reinforcements from General Wise's column had come up when ordered." Wise responded by calling Floyd that "bullet-hit son of a bitch."

Judah Benjamin, the Confederates' acting secretary of war, congratulated Floyd "on this brilliant affair," but deplored the fact that reinforcements hadn't reached him in a timely manner. On September 20, prodded by Lee, he instructed Wise "to turn over all the troops heretofore immediately under your command to General Floyd, and report yourself in person to the Adjutant-General" in Richmond.

So that was Floyd's greatest triumph; he had finally defeated Henry Wise. The egregious Floyd marched on, suffering that truly catastrophic defeat by Grant at Fort Donelson the following year.

Hayes was under no illusions that he had done anything special at Carnifex Ferry. "My little detachment did as much real work—hard work—as anybody," he told Lucy, and he took comfort in that. It was his first battle, and he performed credibly; the picture lingers of Hayes, stumbling through the thick underbrush, waving his sword at an invisible enemy.

Hayes managed to pick up an abandoned rebel Bowie knife on the field—"awful to look at"—along with some bed quilt material from an abandoned wagon. He sent a piece of it along to Lucy as a souvenir.

The rebels he had faced at Carnifex Ferry were far from the pick of the Confederate Army, and Hayes was badly misled by the encounter. "The young men in Floyd's army of the upper class," he told Uncle Sardis, "are kind-hearted, good-natured fellows, who are [as] unfit as possible for the business they are in. They have courage but no endurance, enterprise, or energy. The lower class are cowardly, cunning, and lazy. The height of their ambition is to shoot a Yankee from some place of safety." In the months ahead, Hayes would revise his thinking on the fighting qualities of an implacable enemy.

Lee made a half-hearted attempt to renew the attack on the Union forces after Carnifex Ferry, but nothing much came of it. Rosecrans then tried to cut off Floyd's army, but nothing much came of that either. As winter approached, both commanding generals—Lee and Rosecrans—moved on to other commands. That left West Virginia to Floyd and Cox.

Hayes was temporarily given the job of judge advocate, presiding over trials of the army's various miscreants. It was not something he enjoyed very much. "I dislike the service," he said, "but of course must obey."

One of the pleasures of serving with the 23d was listening to the regimental band. It was a good one, and it stayed in service long after most regimental bands had been broken up and sent home. Hayes swore he could recognize his band almost anywhere. "I was sitting in the court-house at Buckhannon one afternoon, with windows open, a number of officers present, when we heard music at a distance. No one expected any regiment at that time. I never dreamed of the Twenty-third being on the road, but the music struck me like words from home. 'That is the band of my regiment,' was my confident assertion. True, of course."

In the evening, when the men were gathered around their camp-fires, the band would serenade them with old favorites that reminded them of home. Bands were an extravagance, perhaps, but a welcome one. (They should not be confused with field music—the drummers, many of them boys, who beat out various drum rolls during battle, each of which had its own meaning. These drum messages were the only way battle leaders could signal their intentions in the sound and fury of combat.)

Stanley Matthews, the regiment's lieutenant colonel and Hayes's old friend, tried hard to be a good soldier, but he never earned the respect of the men under his command. Hayes understood that and probably wasn't disappointed when Matthews left the regiment to take command of a newly recruited volunteer regiment. That didn't work out either, and Matthews, recognizing his own shortcomings, resigned his commission and went home to Cincinnati. Hayes was promoted to lieutenant colonel, taking Matthews's place, on October 31. That meant he no longer had to travel all over West Virginia holding courts-martial.

Back home, Lucy was still aflame with war ardor and was keenly disappointed that the war effort was lagging. Lincoln, she told Ruddy, "lacks decision—he is too easy," and she was furious that her hero, General Fremont, one of the most useless of all Civil War generals, wasn't being properly recognized by the authorities in Washington. Hayes cautioned Lucy that Lincoln "is honest, patriotic, cool-headed, and safe. I don't know any man that the nation could say is under all the circumstances to be preferred in his place." He constantly urged both Lucy and his mother, Sophie, to be patient.

Like Garfield, he was also becoming disenchanted by West Pointers. "I am less disposed to think of a West Point education as requisite for this business than I was at first," he said. "Good sense and energy are the qualities required." He went on to say that "old enterprises are the successful ones. Take counsel of hopes rather than of fears to win in this business." The one thing he may have failed to consider was that at the very top, a touch of genius didn't hurt.

War and the death of so many promising young men also made Hayes, a self-described "unbeliever," think of his own mortality. He wrote this moving passage in his diary on October 29:

We fret our little hour, are happy and pass away. Away! Where to? "This longing after immortality! These thoughts that wander through eternity!" I have been and am an unbeliever of all these sacred verities. But will I not take refuge in the faith of my fathers at last? Are we not all impelled to this? The great abyss, the unknown future,—are we not happier if we give ourselves up to some settled faith? Am I not more and more carried along, drifted, towards surrendering to the best religion the world has produced? It seems so. In this business, as I ride through the glorious scenery [of] this loveliest season of the year, my thoughts float away beyond this wretched war and all its belongings.... I think of the closing years of the down-hill side of my life, and picture myself a Christian, sincere, humble, devoted, as conscientious in that as I now am in this—not more so. My belief in this war is as deep as any faith can be;—but thitherward I drift. I see it and am glad.

The little army settled down for the winter at Fayetteville, not far from Gauley Bridge. There, Hayes had a comfortable room in a house abandoned by its rebel-sympathizing owners. On November

22, he reported in his diary, he had dinner at Gauley Bridge with a number of prominent officers. "Always treated well there," he said. "Ate pickled oysters immoderately and foolishly; drank mixed drinks slightly but foolishly." A few weeks later, he reported he had a severe headache. "Drank a little bad wine last night."

Hayes wasn't an alcoholic; he never had the problems of Grant, who couldn't handle more than a glass or two of whiskey. But every now and again he reported in his diary uncomfortable results from imbibing too freely. Lucy's family had a long history of supporting the temperance movement, and she no doubt tried to nudge her husband in the direction of abstemiousness. (The whole drinking business would come to a head when Hayes was president; he and Lucy banned alcohol at White House dinners and became the target of ridicule in the popular press.) Hayes, a member of Sons of Temperance, may have worried more about his own drinking than conventional wisdom about him suggests.

At dinner on Monday, December 23, Hayes was handed a telegram from Dr. Joe, home on leave in Cincinnati. "Wife and boy doing very well. Stranger arrived Saturday evening, nine o'clock P.M." The stranger, Joseph Thompson Hayes, was the couple's fourth child, a boy like the others. "The little fellow, I hope, is healthy and strong," he wrote Lucy the next day. "It is best it was not a daughter. These are no times for women," an opinion the tough-minded Lucy Webb Hayes may not have shared.

The regimental band serenaded him in honor of the little stranger Christmas morning. "A fine band and what a life in a regiment," he said.

With both armies hunkered down for the winter, members of the 23d were given leave to spend a few days at home with their families. One of them, Sergeant John McKinley (no relation to William) stopped by to say hello to Lucy. "Your Sergeant McKinley is a curiosity," Lucy wrote Hayes. "Don't say anything about the sergeant's condition when he called, for getting home had overcome him and it did not affect me in the least."

"Heard from home," Hayes wrote in his diary. "Sergeant McKinley with letter and watch [from Hayes]—tight, drunk, the old heathen, and insisting on seeing the madame. I didn't dream of that. He must be a nuisance, a dangerous one too, when drunk. A neat disciplined soldier under rule, but what a savage when in liquor! Must be careful who I send home."

What concerned Hayes most about drinking too much alcohol was the possibility of losing control. He couldn't bear even thinking about that. Sergeant McKinley, the old heathen, was one of the examples he had in mind.

Union camps almost always drew escaping slaves looking for sanctuary, freedom, or something to do. Hayes's camp at Fayetteville was no exception. "Twelve or fifteen contrabands [the euphemism for slaves] arrived," Hayes wrote in his diary on January 2, 1862. "Officers and soldiers employ them as cooks and servants. Some go to Ohio. Nobody in this army thinks of giving up to Rebels their fugitive slaves."

Pondering the broader question, Hayes wrote that he didn't want "to see Congress meddling with the slavery question. Time and the progress of events are solving all the questions arising out of slavery in a way consistent with eternal principles of justice. Slavery is getting deathblows. As an 'institution,' it perishes in this war. It will take years to get rid of its debris, but the 'sacred' is gone."

Hayes managed to slip home himself on February 1, visiting Lucy and the boys in Cincinnati and Uncle Sardis in Delaware, Ohio. He had gone off to war clean-shaven. He came home on leave with a full beard.

He was back in camp on February 28. "Found the Twenty-third men pleased to see me; felt like getting home," he wrote in his diary. "Darling," he wrote Lucy on March 1, "you will be pleased to know, and so I tell you, I never loved you more than I do as I think of you on my late visit, and I never admired you so much."

But it was life in the army that truly inspired him. He and some companions went for a "glorious ride" to see the scenery along the

New River on March 8. "How the blood leaps and thrills as we race over the hills!" he wrote in his diary. "Physical enjoyments of this sort are worth a war. How the manly, generous, brave side of our people is growing! With all its evils war has its glorious compensations." Spring was now coming to the mountains in West Virginia, and it was time to resume campaigning.

"We are getting ready to move south," Hayes wrote Uncle Sardis on April 8. "Our first stop, unless the enemy stops us, will be at Princeton, . . . the county-seat of Mercer County. We shall stop there for supplies, etc., etc., and to suppress Rebel recruiting and guerrilla bands probably a fortnight, then on to the [Virginia & Nashville] railroad at Wytheville, Dublin, or some other point. The enemy will try to stop us. They will do their best, as the railroad is of the utmost importance to their grand army in eastern Virginia."

By this time Colonel Scammon had been promoted to command of a full brigade—the 23d, 30th, and 37th Ohio regiments, an eight-gun artillery battery, and a small force of cavalry. That meant that Hayes was in command of the 23d.

General Fremont, who had been in charge of all troops in the western command, had been demoted for military and political incompetence and was now being given a second chance—command of all the troops in western Virginia, perhaps 35,000 in all. Fremont proposed to advance on two fronts. He would lead a column up the Shenandoah Valley on the eastern side of the mountains, where he would meet—and be completely outclassed by—Stonewall Jackson, bringing an end to his sorry military career.

Cox, on the western side of the mountains, would lead the other column south to Princeton and then cross into Virginia and strike the strategic railroad line at either Dublin or Wytheville. Hayes, in his letter to Uncle Sardis, fully understood the plan and was itching to get on with it.

After a rain delay, Cox's little army—fewer than 10,000 men in all—began its advance on April 24, led by the impatient Hayes and the 23d Ohio. Five days later they were camped "in a beautiful healthy place" at the foot of Flat Top Mountain, on the line dividing Raleigh and Mercer Counties, north of Princeton, when Hayes heard from his scouts that a gang of bushwhackers was operating near Camp Creek, fifteen miles away. He sent Lieutenant James L. Bottsford and Company C to track them down.

Bottsford didn't find the rebels, but they found him. Colonel Walter Jenifer, commanding about 300 men in Princeton, heard that Bottsford and his company of fewer than 100 men were poking around a hamlet called Clark's Hollow looking for the bushwhackers, who had him under observation all the time. He decided to capture the lot.

The rebels attacked the morning of May 1, taking Bottsford completely by surprise. Badly outnumbered, he moved his men into a farmhouse, where he hoped to hold off the rebels until reinforcements could arrive. Hayes, in fact, was on his way. He and the rest of the 23d broke camp at 6:00 A.M. and soon heard firing in the distance. "Turned out to be Company C in Camp Creek," Hayes wrote in his diary. When the 23d arrived in a clearing near the farmhouse, the rebels, seeing they were now outnumbered, retreated to Princeton.

Bottsford had lost one man killed, another mortally wounded, and eighteen wounded, a heavy toll for one company. One of the wounded, Hayes said, was a Sergeant Ritter, shot in the head, the bullet lodging between the scalp and skull. "He fell, but instantly jumped up saying, 'You must shoot lower if you want to kill me.'"

Hayes said he came up to the farmhouse soon after the shooting stopped. "I couldn't speak when I came up to the gallant little company and they presented arms to me. I went around shaking hands with the wounded. They all spoke cheerfully." As he looked "at the glow of pride in their faces, my heart choked me, I could not speak, but a boy said, 'All right, colonel, we know what you mean.'"

Hayes was now in full battle cry. He chased the rebels for thirteen hours, all the way to Princeton. "On approaching the town," he wrote in his diary, "we saw great clouds.... Within two miles we knew the Rebels were burning the town. We hurried forward; soon reached an elevated ground overlooking the place. All the brick buildings, court-house, churches, etc., were burning. I ordered up the howitzers to scatter out the few Rebel cavalry who were doing it; deployed the regiment by a file right into a field and marched forward by battalion front. The town was soon overrun.... And so ended the first of May—twenty-two miles in mud and rain. An exciting day. Five enemy killed, nine badly wounded that we got.... A good day's work."

Scammon didn't think so. In a severe letter to General Cox, he criticized his headstrong subordinate for sending Bottsford so far ahead of the rest of the column, putting him and his company in what could have been a fatal situation. Hayes, deeply affronted by the criticism, told Scammon he thought the expedition had been a huge success. "I thought that a most meritorious thing had been done," he said. "Upon the whole, I think that the affair deserves commendation rather than censure."

Scammon backed down and Fremont said kind things about Hayes in a dispatch to the War Department. Newspapers back home, desperate for good news from the front, even an incident as minor as this one, celebrated Hayes's courage and enterprise.

Hayes knew he had been put on a leash, and he promised his superiors that from now on he would do nothing rash or impetuous. But he was still in a fighting fury, urging Scammon and Cox to push on to the New River Narrows and Giles Court House.

Hearing from scouts and fugitive slaves that the Narrows—a two-mile-wide gap through the mountains—was lightly defended, Hayes pleaded with Scammon to allow him to move forward. "I wish to send three companies or so to the Narrows immediately to see if we can catch the [rebel] guard and baggage left behind. If you approve send me word back immediately and I will start the expedition in the morning.... Do send the order."

Too impatient to wait for a reply, he sent Major James M. Comly forward with three companies of infantry and a small detachment of cavalry. At midnight, an anxious Hayes wrote in his diary that he "received a message from Major Comly that the party finding the Narrows deserted and all property gone had gone on to Giles [Court House] and taken it completely by surprise, capturing some prisoners and a large amount of stores—two hundred and fifty barrels of flour and everything else. Very lucky! And Colonel Scammon thereupon approved of the whole expedition, although it was irregular and in violation of the letter of orders."

We don't know Scammon's real thoughts about Hayes's impetuous actions, but he must have been very nervous. He was, by his very nature, constantly nervous.

Hayes arrived in Giles Court House, also known as Pearisburg, "a neat, pretty village," about 6:30 P.M. the next day, "after a fatiguing march of twenty-eight miles." Now, he said in his diary, "all safe if we are vigilant." He wrote Scammon the same day, May 7, saying, "We are without artillery and perhaps you would do well to send some."

Hayes was immensely pleased with himself. In another letter to Scammon, he boasted that the expedition was "perfectly impudent ... one of the boldest things of the war." In a letter to Lucy, he said the expedition was "bold and impudent."

Impudent it was, and also imprudent. For the second time, Hayes had extended the Union lines too far into rebel territory. His position wasn't nearly as secure as he said it was.

Hayes was no fool, and he was beginning to get a little nervous himself. The enemy, he told Scammon, was concentrating thirteen miles away at Cloyd's Mountain—three Virginia regiments as well as some cavalry and artillery. "It is certain," he said, "we ought to be promptly and heavily reinforced."

"No reinforcements yet," he wrote in his diary on May 9. "Have asked for them in repeated dispatches. Strange. I shall be vigilant. Have planned the fight if it is to be done in the houses at night, and the retreat to the Narrows, if in daylight with the artillery against us. The town can't be held if we are attacked with artillery. Shameful! We have rations for thirty days with a brigade and tents and other property."

In a letter to Scammon that same day, Hayes sounded a little desperate. "The enemy is recovering from his panic," he said, "is near the railroad and getting reinforcements. He is already stronger than we are, at least double as strong."

The rebel commander was General Harry Heth, and, just as Hayes thought, he had been reinforced. He now had 5,000 men fit for duty, and he hoped to attack Hayes at Giles Court House and gobble up the entire 23d Ohio.

"We are attacked at 4 o'clock this morning," Hayes wrote in his diary on May 10. He went on:

I got up at the first faint streak of light and walked out to see the pickets in the direction of the enemy. As I was walking along I heard six shots. "No mistake this time," I thought. I ordered Captains Drake and Sperry to skirmish before the enemy and keep them back; the rest of the regiment to form in their rear. Led the whole to the front beyond the town; saw the enemy approaching—four regiments or battalions, several pieces of artillery in line of battle approaching. The artillery soon opened on us. The shell shrieked and burst over [our] heads, the small arms rattled, and the battle was begun. It was soon obvious that we would be outflanked. We retreated to the next ridge and stood again. The men of the Twenty-third behaved gloriously, the men of Gilmore's cavalry, ditto; the men of Colonel Paxton's cavalry, not so well.

I was scratched and torn on the knee by a shell or something, doing no serious injury. I felt well all the time. The men behaved so gallantly! And so we fought our way through town, the people rejoicing at our defeat, and on for six hours until we reached the Narrows, five and one-half miles distant. The time seemed short.... We had three men killed; a number wounded none severely, and lost a few prisoners.

But it wasn't safe at the Narrows either, as the boys from Ohio once again came under fire from the rebel guns. They had to fall back another five miles, to East River, where the next day they were joined by Scammon and reinforcements.

Hayes had no regrets. "A well-ordered retreat which I think was creditable," he said in his diary. "Masterly," he added, on second thought. In his official report to Colonel Scammon, he said "it is much to be regretted that reinforcements which I had so frequently requested could not be sent in time to save Parisburg [Pearisburg], as the loss of position and property is very serious." Scammon asked him to delete the paragraph, and Hayes agreed. "I did not want to embarrass him," he explained.

In a long letter to Lucy on May 11, Hayes noted that in the battle he got a scratch on his knee, "just drawing blood but spoiling my drawers." And, to Lucy if to no one else, he admitted it had been a close thing. "We got off as by a miracle," he said. And then he added that he had just received information indicating that "it was probably well we were not reinforced. There would not have been enough to hold the position we had against so great a force as the enemy brought against us."

McKinley was with the 23d during the engagement, but he was no longer at the front as a private in Company E. He had been promoted to regimental commissary sergeant on April 15. As commissary sergeant, he was responsible for providing rations for the troops under his care. Slaughtering and butchering cattle and sheep was sometimes a part of his job. Packing supplies on the backs of stubborn mules was also one of the conditions. We don't know very much about his daily life as a commissary sergeant because he stopped writing his diary late in November 1861. He also stopped sending stories back to his hometown newspapers.

It was a "bombproof" job, and soldiers often derided the men who performed those rear-echelon duties. But McKinley—"Mack," the other soldiers now called him—was by all accounts good at his job.

The campaign had not been a success. Jackson routed Fremont

in the Shenandoah Valley, and Cox failed to reach the Nashville & Virginia Railroad. Hayes was no longer euphoric. "I was much vexed that we were not reinforced," a humbler Hayes wrote Uncle Sardis. "Perhaps I was wrong. It is now believed that the enemy ... have been sending heavy bodies of troops this way; that our force is wholly inadequate to its task, and must wait here until largely strengthened. I am not sure about this, but accept it without much grumbling."

"My command," he continued, "had a narrow escape." It got away, he said, only because he had taken special precautions. Hayes was learning that impudence and boldness weren't all that a good soldier needed to be successful.

On June 1—at last—the boys of the 23d got their new rifled muskets. Hayes and some of the others in his command tried them out a half-mile from camp. "The ball at one-fourth mile passed through the largest [fence] rails," he said. "The hissing of the ball indicates its force and velocity, I think it is an excellent arm."

They were camped at Flat Top Mountain, twenty miles south of Raleigh. Hayes called it "the boundary line between America and Dixie."

One day, Hayes said, General Cox called him in and read a letter he had just received from his old roommate in Columbus, General Garfield. Garfield was off once again on a tirade about the questionable loyalty of many Union generals and politicians. "These semi-traitors must be watched," Hayes agreed. "Let us be careful who become army leaders in the reorganized army at the end of the rebellion. The man who thinks that the perpetuity of slavery is essential to the existence of the Union, is unfit to be trusted. The deadliest enemy the Union has is slavery—in fact, its only enemy." Yet there were still rebel armies in the field, and they were still pretty deadly.

Cox's Army of the Kanawha lingered on Flat Top Mountain for weeks, seemingly forgotten by Union strategists in Washington. It wasn't until August 14 that they began moving out. The band played the same old hymn Garfield's troops had heard when they finally left eastern Kentucky—"Oh, ain't I glad to get out of the wilderness."

In the fighting in West Virginia, Hayes had demonstrated, to himself if to no one else, that he had something of a flair for leading volunteers. They liked him and trusted him. He also had shown a quality in great demand in these early Union armies—aggressiveness. Like Grant and Garfield, he was hell-bent on destroying his enemies.

It was good preparation for what would happen next; Hayes and McKinley were heading east to the big war, to South Mountain and Antietam, and some of the hardest fighting they would ever know.

Chapter 8

SOUTH MOUNTAIN, ANTIETAM, AND THE GREAT DUBLIN RAID

HAYES AND McKINLEY and the 23d Ohio moved down from the mountains to a new camp at a lower elevation in mid-July, but a new campaign seemed far away. "I feel dourish today," Hayes wrote in his diary on July 18. "Inaction is taking the soul out of us."

One of Hayes's problems was Colonel Scammon, still technically in charge of the 23d Ohio although commanding a brigade. Hayes made no bones about his ambition to lead a regiment and worried that Scammon was so incompetent he might never be promoted to brigadier general (and a posting somewhere else). He began toying with the idea of leaving the 23d to take command of one of the new Ohio regiments.

An incident late in July underscored his distaste for his commanding officer. It started on July 24, when he was asked by a loyalist, Mr. Caldwell, to send some troops into rebel-held territory to rescue his wife and four children. It seemed a simple enough errand of mercy, and Hayes was eager to undertake it. But Scammon wasn't so sure. "I got a lame, halting permission from Colonel

Scammon," Hayes wrote in his diary. "The colonel says I may go if and if; warning me of the hazards, etc., etc., shirking all responsibility. It is ridiculous in war to talk this way. If a thing ought to be done according to the lights we have, let us go and do it, leaving events to take care of themselves. This half-and-half policy, this do-less waiting for certainties before action, is contemptible."

Still seething over Scammon's conduct, he took some infantry and cavalry across the New River into Mercer County and rescued Mr. Caldwell's family without trouble of any kind. "A merry little expedition," he wrote.

At daylight on August 7, Hayes was aroused by a courier "saying our most distant picket had been fired on and as no one had come in, they were believed to be all cut off. I got out two companies to see to it." Twenty minutes later, another courier reported the rebels were attacking Major Comly and four companies from the 23d in force at Pack's Ferry. There were as many as 4,000 of them, the courier said, and they had artillery.

Hayes set out to relieve Comly with all the troops he could muster, the band leading the way, blaring martial tunes, hoping to convince the rebels an enormous force was headed in their direction. "Fighting battles is like courting the girls," Hayes told his troops. "Those who make most pretension and are boldest usually win. So, go ahead, give good hearty yells as you approach the ferry, let the band play. But don't expose yourself, keep together and keep under cover. It is a bushwhacking fight across the River. Don't expose yourself to show bravery; we know you are all brave."

Hayes and his reinforcements easily saved the day at Pack's Ferry, routing the Confederate force, which probably numbered fewer than 2,000 men. "Tents were torn and many narrow escapes made," Hayes said, "but strangely nobody on our side was hurt. With our long-range muskets, the enemy soon found they were likely to get the worst of it." Scammon reached the ferry about four hours after the fighting had ended. "The colonel is too nervous and fussy to be a good commander," Hayes wrote. "He cut around like a hen with one chicken after getting news of our being attacked," wasting three or four hours before advancing to the scene of the fighting.

"You will see in the newspapers, I suppose," Hayes wrote Lucy on August 18, "that General Cox's division (the greater part of it) is going to eastern Virginia. We left our camps Friday, the 15th, making long and rapid marches from the mountains to the head of navigation on this [the Kanawha] river. We now go down to the Ohio, then up to Parkersburg, and thence by railroad eastwardly to the scene of operations."

The men, Hayes said, "are delighted with the change. They cheer and laugh, and the band plays, and it is a real frolic. During the hot dusty marching, the idea that we are leaving the mountains of West Virginia kept them in good heart."

With action approaching in what he and most of his men agreed was the big war, Hayes's heart lifted too, and there was less talk about leaving the 23d to command a new regiment.

Cox had been primarily responsible for the move, arguing to his superiors in Washington that his hard-marching mountain men would be an asset in the east. He made his case, and he was assigned to make the long trip by foot, by boat, and by train with 5,000 men, the Kanawha Division, to join a new command, the Army of Virginia, under General John Pope.

Pope met Lee, Jackson, and Longstreet on August 29 and 30 at the Second Battle of Bull Run and was badly beaten. His troops came scurrying back toward the capital. Hayes watched as they passed his position near Alexandria. "The great army is retreating, coming back," he wrote. "The Eastern troops don't fight like the Western. If the enemy is now energetic and wise, they can take great advantages of us. Well, well, I can but do my duty as I see it."

Hayes no longer underrated the Confederate Army. "The enemy here," he said, "has a large force of gallant and efficient cavalry. Our cavalry is much inferior. The Rebel infantry is superior to ours gathered from the cities and manufacturing villages of the old states. The Western troops are, I think, superior to either.... In generalship and officers they were superior to us. The result is we must conquer in land warfare by superior numbers. On the water we have splendid artillery [in Navy gunboats], and are masters. High water, deep rivers, heavy rains are our friends."

Lincoln fired Pope and gave the command of all troops in and around Washington to George McClellan. Lee's confident army then crossed the Potomac River into Maryland and created pandemonium in the nation's vulnerable capital. McClellan was ordered to do something about it.

Hayes, at least, maintained his optimism in the face of truly discouraging events. "I don't give it up," he said. "Something far more damaging than anything which has yet happened must occur, or these attempts to carry the war into our territory must recoil heavily on the Rebels. Failing to hold their advanced conquests, they must go back vastly weakened and disheartened, while our following wave will be a growing and resistless one." He had been a soldier for only sixteen months, but already he was becoming a pretty decent military analyst.

"McClellan is loved," he said. "Not thinking him a first-class commander, I yet in view of this feeling, think him the best man now available." That was more sound analysis.

Cox's Kanawha Division was attached to Ambrose Burnside's Ninth Corps, but on September 7 it was temporarily under the command of a stubborn West Pointer, Jesse L. Reno. It was late that day, camped near the Leesboro Road, that Reno and Hayes tangled in one of the Civil War's classic encounters between a West Point professional and an amateur volunteer. Here's how Hayes told the story in his diary.

Road full of horse, foot, and artillery, baggage and ambulance waggons. Dust, heat, and thirst. "The Grand Army of the Potomac" appeared to bad advantage by the side of our troops. Men were lost from their regiments; officers left their commands to rest in the shade, to feed on fruit; thousands were straggling; confusion and disorder everywhere. New England troops looked well; Middle States troops badly; discipline gone or greatly relaxed.

On coming into camp Major-General Reno, in whose corps we are, rode into the grounds occupied by General Cox's troops in a towering passion because some of the men were taking straw to feed horses in McMullen's Battery and to cavalry horses; some in the Twenty-third regiment were taking it to lie on. The ground was a stubble field, in ridges of hard ground. I saw it and made no objection. General Reno began on McMullen's men. He addressed them: "You damned black sons of bitches." This he repeated to my men and asked for the colonel. Hearing it, I presented myself and assumed the responsibility, defending the men. [Scammon was nearby and heard the whole thing but did not step forward.] I talked respectfully but firmly; told him we had always taken rails, for example, if needed to cook with; that if required we would pay for them.

He denied the right and necessity; said we were in a loyal state, etc. Gradually he softened down. He asked my name. I asked his, all respectfully done on my part. He made various observations to which I replied. He expressed opinions on pilfering. I remarked, in reply to some opinion, substantially, "Well, I trust our generals will exhibit the same energy in dealing with our foes that they do in the treatment of their friends." He asked me, as if offended, what I meant by that. I replied, "Nothing—at least, I mean nothing disrespectful to you."

Hayes's volunteers were agog. As the angry general rode away, Hayes said, "the men cheered me." Later, Hayes said, some of his men reported that while talking to him, Reno had "put his hand on his pistol," causing many of the Ohio boys to reach for their own weapons. It might have led to some serious trouble for Hayes, but a week later, Reno was killed in battle.

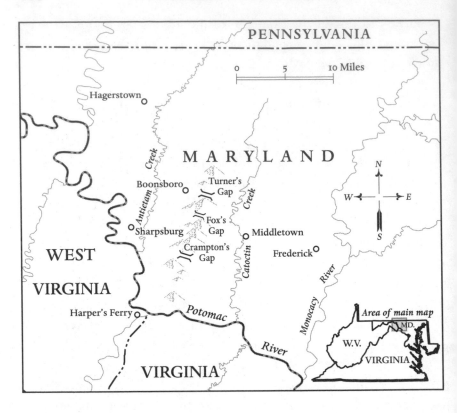

McClellan's troops marched into Frederick, just behind the retreating rebels, on September 12. "We marched in just at sundown," Hayes said, "the Twenty-third a good deal of the way in front. There was no mistaking the Union feeling and the joy of the people—fine ladies, pretty girls, and children were all in the doors and windows waving flags and clapping hands.... The scene as we approached across the broad bottom-lands in line of battle, with occasional cannon firing and musketry, the beautiful Blue Ridge Mountains in view, was very magnificent."

"The enemy has gone northwest," Hayes wrote Uncle Sardis, "filthy, lousy, and desperate. A battle with them will be a most terrific thing. With forty thousand Western troops to give life and heartiness to the fight, we should, with our help, whip them, at any rate, but it is by no means a certainty."

Lee was hoping to sweep into Pennsylvania after disposing of McClellan's army and a large federal garrison at Harper's Ferry. He sent Jackson with his corps to take Harper's Ferry, expecting those legendary soldiers would be back in time to deal with McClellan. What he didn't know was that McClellan was in possession of his Order No. 191, spelling out, in detail, all of his plans. A Union corporal had found a copy of the orders in a corn field near Frederick and, sensing he was on to something big, had made sure they found their way to headquarters. "Now I know what to do," McClellan said after reading them.

The bulk of the rebel army—Longstreet's command—was positioned behind South Mountain, really a series of ridges, with crests 1,300 feet high, running for fifty miles in a northerly direction from the Potomac River. There were three gaps through the ridges— Turner's and Fox's to the north, and Crampton's farther south. The Union Army needed to crack through one or more of those gaps to get at Lee's army.

Lee knew his enemy, and the last thing he expected from McClellan was enterprise. But with the captured orders in his hands, McClellan pushed his troops forward toward South Mountain with uncharacteristic speed and determination. Lee, as usual, was up to the challenge. He reacted quickly and pushed his own troops forward to contest the gaps. He decided to form his main defensive line at a village called Sharpsburg, near Antietam Creek.

But for all his advantages, McClellan was still McClellan; he hesitated on September 13, when he could easily have swept through any of the gaps, and decided to make his attack the next day, the 14th, by which time some of Lee's troops had been rushed into position.

Cox's Kanawha Division was ordered to lead the attack at Fox's Gap. September 14 was a Sunday, a clear and beautiful day, and the fighting began at approximately 9:00 A.M. In his diary, written several days after the battle, Hayes said, "I am sent with the Twenty-third up a mountain path to get around the Rebel right with instructions to attack and take a battery of two guns supposed to be

posted there. I asked, 'If I find six guns and a strong support?'
Colonel Scammon replies, 'Take them anyhow.' It is the only safe
instruction." As usual, Hayes told the story better than anyone else:

> Went with a guide by the right flank up the hill, Company A
> deployed in front as skirmishers. Seeing signs of rebels [I] sent
> [Company] F to the left and [Company] I to the right as
> flankers. Soon saw from the opposite hill a strong force coming
> down towards us; formed hastily in the woods; faced by the rear
> rank (some companies inverted and some out of place) towards
> the enemy; pushed through bushes and rocks over broken
> ground towards the enemy; soon received a heavy volley,
> wounding and killing some. I feared confusion; exhorted,
> swore, and threatened. Men did pretty well. Found we could
> not stand it long, and ordered an advance. Rushed forward with
> a yell; enemy gave way. Halted to reform line; heavy firing
> resumed.

"Now, boys," he told his troops, "give them hell." Others recall
that what he really said was, "Give the sons of bitches hell." He was,
once again, in a fighting rage. His diary continued:

> I soon began to fear we could not stand it, and again ordered a
> charge; the enemy broke, and we drove them clear out of the
> woods. Our men halted at a fence near the edge of the woods
> and kept up a brisk fire upon the enemy, who were sheltering
> themselves behind stone walls and fences near the top of the
> hill, beyond a cornfield in front of our position.
>   Just as I gave the command to charge I felt a stunning blow
> and found a musket ball had struck my left arm just above the
> elbow. Fearing that an artery might be cut, I asked a soldier
> near me to tie my handkerchief above the wound. I felt weak,
> faint, and sick at the stomach. I [lay] down and was pretty
> comfortable.

It was at this point, Hayes remembered later in his diary, that he had a long talk with a wounded Confederate soldier, lying nearby. "I gave him messages for my wife and friends in case I should not get up. We were right jolly and friendly; it was by no means an unpleasant experience."

"You came a good ways to fight us," Hayes told the rebel, who then asked where Hayes came from. "Ohio," Hayes replied. "Well," said the young Confederate, "you came a good ways to fight us." Hayes went on in his diary:

I was perhaps twenty feet behind the lines of my men, and could form a pretty accurate notion of the way the fighting was going. The enemy's fire was occasionally very heavy; balls passed near my face and hit the ground all around me. I could see wounded men staggering or [being] carried to the rear; but I felt sure our men were holding their own. I listened anxiously to hear the approach of reinforcements, wondering they did not come.

I was told there was danger of the enemy flanking us on our left, near where I was lying. I called out to Captain [J. L.] Drake, who was on the left, to wheel his company backward so as to face the threatened attack. His company fell back perhaps twenty yards, and the whole line gradually followed the example, thus leaving me between our line and the enemy. Major Comly came along and asked me if it was my intention the whole line should fall back. I told him no, that I merely wanted one or two of the left companies to wheel backward so as to face the enemy said to be coming on our left. I said if the line was now in good position to let it remain [so] and to face the left companies as I intended. This, I suppose, was done.

The firing continued pretty warm for perhaps fifteen or twenty minutes, when it practically died away on both sides. After a few minutes' silence I began to doubt whether the enemy had disappeared or whether our men had gone father back. I called out, "Hallo, Twenty-third men, are you going to

leave your colonel here for the enemy?" In an instant a half
dozen or more men sprang forward to me saying, "Oh, no, we
will carry you wherever you want us to." The enemy immediately opened fire on them. Our men replied to them, and soon
the battle was raging as hotly as ever. I ordered the men back to
cover, telling them they would get me shot and themselves too.

They went back and about this time Lieutenant [Benjamin
W.] Jackson came and insisted on taking me out of the range of
the enemy's fire. He took me back to our line and, feeling faint,
he laid me down behind a big log and gave me a canteen of
water, which tasted so good. Soon after, the firing having died
away, he took me back up the hill, where my wound was dressed
by Dr. Joe. I then walked about half a mile to the house of
Widow Kugler. I remained there two or three hours when I was
taken with Captain [John W.] Skiles in an ambulance to Middletown—three and a half miles—where I stopped at Mr. Jacob
Rudy's.

What the wounded Hayes couldn't have known was that the
charge he had so gallantly led carried the day, or at least that part
of the day. The charge ended in a fierce hand-to-hand melee with
bayonets and clubbed muskets, forcing the rebels, finally, to turn
and flee. About a third of the men commanded by rebel general
Samuel Garland had been killed or wounded and the rest, one rebel
commander said, were "too roughly handled to be of any further
use that day."

Cox's troops were reinforced later in the day, but so were the
Confederates. The fighting went on, and on. To observers down
below in the valley, the whole crest of the mountain appeared to be
on fire. With Union troops applying almost unbearable pressure at
nearby Turner's Gap, Lee decided during the night to withdraw all
of his troops from South Mountain.

Hayes, in the tender care of the Rudy family in Middletown, sent
telegrams to Lucy, Uncle Sardis, and one or two friends saying he had

been wounded and was recuperating nicely. He urged Lucy to come to him, to give him comfort and to tend his wound. Lucy received her telegram in Chillicothe. "I am here," it said, "come to me. I shall not lose my arm." But where was "here"? Hayes hadn't said, and Lucy could only presume from the fact the telegram originated in Washington that he was in a hospital somewhere in the capital.

She was still nursing her baby, Joseph, and so had to hope her mother or one of her friends would be able to find a wet nurse while she was away. She left Chillicothe on the morning stage to Columbus. There she was joined by William Platt, a family friend, who accompanied her on the railroad cars to Washington.

Hayes had told her earlier that if anything happened to him, he would be at the Kirkwood House. She checked in there, but the hotel knew nothing of Hayes's whereabouts. Then she began making the rounds of the hospitals, all of them filled with wounded men, surrounded by their friends and families. The city was even more chaotic than usual.

At the Patent Office, operated during the war as a military hospital, she was treated by personnel in what she described as a "cruel and unfeeling manner." She then turned to the surgeon general's office at the Capitol. They were just as unhelpful. Platt finally had a smart idea. He tracked down the man who had sent the original telegram and discovered that it had originated in Middletown, but for reasons known only to the telegraph service the point of origin had been changed to Washington. Mrs. Hayes and Platt returned to the Patent Office, hoping to uncover more information. There, she noticed several boys with the numbers "23" on their caps. Immediately, Lucy called out, "Twenty-third Ohio!" "Why, this is Mrs. Hayes," one or more of them responded. They told her that Middletown was the place, and it was there that she would find her husband. "By noon," biographer Emily Apt Geer says, "Lucy and William Platt were on their way to Frederick, Maryland, as close as the railroad could take them to Middletown." Lucy stood all the way, for three hours, next to the water cooler.

Waiting for them at the Frederick station was Lucy's brother, Dr. Joe. He had ridden from Middletown to Frederick every day, hoping to see his sister. Dr. Joe spotted Lucy sitting on the steps of the station. "With my bundle in my hand," Lucy said, she must have looked "very forlorn."

On the road to Middletown, Lucy was puzzled by the way the carriage veered this way, then veered the other. The carriage driver explained he was trying to avoid dead horses lying in the road. They finally arrived at the Rudy house in Middletown. Hayes joked that his wife had always said she wanted to visit Washington.

Weeks later, Lucy wrote her "dearest Ruddy" that she had just finished reading the senior Oliver Wendell Holmes's poignant article in the December issue of *The Atlantic Monthly*, "Search After the Captain," about his own experience in trying to locate his wounded son, the future Supreme Court justice, on the battlefield. Now, Lucy told Hayes, she didn't want to hear any more jokes about her search for her wounded husband.

From his comfortable bed in the Rudy home, Hayes finally learned that the Union troops, including his own, had broken through the South Mountain gaps. Casualties in the 23d, heaviest in Cox's division, were 130, including thirty-two killed. Hayes was pleased that both Cox and Scammon mentioned his and his regiment's performance in their official reports. Hayes, Scammon said, had "gallantly and skillfully brought his men into action."

Confined to his bedroom, Hayes was frantic to learn how the campaign was going. He paid one of the Rudy boys a dollar a day to post himself at a front window and describe the troops marching past, where they were from and how they looked.

"Lucy is here and we are pretty jolly," he wrote Uncle Sardis on September 26. "She visits the wounded and comes back in tears, then we take a little refreshment and get over it."

Hayes missed the great battle at Antietam between Lee and McClellan on September 17, the single bloodiest day in the Civil War, but McKinley, the commissary sergeant, was there, and what he did that day became a key part of his personal and political story, much admired by his campaign biographers. Sergeant McKinley was a hero at Antietam.

Much of the fiercest fighting raged around a bridge over Antietam Creek that became known to history as Burnside Bridge for the general who tried to get across it. Scammon's brigade, including the 23d, managed to ford the creek just a little below the bridge at approximately 1:00 P.M., the same time Burnside's troops, in their third try, finally got across.

Scammon's brigade had begun the day without breakfast because of the failure of the Ninth Corps' commissary wagons to reach them. By 2:00 P.M., hunkered down on the far side of Antietam Creek, with no supplies in sight, they were tired and hungry. McKinley, acting commissary sergeant for the brigade that included the 23d, decided to take things into his own hands. Without asking anyone, he recruited some of the stragglers and ordered them to collect rations—cooked meat, pork and beans, crackers, and a barrel of ground coffee—and load them on a wagon.

Then he asked for volunteers to take the rations to the men at the front, two miles away. Only one soldier, John A. Harvey of the 23d's Company I, answered the call. He and McKinley set off together for the battlefield in a wagon pulled by two horses. Harvey described the ride that became such a key part of the McKinley legend (just as Garfield's ride at Chickamauga became a part of his).

We started by the way of a by road through a heavy piece of woods. After driving along the road for some distance from the camp, we met an Army officer with his staff and he told McKinley that he must not try to go to the Regiment as it would be impossible to run the blockade, as the Rebel forces had command of an open strip in the woods. The road being so narrow that we could not turn around, Sergeant McKinley thought that we had better try to go on a little farther. Before we came to an open space in the woods, and close to the brow of a hill we met another Commanding Officer who ordered us to immediately turn back. We stopped and considered the matter and the Officer and his body guard went in the opposite direction. This left Sergeant McKinley to decide what was best to do. The Regiment was almost in sight of us and Sergeant McKinley was so anxious to carry out his point and give the half-starved boys something to eat. He made one more appeal to me to run the blockade; he himself risking his life in taking the lead, I following and the horses going at full speed past the blockade. We had the back end of the wagon shot away by a small cannon shot. In a very few minutes we were safe in the midst of the half-famished regiment.

Harvey's account was written thirty-five years later, in 1897, just as McKinley was taking office as president of the United States. But no one ever seriously challenged it. McKinley did bring cooked rations to the troops, and they were grateful. Major Comly, in command of the 23d in Hayes's absence, remembered his men cheering as McKinley's wagon arrived with the rations. Others remembered one old veteran saying, "God bless the lad." McKinley always said those were the sweetest words he ever heard. Comly wrote a note to Hayes full of praise for McKinley. The sergeant "showed ability and energy of the first class," Comly said, "in not only keeping us *fully supplied* with rations throughout the fight, but in having them fully prepared for eating, also. We had *plenty* when every body else was short. He delivered them to us *under fire.*" Comly said McKinley deserved a promotion to second lieutenant.

Years later, some of McKinley's old comrades-in-arms argued he deserved a Congressional Medal of Honor for his valor on the Antietam battlefield. McKinley, sensibly, scoffed at the idea.

Antietam was a battle fought by tested veterans on both sides, and the result was carnage of a kind never experienced again in a single day by American boys. The final count, killed and wounded, was 12,410 on the Union side, 10,700 on the Confederate side.

Technically, it was a draw, but in fact it was a Union victory, for Lee had been thwarted in his effort to bring the war to the north, and he had lost one-fifth of his army. It gave Lincoln all he needed to announce a preliminary Emancipation Proclamation.

After the battle, the nineteen-year-old McKinley returned to Ohio to recruit replacements for the 23d and other Ohio regiments. There he learned from Governor David Tod that thanks to Colonel Hayes, he had won his promotion. He stopped in Cleveland on his way home to see Captain Hastings, who was there on recruiting duty. "It took me but a few minutes to find out that he had only enough money to buy a soldier's railway ticket to his home in Poland, Ohio," Hastings recalled. "I said, 'McKinley, how would you like to go home to your mother in your second lieutenant's uniform, with your sword by your side?' How his eyes sparkled when I said, 'You ought to and you shall. Stay with me two or three days, and I will fit you out.' What a proud boy he was (then 19) when he donned his uniform; I could not have enjoyed it more if I then had known he was later to become President of the United States. He was a very lovable boy, and in later years.... I grew to love him past all understanding. He always rode a little brown horse [after he became an officer], and Webb C. Hayes [Colonel Hayes's son], then an urchin of perhaps six years, used to call out to McKinley, 'Hullo Billy McKinley on a bob-tail nag.'" (At the time Hastings wrote his recollections, Webb Hayes was a lieutenant colonel in the army, serving in the Philippines.)

As an adult, McKinley appeared to be stiff and formal, nothing like the lively teenaged soldier his army comrades remembered. Hayes became very attached to him. "One of our new lieutenants— McKinley—a handsome bright, gallant boy, got back [to camp] last night," Hayes wrote Lucy. He suspected McKinley might be one of "the generals of the next war." Indeed he might; he was the commander-in-chief.

Two weeks after Lucy's arrival in Middletown, Hayes was deemed fit enough to make the journey home. With six or seven disabled soldiers from the 23d, they began their tiresome journey to Ohio by train. Lucy, finding no seats, led the way into the Pullman car, occupied by a fashionable crowd returning from the health spa at Saratoga, New York, her biographer Emily Apt Geer says. "Oblivious to resentful glances, Lucy helped her 'boys' into empty seats. When a telegraph messenger came through the car paging Colonel Hayes, the 'society folk' became interested in the group and offered them grapes and other delicacies. Lucy disdainfully declined them." Lucy was a woman of character.

To Hayes's delight, Scammon was finally promoted to brigadier general, and Hayes took his place, with the rank of full colonel, commanding the 23d Ohio. He rejoined his regiment in West Virginia in late November. "It was like getting home again after a long absence," he wrote Lucy. It was not just that he was back with his old regiment; it was that he was back in West Virginia. The regiment was camped near one of the newly formed volunteer regiments, the 89th Ohio. Officers in the 89th warned their men that the tough old veterans of the 23d would steal everything they had if they didn't nail it down. Like every veteran regiment ever stationed in swiping range of fresh recruits, the 23d lived up to its reputation. The veterans stole stoves, blankets, and even, on one notable occasion, a tent sheltering a number of sleeping tenderfeet. "Our men sympathized, our camp was searched, but, of course, nothing was found," Hayes wrote in his diary. "After the Eighty-ninth moved, men were seen pulling out of the river stoves and other plunder by the quantity. The Eighty-ninth's surgeon was a good friend of Captain [Israel] Canby. He called on the captain a few days ago and was surprised to find his cooking stove doing duty in Captain Canby's tent."

On January 4, 1863, Hayes gave a brief speech to the boys of the 23d, summing up the regiment's record in 1862—Clark's Hollow, Princeton, Giles Court House, South Mountain, Antietam. Those actions, he said, "amply justify the satisfaction and pride with which I am confident we all feel in the regiment to which we belong. We

A serious Major General Grant, photographed after the capture of Fort Donelson.

Grant, in his first Civil War battle, audaciously attacks rebel troops at Belmont, Missouri. Columbus, the enemy stronghold, is on the far side of the Mississippi River in Kentucky.

Grant, on his horse, watches patiently as his soldiers prepare to advance against Southern troops in his first great victory, at Fort Donelson, early in 1862.

*Humphrey Marshall, Garfield's foe,
"big as hell, brave as a hoss."*

*Garfield, in his brigadier general's
uniform, late in 1863.*

*Garfield leans over to talk to
an aide in the wild and
treacherous Big Sandy Valley
in eastern Kentucky.*

Hayes, at left, with his best friend in the regiment, his brother-in-law, "Dr. Joe" Webb, in 1864.

Hayes said he could identify his regimental band from the splendid music they made, sight unseen. Here they are, lined up, in West Virginia in 1863.

Members of the 23rd Ohio's color guard had their picture taken at the end of the war. The flags were shredded by rebel fire in more than a dozen battles.

A rare portrait of McKinley in uniform, young and touchingly vulnerable, early in the war.

Hayes, in his general's uniform, poses for a formal portrait.

*Harrison, almost smiling,
in his formal portrait.*

*Harrison, at far left, with his bibulous "incubus," General William Ward, seated,
and two other officers.*

In a splendid Kurz and Allison campaign sketch published in 1888, called "Come on, boys!" Harrison is shown leading his Hoosiers at Resaca.

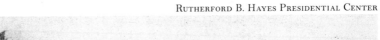

Generals Lee and Grant shake hands in the surrender ceremony in Mr. McLean's parlor at Appomattox. Lee's lone aide, Colonel Charles Marshall, is at far left.

Hayes's 23rd Ohio, being mustered out in 1865 in Cleveland. Not many were left from among those who had marched off to war in 1861.

recall these events and scenes with joy and exultation. But as we glance our eyes along the shortened line, we are filled with sadness that we look in vain for many forms and faces once so familiar! We shall not forget what they gave to purchase the good name which we so highly prize. The pouring out of their lives has made the tattered old flag sacred."

During the year, he wrote in his diary, the regiment received sixty-eight recruits and discharged sixty-six. It had forty-seven men killed in action, and another twenty died of wounds. Fifteen men died of disease. Total loss, he said, "aggregates one hundred and forty-eight. Net loss 80."

It was at about this time he was notified that he was the new commander of the First Brigade of the Second Kanawha Division, commanded by his old nemesis, General Scammon. That gave him command of the 89th Ohio, the same regiment his boys had thoroughly dismantled just a few weeks earlier, along with two small cavalry detachments. One of the first things he did as brigade commander was to appoint Lieutenant McKinley the brigade's acting quartermaster. That meant McKinley was responsible for supplying everything the brigade needed, except guns. McKinley was a careful, deliberative young man, and those qualities helped to make him a good quartermaster.

Lucy and the two older boys, ten-year-old Birchard and eight-year-old Webb, arrived at Hayes's log-cabin headquarters, Camp Reynolds, near Gauley Bridge, for a long visit on January 24. It was a difficult journey, and not many mothers would have undertaken it with two small boys. They were reasonably comfortable traveling by boat from Cincinnati to Charleston, but the next twenty-eight miles were by wagon on deeply rutted, muddy roads that passed through mountain gaps that conceivably could have hidden bushwhackers.

"We have had a jolly time together," Hayes wrote in his diary. "The boys," he said, "rowed skiffs, fished, built dams, sailed little ships, played cards, and enjoyed camp life generally." When Hayes was busy, Lucy went off riding with her brother, Dr. Joe. One day, they ventured too far and had to race back to camp with, they believed, rebels not far behind.

With spring approaching, Hayes and the 23d moved from Camp Reynolds to Camp White, across the river from Charleston. Lucy and the two boys returned to Ohio. When it appeared nothing was going to happen anytime soon, Hayes asked Lucy, her mother, and all four boys to come on back. "They are housed in a pleasant little cottage on the river bank—plenty of fruit and flowers and not over fifty steps from my tent," he said. Then, on June 25, this tragic entry in his diary.

> A few happy days, when little Joseph sickened and died yesterday at noon. Poor little darling! A sweet, bright boy, "looked like his father," but with large, handsome blue eyes much like Webb's. Teething, dysentery, and brain affected, the diseases. He died without suffering; lay on the table in our room in the Quarrier cottage, surrounded by white roses and buds all the afternoon, and was sent to Cincinnati in care of Corporal Schiremes ... this morning. I have seen so little of him, born since the war, that I do not realize a loss; but his mother, and still more his grandmother, lose their little dear companion, and are very much affected.

Garfield, a more worldly and ambitious man, had been devastated by the death of his daughter, Trot. But Garfield had known her and loved her. Joseph was one of four Hayes boys, and he hardly knew the little fellow. "The visit has been a happy one," Hayes wrote, unaccountably, on July 1, "saddened though it is by the death of our beautiful little Joseph. Lucy has been cheerful since— remarkably so—but on leaving today [for home] without him she burst into tears on seeing a little child on the boat."

A few days later, Hayes and the boys rusticating in West Virginia heard the news that Grant had taken Vicksburg and that

George Gordon Meade had defeated Lee at Gettysburg. Hayes ordered 100 guns fired to celebrate the victories.

On July 11, Hayes's brigade broke camp and started an expedition to Raleigh County, southeast of Charleston, a rebel stronghold. Hayes didn't think it was a good idea. "We are too weak to accomplish much," he wrote in his diary. He went on to say that his brigade would "run some risks, and I see no sufficient object to be accomplished." They reached Raleigh, the county seat, on July 16. "Found the enemy strongly fortified at Piney River. It was deemed unsafe to assault in front, and [since] fiddling it would take much time to turn the position, it was resolved to leave without attempting to storm the works." Curiously, though, the rebels abandoned their positions that night and ran away. No matter; the expedition, commanded by General Scammon, turned around and headed back towards Charleston. Just as Hayes had predicted, it had been a waste of time and energy.

"Morgan is in Ohio," Hayes wrote in his diary on July 16, and the whole southern part of the state was in a panic. "Morgan" was the ubiquitous rebel raider John Hunt Morgan.

Lucy was visiting friends in Chillicothe when news spread that rebels had invaded Ohio, for the first and only time. "No one could give a description to fully equal the scene," she wrote Ruddy. "All the Militia from adjoining Counties were here.... All these unarmed sheep were drawn up to be reviewed—the few arms that were distributed were carefully marched to the northern end of town. In the meantime the different scouting companies came across each other and mutually seeing Morgans men before them took to their heels ... and on coming to Paint Creek bridge so terrified the guard that they set the bridge on fire—in an instant the whole was in flames—while Morgan had not even a scout near." Lucy, the old campaigner, was vastly amused.

By all accounts, Morgan's column—1,200 troopers in all—was at Gallipolis, on the Ohio River in the southern part of the state bordering West Virginia. Hayes happened to be in a telegraph office when news flashed over the wire that Morgan had moved into Ohio. "Immediately grasping the situation," T. Harry Williams says, "Hayes sent a dispatch to Charleston asking whether any steamboats were there. Two were available, came the answer. Hayes directed that the vessels be sent at once up Loup Creek, a tributary of the Kanawha." He told Scammon what actions he had taken and urged that troops board the steamers and intercept Morgan. "General Scammon wisely and promptly determined to head him [off] by sending me." This order, he added parenthetically, "was after a sharp controversy." Three Ohio regiments, the 13th, the 17th, and the 23d, boarded the steamers and took off in hot pursuit.

They caught up with Morgan's cavalrymen on July 19. "About noon he came," Hayes said in his diary. "The Twenty-third went out to meet him; found him in force; sent for [the] Thirteenth; formed lines of battle. Morgan ditto. Seeing we were 'regulars and not militia,' he hurried off, with some loss. We had one wounded, in his hand,—Clemens, Company B."

T. Harry Williams says that Hayes showed indecision and allowed Morgan to get away. It was, he says, his "worst mistake" during the war. That might be a little unfair, for Morgan didn't get away for very long; he was run down at Buffington's Island a few days later, where he was surrounded by troops from a number of regiments, including Hayes's. More than 700 rebels surrendered, and most of the others, including Morgan himself, were captured later (206 of them by the 23d Ohio). "We had a most glorious time," Hayes wrote in his diary.

Hayes and his troops returned to camp in West Virginia, where they would remain for the next nine months. During that time, Hayes was required to talk his troops into doing two crucial things—one, reenlisting, and, two, voting the straight Republican ticket in elections back home. He succeeded at both.

McKinley had a particularly fine winter at Camp White, located just across the river from Charleston. He was now sharing a tent with Captain Hastings; it was a kind of Mutt-and-Jeff affair, the five-foot-six-inch McKinley and the six-foot-four Hastings, "a clothes pin of an officer." Hastings wrote years later that he and McKinley "became much interested in the young ladies of Charleston and surrounding country" that winter. They had "the entrances to the houses of the aristocracy of Charleston," Hastings said, without elaborating on just what an aristocracy might be in a mountain village. McKinley spent so much time visiting the ladies of Charleston that General Scammon instructed Hayes to put a stop to it. "You will call Lieutenant McKinley's attention to this," he said, and should he disobey the restraining order, he would have been arrested.

But the only arrest that took place that winter was Scammon's—he was captured by rebels. With two aides, Scammon had gone downriver to Point Pleasant to do some army business. He decided at day's end that he wanted to get back to Charleston as soon as possible; he ordered a steamer captain to get under way. The captain protested that such a late departure would mean tying up along the river at nightfall, and that, with bushwhackers lining the route, could mean trouble. Scammon insisted on going ahead, and the steamer tied up at a place called Red House Shoals. Just as the captain had feared, rebel partisans—in this case a detachment of irregular Virginia cavalry—came aboard and took everyone prisoner. Poor Scammon, refusing to accept parole, was hauled off to Richmond and thrown in prison. He remained there for six months before being exchanged. We can only imagine the reaction of the steamer's captain. The rebels burned his boat to the waterline.

"I must be cautious in what I say," Hayes wrote Uncle Sardis, "but to you I can write that his capture is the greatest joke of the war. It was sheer carelessness, bad luck, and accident. . . . General Scammon's great point was his caution. He bored us all terribly with his extreme vigilance. The greatest crime in his eyes was a surprise. Here he is caught in the greenest and most inexcusable way."

General George Crook, a celebrated Indian fighter (he had been wounded by a poisoned Indian arrow before the war), replaced

Scammon. "We all feel great confidence in his skill and good judgment," Hayes said.

"We have been marching now for three days," Hayes wrote in his diary on May 1. We have a considerable force and are setting out on a campaign." Hayes was pleased to be in command of a full brigade—four regiments, the 23d and 36th Ohio, and the 5th and 7th West Virginia. The 36th Ohio, Crook's old regiment, was especially welcome—it had distinguished itself in a number of battles and engagements. He also had 2,000 cavalry troopers under the command of Brigadier General William "Swell" Averell. The Second Brigade, commanded by Colonel Carr B. White, consisted of two Ohio and two West Virginia regiments. The Third, under Colonel Horatio G. Sickel, was the weakest. It was made up of two West Virginia regiments and two regiments from Pennsylvania, the 3d and 4th Pennsylvania Reserves. The Pennsylvanians had enlisted to defend their home state, and many of them were not happy to find themselves campaigning in the mountains of West Virginia.

The campaign was a rough carbon copy of the campaign two years earlier in which Fremont had led one column up the Shenandoah Valley (to be demolished by Jackson) while Cox led his little army south in an attempt to wreck the Virginia & Tennessee Railroad. This time, the Union Army in the valley would be commanded by the German-American Franz Sigel, a favorite with German-American voters (and 1864 was a presidential election year). Unfortunately, Sigel was no better than Fremont.

Grant had taken over as supreme commander in March, and his idea was to start campaigns against all rebel armies simultaneously early in May. While he and Meade concentrated on Lee near Richmond, Sherman with his three armies would advance against Atlanta. Sigel and Cox were the third major component of the all-fronts attack. Grant hoped the two generals would be able to meet at Lynchburg after raising hell with the rebel railroads and salt works. From there, they would threaten Lee's left flank, making the operations of the Army of the Potomac that much easier. But Grant wasn't very optimistic about the chances of either Sigel or Crook. "I do not calculate on very great results from the expedition from West Virginia," he wrote Sherman. And, paraphrasing a well-known Lincoln line, Grant told Sherman that "if Sigel cant skin [the enemy] himself he can hold a leg whilst some one else skins."

Crook decided to divide his force into two parts. The first part, Averell's cavalry, would move against Saltville, site (not surprisingly) of one of the Confederacy's biggest salt works. The salt was crucial to maintaining rebel armies in the field—it was used to preserve the meat that formed the major part of the men's rations (along with crackers). The second part, the infantry regiments, would make their way from Gauley Bridge across 140 miles of rugged hills and mountains to Dublin on the New River, an important railroad depot well to the east of Saltville.

Lucy and the boys had been visiting Hayes, and they left for home the same day, April 28, that he and Crook's 6,200 troops set out on their campaign, remembered for years thereafter as the Great Dublin Raid. They passed over familiar terrain—they had been here before—Raleigh, Flat Top Mountain, Princeton, Giles Court House. They arrived on May 9 in front of Cloyd's Mountain, defended by about 3,000 rebels under the command of Colonel Albert Gallatin Jenkins, a prewar Virginia congressman. John C. Breckenridge, the Democratic Party's breakaway pro-slavery candidate in 1860, was supposed to be in command, but he had moved east to see what Sigel was doing. Jenkins grabbed every soldier he could find, some of whom had been en route to other commands, and rushed them into his front lines. The reinforcements included an entire brigade commanded by Brigadier General John McCausland. Poorly armed and inadequately trained home guards and militiamen added to the eclectic mix. Jenkins also sent an urgent call for help to the rebel raider John Hunt Morgan (he had escaped from his Yankee prison) and his troopers at Wytheville. When he had done everything he could, Jenkins wired Breckenridge, "We will give them a warm reception here.... We will not be driven off."

"Monday, the 9th of May, was ushered in by the bugler's reveille, as the gray light of the morning was faintly appearing in the east," E. C. Arthur, a member of the 23d's band, wrote in a lengthy account of the campaign, "and by sunrise the division was in line, moving south on the Dublin pike." Led by the 14th West Virginia, "the long line of blue stretched itself across Big Walker's creek valley, with the bands playing, the troops cheering and the battle flags flowing in the breeze, and our accoutrements glistening in the morning sun, as it gilded the valley with a flood of liquid gold. The scene presented was that of a holiday parade, rather than that of an army going forth to do battle." Bandsman Arthur had a flair for the dramatic.

In his diary, Hayes gave short shrift to the battle that now took place, perhaps because he was becoming used to this sort of thing, perhaps because he was too tired to write at greater length. "Battle of Cloyd's Mountain," he wrote on May 9, "or as Rebs call it 'Cloyd Farm.' Lasted one hour and a half. The Twenty-third and the Thirty-sixth, under the immediate direction of General Crook, charged across a meadow three hundred yards wide, sprang into a ditch and up a steep wooded hill to Rebel breastworks, carried them quickly but with a heavy loss."

He was much too modest. It was a sharp little battle, a resounding Union victory, and he played a critical role in it. He led his brigade across a broad meadow that allowed all his troops to spread out in textbook formation, shoulder to shoulder two lines deep. As they approached the enemy lines, the rebels opened a deadly fire that tore great gaps in the Union formation. Hayes was all over the field, witnesses said, inspiring his men by his own reckless behavior. One soldier recalled later that the colonel seemed "heated clear through."

They reached the base of the hill, just below the rebel positions, to discover their way was barred by a creek, ten to fifteen feet wide and waist deep, according to Bandsman Arthur. "They were here only a moment, during which time many of the boys threw off their knapsacks, when they were ordered forward and up the steep slope into the woods, bearing to the right." A yell and a rush, Arthur said, "and the enemy is beaten back."

Taking part in that yell and a rush was General Crook himself, but his riding boots filled with water, and some of his soldiers had to give him a hand to get to the other side.

The 23d's Company G charged straight into two rebel guns. The rebels managed to slip one of them away, but the boys from Company G captured the other. Private John Kosht, Arthur said, jumped astride the captured gun, "which was too hot to permit him to remain long, but rammed his cap down the muzzle, for which he has been recorded in history."

It was too much for the rebels; they broke and began skedaddling toward Dublin, five miles away. Hundreds of Confederates surrendered on the field, including General Jenkins, who had been wounded in his left arm near the shoulder (he bled to death a few days later when one of his attendants accidentally knocked away a ligature closing off one of his arteries). The Union soldiers began a wild victory celebration that got out of hand; some defenseless rebel prisoners were killed, stabbed to death by bayonets. Crook should have put a stop to it, but he had become so overcome by the day's exertions that he had collapsed in a dead faint.

The only Union officer on the field who kept his wits about him was Hayes. He collected 500 men from his brigade and two artillery pieces, called for his horse (he had fought the battle to that point dismounted), and started a pursuit of the fleeing rebels.

The pursuit began as a general stampede; it soon became something more serious as rebel reinforcements began arriving on the field. What Hayes now faced were 800 troopers from Morgan's detachment in Wytheville, under the command of Colonel J. Howard Smith. They had been rushed to the front in railroad cars and were in no mood to retreat.

It was a critical moment in the battle. Most Civil War brigade commanders would have halted, reported the presence of the enemy in exaggerated terms, and then waited for reinforcements. But Hayes was not like most brigade commanders; he was an aggressive, fighting soldier. He resolved to continue the attack. It was at this dangerous juncture that Hayes showed his stuff.

With Hayes in the lead, the Ohio boys, under instructions from their commanding officer to "yell like devils," pressed forward. Crook, recovered from his fainting spell, came up with the rest of his little army to support Hayes's brigade. It was too much for the rebels; they scattered almost immediately.

Even though lasting only ninety minutes, Cloyd's Mountain was a surprisingly ferocious battle. Union losses were almost 700 men, killed and wounded. Confederate losses were 540 men, almost a quarter of their command. "The victory of Cloyds Mountain was complete," Hayes wrote Lucy. "This is our best fight." And he was pleased to add, as long as Lucy kept it a secret, that "the Twenty-third was the Regiment."

The Union soldiers entered Dublin about 4:00 that afternoon. "Citizens of Dublin remained behind locked doors," a campaign historian wrote. One of them, Mr. Wysor, overcome by the sight of so many triumphant Union soldiers, ran out his front door and began shooting at the conquering heroes. Union soldiers shot him three times, and he died two days later. A neighbor remembered Wysor's six-year-old twin boys running crying down the street just after the shooting. It was, he said, "a pitiful sight."

The federal troops set fire to the railroad depot, the telegraph office, the water tanks and woodsheds, and a number of Confederate government warehouses. About all that was spared was a warehouse filled with high-grade tobacco—the Union troops "realized" (their word for "liberated") the contents.

Crook's next objective was the New River railroad bridge, eight miles east of town. It was a 700-foot-long wooden bridge, covered with a tin roof and supported by iron piers. The rebels, now commanded by General McCausland, retreated to the far side of the river, taking up positions near fourteen guns already in place to defend the bridge. Crook brought his dozen guns forward, placing them on higher, more commanding ground. Shells flew back and forth across the river as the Union bands, led by the 23d's own, broke into the usual repertoire of patriotic tunes.

When the rebel shells began falling, Hayes, who was on horseback, ordered his men to seek shelter. Everybody followed his orders except a dismounted cavalryman from the 5th West Virginia. "Why don't you get off your horse too?" he asked Hayes. Hayes, not amused, ordered the impudent soldier to do as he had been instructed. "I'll get down when you do," the soldier replied. The exchange ended abruptly when a rebel shell exploded, killing the West Virginia private. Dr. Joe rushed to his side to see what he could do—to discover the soldier was a woman. She reportedly had enlisted in the army, disguising her sex, to avenge her father and brother, both killed by bushwhackers.

The cannonade lasted more than two hours, doing very little damage on either side; it ended only when the Confederate gunners started to run out of ammunition. As the Confederate troops began their retreat, taking their guns with them, Union soldiers moved forward and set the bridge on fire. It was a "general jollification," Bandsman Arthur wrote. "The troops on the river banks and bluffs, cheering, cannon booming, bands playing, and the enemy on the run in the dim distance, while the long sought for New River bridge, the capture of which frequent attempts during the war had failed, was now wrapped in flames, and the smacking sound of the timbers as they dropped into the water, and charred and smoking were swiftly borne down the river to tell of its destruction, was an exhilarating picture indeed."

The bridge burned right down to the iron supports. Because Crook had forgotten to bring the kinds of explosives that might have destroyed the iron piers, the best his troops could do was fire cannon balls at them. The cannon balls simply bounced off.

The raid, so far, had been an unqualified success. The rebels had been routed at Cloyd's Mountain, the bridge had been destroyed (although, with the piers intact, rebel engineers put it back together in a few weeks), and it was now time for Crook to finish the job by moving on to Salem and joining forces with Sigel.

But at this critical point, Crook seemed to lose heart. He explained later that he had received word that Lee had whipped Grant—not true—making a forward move inadvisable. He also groused about not hearing either from Averell and his cavalry raiders or from Sigel in the valley. So he turned his army around and began a retreat toward Meadow Bluff, where he could be resupplied from his base at Gauley Bridge.

"His last half rations and forage were issued at Dublin on the 9th," Arthur wrote, "and he was 150 miles from his base of supplies, his ammunition exhausted, his wagon and ambulance trains loaded with wounded and sick soldiers, with about 300 prisoners and two extra pieces of captured artillery and an army of contrabands [slaves seeking freedom], knowing that General Lee could concentrate any number of troops on the railroad."

A brilliant general—a Jackson or a Sheridan—would have pushed forward, short supplies or no. But Crook was no more than a sound general, and he did what he thought best. Hayes found no fault with his commanding general. Crook, he told Lucy, "is a most capital commander." Crook was always his favorite, so much so that he and Lucy would name their next boy for him.

It was a long, hard march, in the rain most of the time and up and over the mountains on muddy roads not much better than footpaths. McKinley, the acting quartermaster, was having a difficult time, for food and everything else was in short supply. As one wagon after another broke down, some of the supplies had to be abandoned. "Out of grub.... Live off the countryside," Hayes wrote in his diary. Guerrillas and bushwhackers lurked on the army's flanks, and Crook himself was slightly wounded by gunfire from one of them.

Years later, McKinley wrote that it seemed "almost unreal and incredible that men could or would suffer such discomforts or hardships."

They reached Meadow Bluff on May 19, and rations and supplies came in from Gauley Bridge two days later. "They had been out 21 days," Harry Williams says. "They had marched 270 miles through 11 counties, they had crossed 17 mountain ridges, they had forded and ferried more streams than they cared to remember, they had experienced 16 days of storm and rain, and they had gone without regular rations for 10 days. It was a rare record, and they felt good about it."

And so they should have. They were now hard, tough soldiers, led by men who knew their business. Hayes called them "a happy little company."

Sigel, on the other hand, was inept ("a fretful, intellectually wizened sort," Bruce Catton says), and his campaign in the valley ended in disaster at New Market in a battle that involved the courageous participation of 247 cadets from the Virginia Military Institute. Grant, less worried about the German-American vote than the politicians in Washington, fired him and named David Hunter to take his place. Hunter took over Sigel's 8,500-man command at Staunton, and on May 21 ordered Crook and his 6,000 men and Averell, now with 4,000 troopers, to join him.

"We reached the beautiful Valley of Virginia yesterday over North Mountain and entered this town [Staunton] this morning," Hayes wrote in his diary on June 8. "We seem to be clear of West Virginia for good."

Hunter, who had served with Garfield in the court-martial of General Porter, was one of the most unpleasant generals to serve on either side in the Civil War. He was prejudiced, grumpy, and subject to violent fits of bad temper. Hardly anyone liked—or respected—David Hunter. Sometimes he was stupid as well. Grant had ordered him to collect his army of 18,000 men and take it east toward Charlottesville and Gordonsville, wrecking the Virginia Central Railroad along the way. The idea was that the advance would unsettle Lee and President Davis in Richmond so much that they would divert troops facing Grant to deal with him. Grant also said that if things really went well, Hunter might consider moving on to Lynchburg, wrecking its factories. Unfortunately, Hunter concluded from reading Grant's orders that Lynchburg should be his primary objective.

And so Hunter's army, led by Hayes's brigade, set off for Lynchburg, and disaster, on June 9. It entered Lexington two days later. "This is a fine town," Hayes wrote Lucy. "Stonewall Jackson's grave and the Military Institute are here. Many fine people. Secesh are not at all bitter and many are Union." But, he said, "some things done here are not right." Hunter, he said, had set fire to the Institute, along with many other homes and buildings in the town. "General Hunter will be as odious as Butler or Pope to the Rebels and not gain our good opinion either. You will hear of it in Rebel papers, I suspect."

One of the buildings destroyed was the home of Major William Gilham, a VMI instructor. A sympathetic McKinley helped Mrs. Gilham remove her furniture and then helped find a wagon to take her furnishings and goods to a place of safety.

Hunter's army marched on to Lynchburg, now being rapidly reinforced by veteran Confederate troops, some of them commanded by one of the South's shrewdest generals, Jubal Early. Hunter made a half-hearted attack the afternoon of June 18, which was easily repulsed by the rebels. Hunter had no choice but to retire in a retreat that took his army all the way back to West Virginia and the Kanawha Valley. "Our raid has done a great deal," Hayes wrote Uncle Sardis, "... but failed in one or two things which could have been done with a more active and enterprising commander than General Hunter. General Crook would have taken Lynchburg without doubt."

Lucy, as warlike as ever, had complained in a letter to Ruddy that "brutal rebels" should be dealt with severely. But Hayes had just seen what brutal Yankees could do. He told Lucy about the way General Hunter had turned the wife of Governor John Letcher and daughters "out of their home at Lexington and on ten minutes' notice burned the beautiful place in retaliation for some bushwhackers burning out Governor [Francis] Pierpont [of West Virginia].

"You use the phrase 'brutal rebels.' Don't be cheated in that way. There are enough 'brutal Rebels' no doubt, but we have brutal officers and men too. I have had men brutally treated by our own officers on this raid. And there are plenty of humane rebels. I have seen a good deal of it on this trip. War is a cruel business and there is brutality in it on all sides, but it is very idle to get up anxiety on account of any supposed particular cruelty on the part of Rebels. Keepers of prisons in Cincinnati, as well as in Danville, are hardhearted and cruel."

More than most of his fellow officers, Hayes shared Lincoln's belief that one day the winners and the losers would need to seek a reconciliation if the Union were ever to be restored. Rutherford Hayes was a good soldier and a decent man.

Chapter 9

CROOK'S DEVILS

HAYES AND HIS Ohio boys had been hustled to the eastern front in August 1862 to bolster panicky forces trying to cope with Lee's invasion of Maryland, and they took part in the terrible battles at South Mountain and Antietam. Now, two years later, with David Hunter's army back in West Virginia, the Confederate general Jubal Early found the way wide open to proceed unmolested down the Shenandoah Valley and to threaten Washington again. And so, with barely any rest from its exertions in May and June in the Great Dublin Raid and the advance on Lynchburg, Crook's little army was ordered east to deal with Early.

Crook's army—about 12,000 men in all, counting cavalry—entered Winchester, the unofficial capital of the valley and perhaps the most fought-over town in the Civil War (it changed hands seventy-two times), on July 22, 1864.

The entry in Hayes's diary for Sunday, July 24, is succinct. "Defeated badly at Winchester near Kernstown by Early with a superior force. My brigade suffered severely. Rebels came in on my

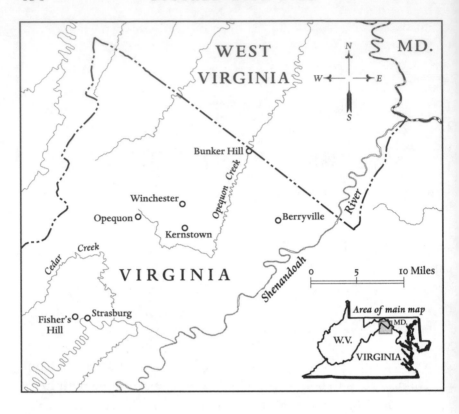

left. Poor cavalry allowed the general to be surprised.... My brigade covered the retreat."

Because the cavalry had not done a good job scouting the enemy, Crook and the other Union commanders were unaware that they were facing Early's entire army. Hayes's brigade and one commanded by Colonel James A. Mulligan had been ordered to move forward against what they believed to be an enemy "reconnaissance in force." Just as Hayes was about to carry out his orders, Dr. Joe rode up and told his brother-in-law the surrounding hills were covered with rebel soldiers. Hayes sent word to Mulligan about the situation. Mulligan replied that he had seen the same thing. They both agreed they were in a tight corner, but still they went forward. Almost immediately, Mulligan, a hero to his men and highly visible with his green scarf, fell mortally wounded, struck by five bullets. His demoralized troops refused to advance any farther.

The two brigades were receiving a punishing fire from both flanks, and Hayes realized it would be folly to continue the attack. He ordered a withdrawal. As the movement began, Hayes told Lucy, his map, an almanac, and a little photographic album fell out of his pocket. "We charged back ten or twenty yards and got them!" It was almost surely at this point that Hayes's horse was killed and Hayes himself wounded very slightly in the shoulder by a spent ball (his third wound of the war).

Now on foot, he rallied his men behind a stone wall. "Hayes's stand at the stone wall not only enabled Crook's army to escape capture by Early's 17,000-man force but also to withdraw in an orderly fashion," Hayes's biographer, Ari Hoogenboom, says, perhaps giving his subject a little more credit than he deserved.

One of Hayes's regiments, Colonel William R. Brown's 13th West Virginia, had been posted as a reserve in an orchard behind the Union lines, and no one had thought to tell Brown what was happening. Hayes suddenly remembered the missing regiment and ordered Lieutenant McKinley, as quartermaster a member of his staff, to find Brown and to order him to join in the withdrawal.

"None of us expected to see him [McKinley] again, as we watched him push his horse through the open fields, while a well-directed fire from the enemy was poured upon him, with shells exploding around, about and over him," Captain Hastings recalled. "Once he was completely enveloped in the smoke of an exploding shell, and we thought he had gone down; but no, he was saved for better work for his country in his future years. Out of this smoke emerged his wiry little brown horse, with McKinley still firmly seated, and as erect as a hussar. Now he had passed under cover from the enemy's fire, and a sense of relief came to us all."

McKinley found Brown and told him to join the retreat. But, Brown told McKinley, "I 'pintedly' believe I ought to give those fellows a volley or two before I go." And so he did. McKinley led the

West Virginia boys through the woods and then returned to Hayes's side. Hastings said he remembered Hayes telling McKinley, "I never expected to see you in life again."

"There were some splendid things done by those around me," Hayes wrote Lucy. "McKinley and Hastings were very gallant. Dr. Joe conspicuously so." The Union cavalry, especially "Swell" Averell's, was not at the top of his list, however. "The real difficulty," he said, "was our cavalry was so inefficient in its efforts to discover the strength of the enemy that General Crook and all the rest of us were deceived until it was too late." Dr. Joe wasn't pleased either. "Our cavalry is a miserable farce," he wrote his mother.

Crook's army retreated, in fairly good order, through Winchester. Most of the inhabitants were Southern sympathizers, Captain Hastings wrote, who were happy to see the bluecoats humbled. "The jubilant faces outnumbered the sad ones. One dear old Quaker lady, whom we all knew, stood at her door as we passed by, tears running down her cheeks, caused by sympathy for our misfortune. For her own safety with her Confederate neighbors looking on we did not dare to make any effusive display of our sorrow at her condition, but Lieutenant William McKinley, in his great kindness of heart, reined in his horse to the curbstone and in a low voice said, 'Don't worry, my dear Madam, we are not hurt as much as seems, and we shall be back in a few days.'"

A promotion for McKinley had been recommended earlier, and it came through a week after the battle. Crook must have heard about McKinley's good works because he asked Hayes if could spare him. Hayes could hardly refuse, and so Captain McKinley, at twenty-one years of age, became the acting adjutant general of Crook's army.

Hayes was back in Middletown, Maryland, on July 31, and wrote his diary entry that day "at the table of my old home when wounded—Jacob Rudy's. They are so cordial and kind. Dr. Joe and I are at the breakfast table. All inquire after Lucy and all."

On August 8, Hayes told Lucy that "we are, for the present, part of a tolerably large army under Sheridan. This pleases General Crook and suits us all. We are likely to be engaged in some of the great operations of the autumn."

Grant had finally put his foot down and insisted that all the scattered armies and detachments in and around Washington and the valley be placed under a single, unified command, and he gave the job to his old comrade, Phil Sheridan, on August 7. With the terrible-tempered Hunter out of the way, Sheridan now commanded 31,000 infantry and 6,000 cavalry. His army, called the Army of the Shenandoah, was divided into three corps—the Sixth, under Horatio G. Wright, veterans from the Army of the Potomac but a little battle-weary from their encounters with Robert E. Lee; the Nineteenth, under William H. Emory, veterans who had seen service but not a whole lot of fighting in Louisiana; and finally the Eighth, Crook's little army. The last was the smallest of the three corps, the "mountain creepers," the ragtag outfit eastern soldiers knew almost nothing about.

"Little Phil" Sheridan's instructions were simple enough—move up the rich and fertile valley and pulverize Early's army, while at the same time destroying everything—crops, barns, livestock—that could sustain the rebel cause. Just like Sherman, already marching to Atlanta and the sea, Sheridan was special. Shelby Foote called him a "bandy-legged Ohioan with heavy crescent-shaped eyebrows, cropped hair, and a head round as a pot, he looked more like a Mongolian than like the Irishman he was." More than any other Civil War general, he knew the value of cavalry (he had been the Army of the Potomac's cavalry commander), and he would demonstrate in the valley what men on horseback could do.

Late in August, Hayes learned that his friends back home in Cincinnati had put his name forward for a seat in the House of Representatives. He wrote to one of those friends, William H. Smith, on August 24. "I cared very little about being a candidate," he said, "but having consented to the use of my name I preferred to succeed. Your suggestion about getting a furlough to take the stump was certainly made without reflection. An officer fit for duty who at this crisis would abandon his post to electioneer for a seat in Congress ought to be scalped. You may feel perfectly clear I shall do no such thing."

The words had such a nice patriotic ring to them that they were widely used in campaign pamphlets in Hayes's presidential campaign in 1876. What Garfield, who gave up his army job to take a seat in Congress, thought about the scalping remark can only be guessed.

The first thing Hayes noticed about Sheridan was the cavalry. "Sheridan's cavalry is splendid," he wrote Uncle Sardis. "It is the most like the right thing that I have seen during the war." Hayes was generally pleased with everything. "We are having capital times in this army—commanders that suit us (we are rid of Hunter), plenty to eat and wear, and beautiful and healthy camps, with short marches. The best times we have had since our first raid under Crook."

Crook's corps was making a routine move—taking a new position near Berryville—when it unexpectedly ran into a large element of Early's army. "We had one of the fiercest fights yesterday I was ever in," Hayes wrote Lucy on September 4.

It was between the South Carolina and Mississippi divisions under General Kershaw and six regiments of the Kanawha division. My brigade had the severest fighting, but in loss we none of us suffered as much as might have been expected. We were under cover except when we charged and then darkness helped. We whipped them, taking about one hundred prisoners and killing and wounding a large number....

I was never in so much danger before, but I enjoyed the excitement more than ever before. My men behaved so well. One regiment of another division nearly lost all by running away. The Rebels were sure of victory and run at us with the wildest yells, but our men turned the tide in an instant.

McKinley was there too, in his first battle as a general's staff officer. In battle, staff officers were used as high-grade messengers, dashing back and forth with new or revised orders. It was often dangerous work. At Berryville, McKinley's horse was shot from under him.

Union losses in the fierce little battle were 166, sixty-three of them from Hayes's brigade. One of those killed was George Brigdon, Hayes's color bearer, the man who carried the brigade's distinctive flag.

Sherman's army had entered Atlanta on September 2. What "a glorious career" they have had, Hayes told Uncle Sardis. A little earlier, on August 5, David Glasgow Farragut had steamed past rebel batteries and captured Mobile. They were both huge Union victories, in both military and political terms. Now it was up to Grant, facing Lee, and Sheridan, facing Early, to finish the job.

On September 17, Hayes noted in his diary, Grant was in camp in his capacity as the Union Army's supreme commander, conferring with Sheridan and his top leaders. Grant had brought a campaign plan with him, but as Sheridan explained what he intended to do, Grant saw no need to pull it out of his pocket. "Go in," he told Sheridan.

The two armies met in a crucial battle known in the north as Opequon and in the south as Winchester (the third battle with that name) on September 19. It was Rutherford Hayes's greatest single moment in the war, the most dramatic event in his entire life. More than anyone else, Hayes was responsible for Sheridan's first great victory.

The fighting began early in the day. Sheridan pushed forward, through a narrow, two-mile-long gorge—the Berryville Canyon— with his two big corps, the Sixth and the Nineteenth, leaving Crook's corps, the Eighth, in reserve at the rear end of the gorge. Crook's artillery commander, Captain Henry A. DuPont, one of the wealthy Delaware DuPonts, was up front on a small knoll with Sheridan as the battle began. "Our infantry lines moved across the fields and were quickly lost to sight as with lusty cheers they entered the woods," he wrote. "In a few moments the firing began—at first a continuous rattle of musketry and booming of cannon, rapidly increasing in volume, then at various points great bursts of infantry fire—which repeatedly rose and fell above the general din of battle. It was not long before a small number of men belonging to the Nineteenth Corps on our extreme right began to emerge from the woods, their dark blouses looking like black spots on the sunburnt vegetation; many others soon followed and in a few minutes the four brigades of the Second Division of that corps, which constituted the first line of battle, broke to the rear and came pouring out of the woods in disgraceful confusion."

To make it even worse, units of the Sixth Corps, on the Nineteenth's left, were also behaving badly. That meant the two corps that Sheridan valued the most were breaking to the rear. He figured the time had come to bring his mountain creepers—Crook's Eighth Corps—forward.

"By noon," Hayes wrote, "the battle was rather against [us]. We were sent for. General Crook in person superintended the whole thing." DuPont—a regular army man—was very precise. He said it was 1:50 P.M. by his watch that "the head of Crook's column emerged from the gorge," its forward movement having been seriously hampered by the stragglers, guns, and wagons clogging the road running through the gorge.

McKinley had been sent to the rear to expedite the passage of Crook's reinforcements. He saw the chaos on the road—all the stragglers and wagons and guns—and decided on his own that Duval's Second Division would do better by marching along both banks of a creek that ran parallel to the road. Colonel Isaac H. Duval said he would take the creekside route only if he was ordered to do so by General Crook himself. "Then," said McKinley, "by order of General Crook, I command you." McKinley said in later years that the next hour or two were nerve-wracking—but the creekside route worked just fine, and Duval's men arrived on the field of battle in good shape.

"Having passed around on the rebel left," Hayes said, "we passed under a fire of cannon and musketry and pushed direct for a battery on their extreme flank.... My brigade in front supported by Colonel White's old brigade. As soon as we felt their fire we moved swiftly forward going directly at the battery. The order was to walk fast, keep silent, until within about one hundred yards of the guns, and then with a yell to charge at full speed. We passed over a ridge and were just ready to begin the rush when we came upon a deep creek with high banks, boggy, and perhaps twenty-five yards wide. Of course the line stopped."

The obstacle—Red Bud Run, feeding into Opequon Creek— was unexpected. It was a "deep, miry pool," Hayes said, and he wasn't at all sure that he and his men could get across it. "If the earth had opened to engulf us," Captain Hastings said, "no more fearful surprise could have seized upon our minds. This morass, totally unexpected and dreadful in its appearance, staggered our line for a moment. Now was needed quick decision on the part of our leaders, which came instantly from Hayes, who, spurring his horse into the morass called out in a voice clearly heard above the hellish sound of the battle, 'Come on, boys!'" Hayes was a little less dramatic:

On we started again. My horse plunged in and mired down hopelessly, just as by frantic struggling he reached the middle of the stream. I jumped off, and down on all fours, succeeded in reaching the Rebel side—but alone. Perhaps some distance above or below some others were across. I was about the middle of the brigade and saw nobody else, but hundreds were struggling in the stream.

Soon they came flocking; all regiments mixed up—all order gone. [There was] no chance of ever reforming, but pell-mell, over the obstructions, went the crowd. Two cannons were captured, the rest run off. The whole of Crook's Command (both divisions) were soon over, with the general swinging his sword, and the Rebel position was successfully flanked, and victory in prospect for the first time that day.

Several years later, Hastings said, he met one of the rebel generals that day, the exemplary John B. Gordon, who pointed to a scar on his cheek and said, "I am indebted to Hayes's boys for this beauty spot. When we first saw Hayes and his men coming over the hills, we rather laughed the movement to scorn, knowing of this morass on our left, but when in you came, plunging into the morass as though it were mere pastime, we began to wonder of what metal such men were made. One of my staff officers remarked, 'they must be devils....' After that charge my men always spoke of your corps as 'Crook's devils.'"

But there was still a lot of fighting to be done. Hayes continued:

We chased them three to five hundred yards, when we came in sight of a second line, strongly posted. We steadily worked towards them under a destructive fire. Sometimes we would be brought to a standstill by the storm of grape and musketry, but the flags would be pushed on and a straggling crowd would follow.

Things began to look dark. The Nineteenth Corps next on our left were in a splendid line, but they didn't push. They stood and fired at long range! Many an anxious glance was cast that way. They were in plain sight. But no, or very little, help came from that handsome line. It was too far off. At the most critical moment a large body of that splendid cavalry, with sabres drawn, moved slowly around our right beyond the creek. Then at a trot and finally with shouts at a gallop [they] charged right into the Rebel lines. We pushed on and away broke the Rebels. The cavalry came back, and an hour later and nearly a mile back, the same scene again, and a third time, and the victory was ours just at sundown.

Throughout the action, Colonel Comly, commanding the 23d, wrote, "as soon as the body of the enemy had been dislodged by us, our cavalry had charged and captured large numbers, cooperating perfectly with us." Sheridan, Comly said, knew what to do with cavalry. So he did: He used them at the precise moment the enemy was beginning to waver from the infantry assaults. We can only imagine, so many years later, the reaction of the rebels, tough soldiers to a man, when they saw these horsemen, sabers flashing, thundering straight at them when they were already beginning to think the day was lost.

Hastings remembered one of the cavalry commanders dashing by, saber flashing, blond hair streaming in the wind. His name was George Armstrong Custer.

Colonel Duval, commanding the division of which Hayes's brigade was a part, was wounded during the fighting. Hayes took his place in the late stages of the battle and remained as the division commander after Duval was sent home to recuperate.

"It was a great victory," Hayes told Lucy. "I certainly never enjoyed anything more than the last three hours.... The sum of it is, [the] Sixth Corps fought well; [the] Nineteenth Corps only so-so. Crook's skill and his men turned the Rebel left making victory possible, and the cavalry saved it when it was in danger of being lost."

Hayes always had this exaggerated notion of Crook's skill as a general. But it was Hayes, not Crook, who made the critical decision on September 19. Without hesitation, he led his men across that "dreadful" bog. Hayes, one of the good colonels, commanding no more than 1,200 men, decided the battle's outcome.

McKinley was all over the battlefield on September 19. At one point, Captain Hastings wrote, he was ordered to see if all those troops on a nearby hill were gray or blue. What ensued was another of those daring rides (not unlike the ones he had already performed at Antietam and Kernstown) that charmed so many patriots during, and after, the Civil War.

"Away went McKinley," Hastings said, "accompanied by his orderly, down the hill, through a cornfield, over an open field, getting closer and closer to this body of cavalry. Soon he was seen to halt, hesitate a moment and then turn and ride rapidly away, toward his command. Now there was no need to question who these troopers were, as a heavy carbine fire was opened upon McKinley, and his orderly was seen to reel and fall from his saddle."

The Union Army, led by Hayes, commanding the Second Division—Crook's old Kanawaha division, with its two brigades, 3,000 men in all—entered Winchester later that day. The old Quaker lady who had been consoled by McKinley when they had marched through Winchester must have been delighted to see them return. No better soldiers lived, Hayes told Lucy, than the ones he commanded.

The battles now unfolded at an eye-popping pace.

"We fought the enemy again (yesterday) at Fisher's hill, near Strasburg," Hayes wrote Lucy on September 23. "They had fortified a naturally strong position with great industry. It seemed impregnable, but General Crook contrived an attack, by going up a mountainside, which turned their position. My division led the attack. The victory was [as] complete as possible, and, strangest of all, our loss is almost nothing."

That's pretty short shrift for what really was one of the most complete victories of the war and one in which Hayes played such a crucial role. Dr. Joe, in a letter to his mother dated September 28, gave a much more vivid description of the battle at Fisher's Hill.

[After Opequon] the enemy fell back to Fisher's Hill, some eighteen miles from Winchester. This was supposed to be impregnable, the key to the Valley. Here they fortified themselves and boasted, as you will see by the Richmond papers, that they could not be ousted. We followed on. At this point the Valley is quite narrow, [Little] North Mountain and Middle Mountain approaching each other, say within three miles of each other. The mountainsides are steep and rough. Now, just here, a creek runs directly across the Valley, whose banks are steep and high and on which the Rebels have erected strong earthworks. To attack these would be worse than death. The Rebels felt quite secure. We could see them evidently enjoying themselves.

After looking about a day or so, Crook proposed to flank them on their left again, this time climbing up the side of [Little] North Mountain. So, after marching all day, at four P.M., we found ourselves entirely within their works, and they knew nothing of it. . . . Crook orders a charge, and with yells off they go, sweeping down the line of works, doubling up the Rebels on each other. They were thunderstruck; swore we had crossed the mountain. The men rushed on, no line, no order, all yelling like madmen. Rebs took to their heels, each striving to get himself out of the way. Cannon after cannon were abandoned (twenty-two captured). Thus we rushed on until we reached their right. Here again as on the 19th [at Opequon] darkness saved them once more. Such a foot race as this was is not often met with. The Rebs say Crook's men are devils.

It was Crook's idea to circle behind the enemy's lines by crawling up and around Little North Mountain, although Sheridan, his old West Point classmate, took credit for it later. Crook was seconded at the critical meeting that considered the circling movement by Hayes, who served as his spokesman. Hayes said Crook's boys—the "buzzards," the "mountain creepers," whatever people chose to call them—would have no trouble climbing around the mountain in complete silence. They had been doing that sort of thing for three years. In speaking for his commanding officer, Hayes served Crook in almost the same way Garfield had served Rosecrans.

The mountain creepers were unquestionably the heroes of the hour. "In few battles of the war," the historian T. Harry Williams says, "did the appearance of a flanking force have the immediate and total effect on an enemy army occasioned by the emergence of Crook's two divisions from the recesses of North Mountain." They had done their job with skill and enthusiasm, and some of the rebels were still running a day later. Grant, when he heard the news, told Sheridan that Fisher's Hill, coming so soon after Opequon, went a long way toward wiping out "much of the stain upon our arms by previous disasters in that locality [the Shenandoah Valley]."

A week after the battle, on September 29, Lucy gave birth to a fifth son, George Crook Hayes, although Hayes didn't hear news of the birth until October 10. "God bless the boy—all the boys—and above all the mother," he wrote Lucy.

Sheridan's army spent a good part of October ravaging the valley—"brown October," they called it—burning the barns, the crops, and many of the farmhouses. It was the same sort of thing Sherman was doing in his march to the sea. "This valley will feed and forage no more rebel armies," Hayes wrote Lucy on October 10. "It is completely and awfully devastated—a 'belt of devastation,' as Sherman calls it for one hundred and twenty-five miles from our lines."

In the midst of it all, Hayes learned on October 18 that he had been elected to Congress, with a 2,400-vote majority. The next day, he learned to his vast discomfiture that Ole Jube hadn't given up the fight, not by a long shot. "Before daylight," he wrote in his diary, "under cover of a heavy fog Rebels attacked the left."

It was a disaster for the Union troops, for Early had played the same trick here at Cedar Creek that Sheridan and Crook had played earlier at Fisher's Hill. Led by General Joseph Kershaw, silent Rebels squirmed their way along a narrow path between the Shenandoah River and the Massanutten Mountains until they were to the right of Crook's camp. They came yelling and screaming out of the fog and fell on Joseph Thoburn's First Division. The surprise was complete; the First Division was overrun before many of its men could even fire a shot. Thoburn himself was killed trying to rally his troops.

Hayes's Second Division was two miles away, and, veteran soldiers that they were, they filed into line when they heard the gunfire. Hayes thought the position was so secure that he rode over to talk to Colonel J. H. Kitching, commanding a ragtag provisional brigade to his left. "I went to the commander," he recalled years later, "and said to him, 'Can you hold on here?' 'Oh yes,' said he, 'I shall have no trouble. This is a good position, and I can hold here if you can hold on down there.' His was a new command, and I felt that sort of assurance in the presence of a new recruit that I would naturally feel, and I said to him, 'You need not feel afraid of my line. I will guarantee that my line will stand there.' But, happening to turn around, I saw my line breaking. Naturally I was somewhat surprised, and I galloped down to see what was going on."

What was going on was that the rebels, led by General Gordon, had smashed into Hayes's lines and sent his men skedaddling to the rear. Hayes described the scene as follows:

Although I was galloping rapidly, I could not get away as rapidly as they [his own troops] did, and, therefore, got the full benefit of the firing from the Rebel line. My horse rolled over and was dead. I fell, and for a moment I suppose I was bewildered, and was somewhat disabled in one ankle. I lay there some little time, how long I do not know precisely, but the men of the retreating line saw me there, and they carried the report to the rear that I was killed. When I awoke out of a sort of fainting spell, I saw that the rebel line was too near for me to escape, unless I used a good deal of strategy and a good deal of speed. I put out one leg, then the other, and found there was some trouble with my right ankle, but I got myself together, and started up the hill for the little grove. Just then there came a tremendous yelling from those graybacks; I can not repeat the language even in the privacy of the family. The names they called me reflected disrespect upon my parentage. I was in the kindest possible way advised to stop, but I succeeded in getting away, and finally I was on a horse again.

During the retreat, Hayes was struck "fairly in the head by a ball which had lost its force in going (I suppose) through someone else," he told Lucy. It was his fourth and final war wound.

A newspaper reporting Hayes's death actually reached Lucy's family at Chillicothe, and she was just beginning to read it when it was snatched away by one of her uncles. A telegraph messenger arrived not long after with the news that Hayes had only been wounded, "not dangerously, and is safe."

Sheridan, returning from a conference in Washington, had spent the night before the battle at Winchester, twenty miles away. He had been awakened early Wednesday morning by one of his aides, who said he had heard heavy firing in the distance. Sheridan dismissed the report, saying it was no more than patrols blazing away at each other. It wasn't until 8:30, after he had had breakfast, that he began riding to join his command. The gunfire by now was heavy, and Sheridan quickened his pace—this, he knew, was more than skirmishing. Soon the stragglers began streaming past him, joined by wagons and ambulances, cluttering the roadway.

Sheridan put his spurs to his horse, Rienzi, a huge black stallion, and galloped at least part of the last twelve miles to the front lines. "P.M.," Hayes wrote in his diary, "General Sheridan appeared; greeted with cheering all along the line. His enthusiasm, magnetic and contagious. He brought up stragglers. 'We'll whip 'em yet like hell,' he says."

Sheridan's ride from Winchester to Cedar Creek became one of the most celebrated rides in American history. Thomas Buchanan Read's poem "Sheridan's Ride," wildly popular at the time, captured the drama:

> *The first the general saw were the groups*
> *Of stragglers, and then the retreating troops;*

What was done? What to do? A glance told him both.
Then, striking his spurs with a terrible oath,
He dashed down the line 'mid a storm of huzzas,
And the wave of retreat checked its course there,
Because the sight of the master compelled it to pause.

As soon as he reached the battlefield, Sheridan noticed something everyone else had missed—the rebel offensive had stalled. For reasons still disputed by partisans, North and South, Early had failed to push forward. Part of the problem was looting—some of his underfed, underclothed, and underequipped soldiers couldn't resist picking up shoes and coats left behind by the retreating Yankees.

Sheridan's appearance on the battlefield "was the most dramatic example in the war of personal leadership, of what one man could do to change the whole face of a battle," Harry Williams says. "God damn you, don't cheer me!" Sheridan shouted at the stragglers. "Come up, God damn you, come up!" Sheridan, cool as he could be, looked the battlefield over, decided everything was running in his favor, and drove his army forward in one of the war's great storybook charges. Early's army was defeated, utterly routed, and Lincoln's chances of winning reelection soared.

McKinley played a small part in it. He had been sent by Crook to move Captain DuPont's artillery into a more advantageous position. "I had been across the pike to put in position DuPont's battery, by order of General Crook, and as I returned I met Sheridan dashing up," he remembered years later. "I took Sheridan to Crook, and they and their staff went back to the red barn. It was there determined by Sheridan to make the charge. Then it was suggested that Sheridan should ride down the lines of the disheartened troops. His overcoat was pulled off him, and somebody took his epaulettes out of a box. The epaulettes were placed upon his shoulders.... Then Sheridan rode down the lines. He was dressed in a new uniform."

Sheridan ordered the Union troops—soldiers from the Sixth and Nineteenth Corps—to advance on the rebel lines at about 4:00

P.M. He didn't include Crook's Eighth Corps in his plan of attack because he didn't think there was enough of it left to matter. Hayes had rejoined the remnants of his Second Division but was still feeling the effects of his tumble from his horse. He muttered to an officer of the Sixth Corps that he was prepared to advance with his men if that's what was needed. But in fact the shattered Eighth Corps played no part in the Union attack that now sent the rebels flying in what amounted to a general stampede.

For Hayes, Cedar Creek was something of a humbling experience. Soldiers from the other two corps made jokes about the performance of the "mountain creepers," and Hayes, not used to this sort of thing, didn't like it. "Some of the foolish fellows in the Sixth and Nineteenth Corps, feeling envious of our laurels in previous battles, have got the Eastern [newspaper] correspondents to represent the rout of Crook's corps as worse than theirs, etc., etc.," he wrote Lucy. "There is not a word of truth in it. A sentence in General Sheridan's dispatch was no doubt intended to correct this in a quiet way. 'Crook's Corps lost seven pieces of artillery, the Nineteenth, eleven, and the Sixth Corps, six.' We were attacked before them, and of course under more unfavorable circumstances, and yet we lost no more.... My division fell back, but brought everything we had—our two cows, tents, and everything."

The truth is, Hayes's Second Division, along with the rest of the Eighth Corps, was taken by surprise and routed in the early hours of the battle at Cedar Creek. It wasn't really their fault—Crook and others had carelessly positioned them—but it was still a defeat, and it rankled.

Cedar Creek ended Sheridan's campaign in the valley. Early and his army retreated to New Market, no longer a force to be reckoned with. In any event, Sheridan had so completely swept the valley that there was nothing left there to support a rebel army. Colonel Duval, now a general, returned to camp, fully recuperated from his wound, and resumed command of the Second Division. Hayes stepped down and took command of his old brigade.

On Tuesday, November 8, Hayes rode with Generals Sheridan and Crook to a polling place in the camp of the 34th Ohio regiment. "All vote for Lincoln," he said. "General Sheridan's 'maiden vote.'" Lincoln, riding the crest of popular victories by almost all of his armies, easily won reelection. "It gives great satisfaction here," Hayes wrote.

By November 23, Crook's army, camped near Winchester, was beginning to prepare its winter quarters. "Colder than any huckleberry pudding I know of," Hayes said. "Whew, how it blew and friz last night!" Warmer clothing—overcoats, stockings, shirts—arrived later that day, and Thanksgiving turkeys were issued "at the rate of a pound to a man."

On December 9, General Crook stopped by Hayes's tent and gave him "a very agreeable present—a pair of his old brigadier-general straps. The stars are somewhat dimmed with hard service, but will correspond pretty well with my rusty old blouse. I know perfectly well that the rank [of brigadier general] has been conferred on all sorts of small people and so cheapened shamefully, but I can't help feeling that getting it at the close of a most bloody campaign on the recommendation of fighting generals like Crook and Sheridan is a different thing from the same rank conferred—well, as it has been in some instances."

The commission dated from October 19 and was given for "gallant and meritorious services at the battles of Opequon, Fisher's Hill, and Cedar Creek." Hayes was right to think he deserved it. The next night, Hayes, General Duval, Colonel Comly, and various members of their staffs sat around drinking "poor whiskey."

At about the same time, McKinley learned that he had been promoted to major, but only by brevet, meaning he could call himself major but couldn't draw a major's pay. The promotion was awarded for "gallant and meritorious service in West Virginia and the Shenandoah Valley." For the rest of his life, even when he was president of the United States, he liked to be called Major McKinley. "I earned that," he once said. "I am not so sure of the rest."

Chapter 10

THE RAILROAD BUSINESS

THE 70TH INDIANA Volunteer Infantry Regiment, camped out near the old state fairgrounds in Indianapolis, had been issued brand-new twenty-man Sibley tents in late July 1862. It rained one night, and water poured into the tents, soaking the soldiers, their blankets, and everything else. They learned their first vital lesson: always dig a drainage trench around your tent.

They were green as grass but bursting with confidence. "We have the best company that ever left Indianapolis, for the boys in it are all young and from the city," Private Charles Harding Cox of Company E wrote his sister, Katie, on August 8. "It is said we have the best regt that has been raised in Indiana."

The commanding officer was Colonel Benjamin Harrison, and he was not an impressive figure. He was small and narrow-shouldered; his voice, even though powerful, had a curious raspy quality to it. His biggest problem was the burden imposed upon him by his family's history and traditions. He was the grandson of a president and the son of a very demanding father. It may have occurred to him that not very many people actually liked him. That was partly due to his lack of social skills—he was simply incapable of making small talk outside his close circle of family and friends. The Civil War would never make him a Jack Kennedy, but it would make him a confident and successful soldier, and that would be decisive in determining his post-war career.

He and his men were sworn into federal service in the morning of August 12 and marched to the arsenal in the afternoon to pick up their new Enfield rifles. That evening, they took part in a dress parade on the capitol grounds that included a serenade from the 19th Indiana Infantry band. Colonel Harrison, a week away from his twenty-ninth birthday, was given a fancy dress sword by his law partner, William P. Fishback, and the ladies of Indianapolis gave the regiment its own battle flag and a national emblem. Prominent citizens delivered patriotic speeches. Harrison replied, three times.

The next morning, the boys of the 70th, 1,000 strong, marched through the streets of the capital, cheered by its residents, and boarded the railway cars at the depot. "Company E," Major Samuel Merrill, the regimental historian, said, "drew the first blood, when just as the engine was about to pull out, Wm. Cooper taught a citizen not to utter unpatriotic sentiments." Second blood occurred when the locomotive rammed into a large bull that had "planted himself on the tracks and disputed [the train's] passage."

They arrived in Louisville, Kentucky, that evening, the first regiment answering President Lincoln's July 1 call for 300,000 volunteers to step foot in a state actively contested by Union and Confederate armies. "During the march through Louisville," Major Merrill said, "most of the citizens looked on in sullen silence, though from one residence ladies came out bearing ... cakes and pies, which they offered to the boys; and negroes could not restrain their joyous laughter and cheers."

The regiment set up camp in a field three miles south of the city. "Our men were so fatigued," Harrison wrote his wife, Carrie, "that they did not put up their tents but turned in on the ground. Some of them did not take their blankets out of their knapsacks but just used it for a pillow." Harrison, however, was rarely so tired he couldn't write a letter to Carrie. This letter was one of the first of hundreds he wrote during his time in the service, all of them gentle, affectionate, modest, and deeply religious.

> I hope you all remember us at home and that many prayers go up to God daily for my Regiment and for me. Ask Him for me in prayer, my dear wife, first that He will enable me to bear myself as a good soldier of Jesus Christ; second, that He will give me valor and skill to conduct myself so as to honor my country and my friends; and lastly, if consistent with His holy will, that I may be brought "home again" to the dear loved ones, if not, that the rich consolation of His grace may be made sufficient to me and for those who survive.

Harrison and the rest of his officers and company commanders had hoped to stay in Louisville for several weeks, to make up for the training that had been cut short by their early departure from Indianapolis. But it was not to be. "At 3 P.M. the day after our arrival," Harrison told Carrie, "we were suddenly told to start at once for 'active service.' We got off about 6 P.M., all in one train with one engine and arrived at this place [Bowling Green] about 9 A.M. the next day. We are encamped in a beautiful situation and are now getting into grand shape."

The train ride across Kentucky from Louisville, bordering Indiana, to Bowling Green, to the south not far from the Tennessee border, was memorable. The boys of the 70th Indiana rode in "box cars that had been used to convey cattle," Merrill said, "and the author of Knickerbocker's History of New York would have described them as fragrantly cushioned for the military occupants."

In heading south, the regiment was approaching trouble. One of the rebel army's legendary raiders, the ubiquitous John Hunt Morgan, was on the loose in northern Tennessee. He and his 1,200

troopers had ridden into Gallatin, just northeast of Nashville, on
August 12, overpowered its Union garrison, and then proceeded to
rip up Louisville & Nashville Railroad tracks and roll flaming box
cars through a mountain tunnel, setting the support timbers on fire
and forcing a cave-in.

Before getting on the cars at Louisville, Harrison had ordered
his men to load their rifles. "I was ... mortified and amused over the
ignorance of some of our new officers," he told Carrie. "Some of
them got the wrong end of the ball down and some rammed the
paper down with the ball and got it lodged, etc. I got mad and rode
along the line scolding, but finally concluded to take it good-
naturedly and make a joke of it."

And Major Merrill observed, "As we jolted along at night
through an enemy's country, with raw recruits lying on loaded
guns, it might be difficult to decide whether the danger was greater
from within or from without."

It was not just the commissioned officers who were totally in
the dark about being soldiers; the noncommissioned officers, so
often the veteran backbone of small units, were ignorant too. Company E's ebullient Private Cox must have felt some nagging pangs
of inadequacy when he was named the regiment's sergeant major
on August 25. "I am entitled to an Officers Uniform and a Sword,"
he said, "all but the *shoulder straps*." He had just celebrated his eighteenth birthday.

"We have got into pretty close quarters with the enemy," Harrison told Carrie, "and have already turned out the regiment in line
of battle twice. Yesterday morning [August 15] a barn of a Union
man was burned within 300 yards of our camp and we suppose by
some prowlers from Morgan's force. At night one of our guards
stationed near a spring from which we get water ... was shot at five
times with a pistol. These shots took effect in his left arm and one
struck a miniature in his pocket and lodged in it.... His wounds are
serious and may result in the loss of an arm."

But their situation was advantageous. Bowling Green had been a strong rebel position with formidable defenses. Its defenders had been forced to withdraw hastily following Grant's capture of Fort Henry on the Tennessee River six months earlier. Harrison and the 70th, now part of a provisional brigade commanded by Colonel S. D. Bruce, happily moved into the old rebel lines.

Imposing discipline was Harrison's biggest problem, and no company needed it more than Sergeant Major Cox's Company E, commanded by Captain William Meredith. Most of the boys in Company E came from Indianapolis and were tough, mischievous, and disobedient. "He has a good many hard city boys and is a *very poor* disciplinarian himself," Harrison told his law partner, William Fishback. "I have broken two of his corporals, put one of his lieutenants under arrest, and have a large squad [of boys from Company E] in the guardhouse. They are beginning to know me now."

A chastened Captain Meredith wrote a groveling letter to Harrison on August 24. "I am sincerely anxious to reform, Colonel, as you are to have me reform, only let me escape worse disgrace this time. For to such of those who love me let me 'try again.' I will take any obligation you may dictate to abstain entirely from the use of liquor in all shapes during my connection with the army.... I do not pretend to excuse myself, I only ask a chance to redeem myself." Harrison gave him that chance, and Meredith kept his word, serving with distinction for the rest of his time in the army.

On September 5, Harrison wrote Carrie about a "little episode" he had been forced to deal with. "Some ladies of easy virtue from Louisville," he said, "have established themselves near our camp and our boys have been breaking guard to get to them. Tonight I sent out a squad that surrounded the house and they have just reported with a dozen men who are now lodged in the guard house."

One of the problems was that in each of these companies, everybody knew one another. Merrill said they had trouble dealing with orders "that seemed to be unreasonable, or that were given in an imperious manner by the lately commissioned, who had been boon companions at home. Some of the officers felt sincere compunction when obliged to punish refractory subordinates, that could see no fault, nor even impropriety in disobedience. One such officer wrote to his wife: 'The hardest thing about this life, and a thing that often makes me feel like resigning, is the necessity of punishing boys, fine fellows in many respects, who take to disobedience as a duck does to water.'"

Harrison didn't feel any compunction about cracking down on his wayward troops. "Discipline was severe," Merrill said, "for the commander, Colonel Benjamin Harrison, knew that without discipline a thousand men are no better than a mob."

In his letters to Carrie, Harrison recognized the task at hand. "As to the feelings towards me in the regiment now I believe you would find that every officer has come to respect me and that all traces of difficulty have been obliterated," he told her. Respect was the key word; he had earned their respect, but until they had experienced combat together, it would not be much more than that.

The rebel raider, General Morgan, was still the most pressing problem. Late in September, Union scouts heard that some of his men, under a Captain Dortch, were recruiting in Russellville, thirty miles away. Harrison was ordered to take about 500 men from his own 70th, 100 more from the 8th Kentucky Cavalry, and 100 men from Company K of the 60th Indiana to see what was happening.

At 9:00 A.M. on September 30 they set out by train—they rode in freight cars, Harrison up front in the cab—for Russellville. At Auburn, they found the rebels had burned the bridge over Black Lick. These midwestern Union regiments were extraordinary for the number of specialized talents the men in them possessed. Harrison discovered at Auburn that he had several railroad men under his command, including one of his own officers, Captain William S. Fisher of Company I, who had built railroad lines before the war. Harrison set them to work. "The woods furnished heavy timbers for piers and stringers to span the forty feet of space where fire had wrought destruction," Merrill wrote. "The material was cut, carried and placed in position by the men. Crossties and spikes were picked up, crooked iron rails were straightened, and in less than three hours the ravine was passable."

While Captain Fisher and his railroad men worked on the bridge, other members of the patrol searched the village, especially the home of a well-known captain in the rebel army. The captain wasn't there, but his ten daughters, according to Major Merrill, were. The Yankees were followed, he said, "from parlor to bedroom, from cellar to garret by beautiful anathematizing damsels."

Leaving fifty men behind to guard the bridge, Harrison and the rest of his little expedition climbed into and on top of the box cars and resumed their advance on Russellville, twelve miles away. "When within about two miles of the place," Harrison said in his official report, "I saw a negro riding furiously towards us along the side of the track and immediately ordered the train stopped to get what information I could of the situation and forces of the enemy. I learned from him the exact location of the rebel encampment, but could not so definitely learn their number."

Just like Hayes and Garfield, Harrison had spent many long nights reading the standard military manuals, and he too had become enamored of the pincers strategies that always looked good on paper. So, on the spot, he decided to try one of his own. He "threw off" three companies from his own regiment and the one he had with him from the 60th Indiana, all under the command of Major Samuel Vance, "for the purpose of entering the town from the south." He said he then "ran on to within a mile of the town, where I threw off the residue of my troops, and turning off to the right of the railroad, through a cornfield, I deployed Company A, Captain Scott, as skirmishers, and advanced cautiously toward the rebel camp" from the north. Captain Harry Scott was Carrie's brother, making the advance on the rebel camp something of a family affair.

Coming into an open field, the enemy were discovered in their camp, when I ordered the skirmishers to advance and open fire, which they did in fine style, their fire being but feebly returned by the enemy. I brought the battalion forward, close upon the skirmishers, but the enemy retreated so rapidly that we could not come up with them so as to open fire. Seeing from the dust that a portion of them were fleeing along the road leading north on the west side of their encampment. I detached Company H, Captain Cumming, to cut off their retreat, which was effected in good order. A few shots being fired with good effect. Having marched through the rebel camp, we found the enemy had fled in every direction and in the utmost confusion, through the cornfields and into the town.

It was at this point that Major Vance closed the vise. He and his troops came forward "on the double quick, each company taking a separate street, all debouching into that from which the rebels were retreating. As the broken squads of rebel horsemen passed the posts of the respective companies they delivered their fire with great steadiness and precision, killing and wounding a large number."

Thus, in his very first engagement, Harrison accomplished something that had always eluded Garfield—carrying out a successful pincers movement. It was mostly successful anyway, for a good many of the rebels, including Captain Dortch, escaped. Suspecting that many of them had taken refuge in the homes of rebel sympathizers in the town, Harrison ordered his men to search all the houses. They managed to take about ten prisoners.

The catch would have been larger if Harrison hadn't been beguiled by a clever old lady called Aunt Lucy Blakely, who was sheltering at least one of the rebels. She recited passages from the Bible to the devout Harrison and several of his men who were trying to search her house and property. When she ran out of Bible verses, she served tea, including a very nice wine cake. By the time the formalities had all been observed—Harrison was too polite to refuse—the rebels in and around the house had gotten clean away.

But it wasn't a bad day's work. Harrison lost only one man to enemy fire, Howard Hudnut of Company A, shot in the chest. Harrison estimated the enemy lost thirty-five killed and wounded, along with the ten prisoners. He also reported that he and his men had captured forty-two good horses, fifty shotguns and muskets, and sixty saddles. Harrison laid claim to one of the rebel horses, named him Russel, and shipped him home.

"The regiment did splendidly," and Harry Scott "behaved very gallantly," Harrison wrote Carrie. The only fault he could find was that the regiment didn't show as much order as he would have liked in marching from the railroad cars to the scene of the battle, "there being a little too much eagerness to get into the fight." Then, too, he was sorry that Private Jonathan Burns was accidentally shot at Russellville "by a gun which fell from the hands of one of the men as they stood in the street." He said he expected Burns would recover.

It was back then to the routine of camp life, enlivened by singing and instrumental music around the campfires in the evenings. These evenings, he wrote Carrie, "pass as pleasantly as wanderers could hope to have them." He went on:

> But oh! how many earnest desires I have heard expressed to see the loved ones at home. . . . I wonder sometimes if you as often and as earnestly think of me. I think a man of strong domestic and family attachments is made to prize the love and sympathy of a good wife and the unselfish and tender love of children, much higher by a taste of camp life. When I think of the nice cottage at home and its dear inmates, I have been forced to think . . . of the thousands of other homes broken up by this abominable rebellion. I feel malignant towards the accursed authors of it. . . . I love to think that I am in some humble way serving a country which has brought so many honors to my kindred and such untold blessings to those I love.

Back in Indianapolis, however, all was not rosy. A group of folks there seemed to be working hard to deprive Harrison of his elected post as supreme court reporter. When he left for the war, Harrison had named another lawyer, John Caven, to serve as his deputy. Under this arrangement, he could continue to collect the royalties from the sale of the court's papers and decisions. But the Democrats—they were stronger in Indiana than anywhere else in the Midwest—argued that Harrison couldn't hold two money-paying jobs, court reporter and army colonel. They petitioned the court to declare the office vacant and nominated Michael Kerr, Harrison's opponent in 1860, as their candidate for the job. This was bad enough, but Harrison's own party—the Republicans—made it so much worse by choosing a Democrat with the unlikely name of "Pop-gun" Smith to be its candidate. "I think this is *shameful treatment*," Harrison wrote Carrie. Shameful it surely was.

The courts upheld the Democrats, and in the October election, Kerr and the rest of the Democratic ticket were swept into office. Kerr immediately laid claim not only to all future royalties from the court's books but also from two books that already had been published. "I would like to give M. Kerr a caning better than anything I know of," an angry Harrison told Carrie.

Harrison had more trouble with some of his own men. The problem was antiwar Democrats back home—Harrison called them traitors—who had embarked on a letter-writing campaign to the men at the front. These Hoosiers argued that the war was unjust, pointing to Lincoln's September 22 preliminary emancipation proclamation as proof of the fact that it had become an abolitionist's war. Hoosiers generally opposed the breaking up of the Union, but they were often of two minds about slavery. Sergeant Major Cox's racist views weren't entirely atypical. "I do not like the niggers," Cox wrote his sister, "and desire to see them all 'put away' our first opportunity.... I do despise *them* and the more I see of them, the more I am against the whole *black* crew."

Desertion became troublesome, with some of the soldiers arguing that they were free to leave the army because they hadn't been sworn in properly. It was a specious argument put to them by the

Copperheads [antiwar Democrats] back home. In an attempt to deal with sagging morale, Harrison called a mass meeting of the regiment and invited the brigade commander, Brigadier General Eleazer Paine, to address the men. His pro-Union speech was warmly received, but the real stem-winder was delivered by Harrison. He spoke for an hour and "riveted the attention of that mass of men," Major Merrill said, and he "was cheered vociferously when he closed." Merrill wrote that Paine was so impressed that he slapped him on the back and told him that "that Colonel of yours will be President of the United States some day." A likely story, but, apocryphal or not, it underlines the impression that Harrison only became truly animated when he was speaking to large audiences.

The speeches helped, and the morale of the Indiana boys slowly improved. "I hope rebellion at home may never again come to such an alarming extent," Cox, now a second lieutenant, wrote to his sister, "but if it should happen and the *Union* men at home cannot attend to them, a few regiments which have been down in 'Dixie' attending to professed rebels, should be called home and *they* would be *dried up* immediately. I hope we may never be called back on such a mission, but if it is *necessary*, we would willingly go and express to such scoundrels by *ball & powder* the sentiments of the Union soldiers."

What really galled the men of the 70th was that they had been in service long enough to be veterans and yet they had never fought in a real battle. Things seemed to be looking up when Rosecrans succeeded Buell in command of the Army of the Cumberland late in October. Carrie was visiting her husband when Rosecrans rode into camp on November 3 and passed the word that the 70th would be deployed as part of a powerful army that was poised to strike a crippling blow against the South. The 70th was assigned to Brigadier General William T. Ward's brigade, which was part of Brigadier General Ebenezer Dumont's 12th Division, which was part of Major General George Thomas's 14th Corps. The 70th, finally, was in the middle of the action.

Dumont's division moved out, heading south into battle, on November 25. Major Merrill said the chaplain climbed up on a small stone marking the border with secessionist Tennessee and proposed three cheers, "which swelled into bursts of shouting as the men approached the stone and discovered for what they were yelling. The band struck up Dixie, and there was rejoicing, as if new territory had been gained."

When they reached Gallatin in mid-December, Harrison received the bad news that he and his Hoosiers were being detached from the fighting army to set up camp at Drake's Creek and to keep the twenty-six miles of railroad track between Gallatin and Nashville open so that the big army could be provisioned.

"I suppose you have heard of our regiment being in the railroad business," Cox wrote Katie. "Well! it is so. We did not contract the job ourselves, but were forced to guard this railroad from Gallatin to Nashville 26 miles, against the will and wishes of all the officers and men. The regt is scattered at 5 different bridges, from one to four companies at a bridge. Col Harrison is doing all in his power to have us reunited again, whereby we may enter the *field* and stand some chance for *distinction*, as it is *glory* can never be won or never *has been*, guarding 'railroad bridges,' and unless we are speedily brought together again I am afraid the 70th has '*played her hand*.'"

On Christmas Eve, a lonely Harrison wrote another tender and sentimental letter to Carrie:

And this is Christmas eve; and the dear little ones are about this time nestling their little heads upon the pillow, filled with the high expectations of what Santa Claus will bring them, and Papa is not there. How sad and trying it is for me to be away at such a time, and yet I cannot allow my complaining spirit to possess me. There are tens of thousands of fathers separated like me from the dear ones at home, battling with us for the preservation of our noble government, which, under God, has given us all that peace and prosperity which makes our homes abodes of comfort and security. I am enduring very heavy trials in the army, but I believe that I was led to enter it by a high sense of Christian patriotism and God has thus far strengthened me to bear all cheerfully. I can never be too thankful for the heroic spirit with which you bear our separation and its incident trials and hardships. I know you must be very lonesome and oppressed with many anxieties, but God will give you strength to bear them all and will, nay I believe already has, drawn you closer to Himself as the source of all comfort and consolation.

To Harrison's disgust, Morgan was still on the loose. "The railroad has been cut again by ... Morgan," he wrote Carrie. "What a shame it is upon our generalship that he cannot be caught or entrapped." (It would be another seven months before Rutherford B. Hayes and his boys from Ohio would take part in Morgan's capture.) Rain was falling, and Harrison was confined to his tent with nothing to read. "I am lonesome enough to make a Frenchman meditate suicide," he complained.

He and his men could actually hear the guns forty miles away as Rosecrans and Bragg slugged it out at Murfreesboro (or Stones River) for three days, starting December 31. His own brother, John Scott Harrison Jr., and Carrie's brother, Harry, were at the front, where John was severely wounded in his shoulder by a minié ball. Harry, Harrison told Carrie, "was there to help."

"I almost envy John his honorable wound," Harrison said, "and hope we may soon exchange the ease and quiet of our present camp for the hardship and dangers of the field.... Not that I am ambitious of military fame, but because I want to feel that I am accomplishing something for the cause, which I sacrificed to espouse."

Lieutenant Cox felt much the same way. "We are having an easier time than ever before," he wrote his sister, "a beautiful camping ground, plenty to eat, nothing to do and any amount of handsome young ladies in the vicinity, but are not satisfied altogether. We are anxious to go to the *front* and endure the hardships and privations, and share the honor of our brother soldiers who have been standing the brunt of battles."

The boys of the 70th were holed up in blockhouses, structures that hadn't changed much from the French and Indian War. "We have one block house at this post [Drake's Creek]," Cox said, "but each of the other posts have one. They are built of Sweet Gum logs (2 feet in diameter) ... the logs are stood on ends about 12 feet high, the enclosure will accommodate 100 men and have 20 loopholes on each side. One good company can hold it against any odds, until starved out. We have our camp surrounded by breastworks and are perfectly secure against any charge of the enemy."

It was about this time (January 25, 1863) that Garfield came galloping into Rosecrans's camp in Murfreesboro to talk about becoming chief of staff. And it wasn't long after that that Garfield, who became chief of staff on February 3, began growing impatient with Rosecrans's failure to resume his campaign against Bragg. All of that affected Harrison and the 70th Indiana, for, until Rosecrans moved, there was no chance that the 70th would see action.

The regiment made a small move, from Drake's Creek to Gallatin, in mid-February, but the assignment was the same—keep the railroad running. Harrison bought some more military manuals and even began, for the first time in his life, to read novels (he liked Bulwer-Lytton and Dickens). When he was not reading, leading patrols, or drilling his men, Harrison complained about his new brigade commander, Brigadier General Ward. "The administration of General Ward is exceedingly sleepy and lethargic," he told Carrie. "He neither projects any expeditions beyond our lines, nor engages in any work of military enterprise within them."

In March, Harrison and some of his men, along with a small number of Kentucky cavalrymen, did manage to slip away. They went foraging up the Cumberland River, dragging eighty wagons with them. They captured some flour, fifteen horses, and four prisoners. It was "a pleasant and successful trip," Harrison said. "We were in a country filled with bushwhackers and guerrillas, but I took such precautions against surprise they did not attempt to approach the train [of wagons]." The cavalry, however, misbehaved, tending to plunder and straggle. "But I gave them and the officers a lesson in good discipline.... I have long been of the opinion that most of our cavalry did not earn their salt and I am now even more than ever disgusted with them, especially Kentucky cavalry."

"I'm getting tired of Gallatin," he told Carrie in April, "and would like to be on the move again."

It wasn't until August, though, that Harrison and the 70th broke camp. This time, they inched a little closer to the real war, with their new base in Nashville as part of Major General Gordon Granger's reserve corps. Granger had already played a major role in Rosecrans's successful Tullahoma campaign in June (the one that Garfield probably designed), but when Granger marched again— this time to the ferocious encounters at Chickamauga and Chattanooga—it was without Harrrison and the 70th. Once again, they were left behind, guarding trains bound for Chattanooga.

"I've known I was always a *busy body* in my own affairs as a civilian," he complained to Carrie, "and the lazy spiritless life of a garrison soldier ill-agrees with my habits of mind or body.... I feel as if I were a mere *drone* in the army." Adding to his woes, General Ward was just as big a headache as ever. He was "beginning to be almost *intolerable*" to Harrison.

Chickamauga, one of the great battles of the war, was fought on September 19 and 20, ending in near-defeat for Rosecrans and bringing glory to Thomas and Garfield. Rosecrans was replaced by Thomas, and Grant was put in charge of all the western armies. Thomas and his Cumberlanders broke the back of Bragg's rebel army at Missionary Ridge on November 25.

It wasn't until January 2, 1864, that General Ward's brigade was finally removed from its reserve status and ordered to the front as a part of the 1st Division of the 11th Army Corps (soon, through consolidation with the 12th Corps, to be the 20th). The corps commander was Major General Oliver Howard. He met Harrison and his regiment with a brass band. "He seemed very pleased with the Brigade," Harrison told Carrie. It had taken eighteen months, but Harrison was finally in the line of fire.

In some ways, Major Merrill said, the long delay had been a good thing:

This experience had been one of a nature that few, if any other regiments had enjoyed. Many troops entering the service about the same time were hurried into battle without preparation, and were sacrificed in the vain struggle to stop the advance of General Bragg's veterans. Our regiment while cut off from home and from the rest of the army, and for a long period outnumbered by large bodies of the enemy on every side, was taught that there was nothing to depend upon but constant watchfulness, and confirmed in the determination never to be captured, a fate known to be worse than death.

Night after night it was called out and formed in line of battle, and day after day the monotony of drill was relieved by expeditions against and skirmishes with marauders. . . . Colonel Harrison proposed to form a battalion that in the day of battle would move as if animated by one soul. He had the intellect and the will, and he accomplished the work. If vigilance and labor could keep the men supplied with food and clothing, nothing was wanting. . . .

Now a year and a half of invaluable experience in discipline, drill, skirmishing, scouting, bridge guarding, railway and train guarding, provost duty in village and city, picket duty, regimental, brigade and division evolutions in the field, it was ready to take a place at the front.

Merrill was right on all counts. Harrison had whipped the 70th Indiana into fighting shape. He had accomplished that by being a rigid disciplinarian, and some of his troops had resented that, but it had worked. It had worked because the 70th Indiana was made up of patriotic young men who wanted to be good soldiers, and they understood what Harrison was trying to do. And yet they worried how they would work together when they finally took the field in a serious battle.

Chapter 11

MARCHING THROUGH GEORGIA

HARRISON'S BOYS didn't know it, but they were going to play a critical role in one of history's most celebrated (and vilified) campaigns—Sherman's march to the sea.

And along the way, Harrison would finally demonstrate that he was a real soldier and a credit to the family that had already given the nation Old Tippecanoe. His soldiers would not only learn to respect him but even, as memories grew clouded, feel affection for him. By the time he took his uniform off, he would have won the admiration of his father, John Scott Harrison, and little could have meant more to him than that. None of these things would have happened if he had stayed home and allowed someone else to lead the 70th Indiana into battle.

Grant took supreme command of all the Union armies on March 9, 1864, and immediately put Brigadier General William Tecumseh Sherman in command of the armies in the west, directing his good friend "to move against Johnston's army, to break it up, and to get into the interior of the enemy's country as far as you can, inflicting all the damage you can against their war resources."

Sherman soon began moving generals around. Oliver Howard was transferred to the 4th Army Corps, and Fightin' Joe Hooker, the man who had been so severely beaten by Lee and Jackson at Chancellorsville, took his place. "Whisky I fear will be in the *ascendant* now if the stories about Hooker are well founded," Harrison wrote. "I most *earnestly* hope that we may be delivered of the incubus [General Ward] that we have carried so long." Whisky, however, was no bigger a problem with Hooker than it had been with anyone else, and, sadly, Harrison's "incubus" remained on the job. As far as Harrison was concerned, Hooker turned out to be something of a surprise. A disaster as commander-in-chief of a large army in the field, he was a successful tactical commander when he could see with his own eyes what was going on.

Sherman's army was really three armies—Harrison's army, the Army of the Cumberland (led by George Thomas), 60,000 men and 130 field guns; Grant's and Sherman's old Army of the Tennessee (led by James McPherson), 30,000 men and ninety-six guns; and the Army of the Ohio (led by John M. Schofield), 17,000 men and twenty-eight guns. All in all, at 98,000 men, 88,000 of them foot soldiers, a very powerful force.

"Yonder began the campaign," Sherman wrote. "...He [Grant] was to go for Lee and I was to go for Joe Johnston. That was his plan. No routes prescribed."

Johnston and his Army of Tennessee were camped at Dalton, Georgia, 30 miles southeast of Chattanooga, in the mountains, with about 60,000 men and reinforcements—Bishop Polk again—on the way. Johnston was under heavy pressure from Richmond to move against his powerful enemy, but he preferred a defensive strategy, hoping that in doing so Sherman would make a mistake that he could capitalize on. "He made war like an overmatched fencer," Bruce Catton writes, "moving rapidly to meet every thrust and shift, always conscious that his opponent was the strongest, delaying his own riposte until some of that strength had been spent."

He was assisted by two able corps commanders, steadfast

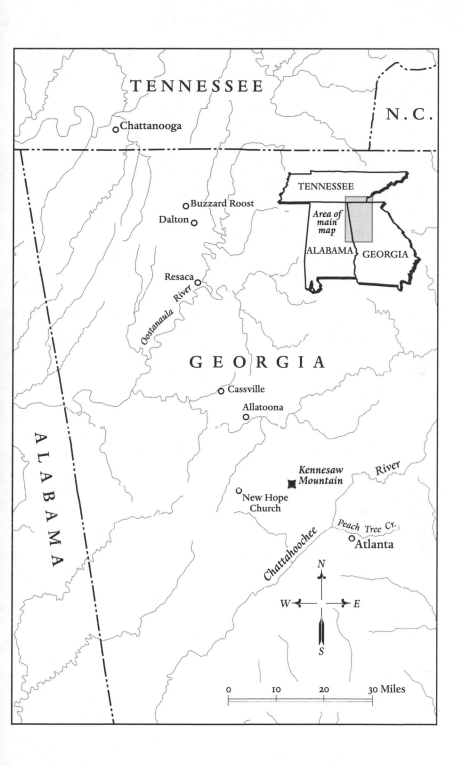

William J. Hardee and John Bell Hood, who had lost the use of his right arm at Gettysburg and his left leg at Chickamauga. Unfortunately, Hood was to his army what Garfield had been to his—a snitch, sending critical and confidential letters back to Richmond, undermining Johnston and his handling of the campaign.

Ward's division, including Harrison's regiment, set off to catch up to the main army, rallying near Nashville for the march to Atlanta and the sea. Ward, Harrison said, had the maddening habit of riding ahead of the main column and getting lost. "Gen. Ward rides on ahead and buys up all of the chickens," he complained. "I think he and his staff must have been tracking chicken when they lost the road yesterday. If we had not stumbled on a house in the hills [where they got directions] we would have been going yet on the Battle Creek road." Ward managed to get lost again the very next day; this time, Harrison blamed his erratic course on heavy drinking. So did Lieutenant Cox. Ward, he told his brother, Frank, was "the poorest excuse for a Genl I ever saw, he keeps eternally *drunk* and has no confidence placed in him either by his superiors or inferiors, the only reason our Brig[ade] has so long been in the rear."

On May 2, Harrison and the regiment passed Chickamauga Creek and a part of the September 19–20 battlefield. "Though time and growing vegetation have obscured most of its horrors," he told Carrie, "we saw very plainly where the fight had raged thick and hot. Great trees three feet through have been shot off by cannon shot."

On May 8, he and the regiment were only six miles from Buzzard Roost and not very far away from Johnston's main position at Dalton. Johnston, a defensive genius, had positioned his men—soon to number 75,000 with Polk's reinforcements—in front of Dalton, mountain peaks on each side. The only way to advance against him directly was through Buzzard Roost, held by Hood's valiant Texans. It was a very strong position. Sherman was perfectly aware of the problem and saw an opportunity to send part of his army out and around Johnston's lines and attack him in the rear at Resaca, through Snake Creek Gap. That would force Johnston to retreat and, cut off from supplies and reinforcements, might lead to his surrender. It was a good plan, and it should have worked. It didn't because the man sent to carry it out, General McPherson, marched to within three miles of Resaca, virtually undefended, and stopped. Johnston, worried by McPherson's flanking approach, withdrew from his position north of Dalton and regrouped at Resaca. Harrison's regiment followed McPherson through Snake Creek Gap and took up a position in front of Resaca. It was here that Harrison and the 70th finally came to grips with the enemy.

The night of Friday the 13th, Harrison crouched around his campfire and wrote another tender letter to Carrie.

I must write you tonight as we look for a battle tomorrow and God only knows who shall come safely through it....

I must say for your encouragement we are admirably situated and that in all human probability we shall attain a decided success over the enemy. May God in his great mercy give us a great victory, and may the nation give him the praise. You will perhaps like to know how I feel on the eve of my first great battle. Well, I do not feel in the least excited, nor any sense of shrinking or fear. I am in my usual good spirits, though not at all insensitive to the grave responsibilities and risk which I must bear tomorrow. I am thinking much of you and the dear children and my whole heart goes out to you in tenderness and love and many earnest prayers.... I send up to God this night that should you lose a husband and they a father in the fight that you may find abundant consolation and in his providence abundant temporal comfort and support. I know you will not forget me ... but let your grief be tempered by the consolation that I died for my country and in Christ. If God gives me strength I mean to bear myself bravely, and come what will, so that you may have no cause to *blush* for me, though you should be forced to mourn.

Farewell, God bless you—
Your devoted husband,

Benj. Harrison.

Early Saturday morning, Harrison and his boys "became engaged in a sharp skirmish fire with the rebs who were posted on a hill about 500 yards from us. One could not show himself on the crest of the hill without at once becoming a target for a dozen rebel sharpshooters and their aim was most provokingly accurate too. The bullets kept whistling over our heads, often striking a tree and falling about our feet."

Early in the afternoon, General Ward, perhaps sober, perhaps not, called Harrison's regiment to attention and ordered them to advance. Harrison figured he was supposed to advance against the rebel works on the opposite hill:

Hearing no command to halt, I went over the hill upon which we were [positioned] and halted at the bottom under cover from a fence to reform my line. While there I saw the Regt to my left had not come down and passed word up to Genl Ward to know what was the matter. He sent me word that he did not intend [me] to pass over the hill, but only advance up to the crest. I was in a position where I could not get back without being exposed to a *terrible* fire and even where we were there was no safety except by lying perfectly flat upon the ground. As I lay there the bullets would strike in the bank just above me and roll the sand down upon my head.

An hour or so later, Genl Ward sent someone to the top of the hill who called to me that the general wanted to see me. I ran a terrible risk of being killed in getting to the hill, but had no other choice than to go. It was very steep, and I could only get up by pulling by the roots and bushes.... I want you to believe I scrambled up pretty *fast*, and the sharpshooters did not fail to pay their compliments to me all the way up.

But he made it safely, and under the cover of darkness the rest of his regiment made it safely back up the hill too. Harrison said that if Ward hadn't been "so maudlin and stupid in his command to me," it never would have happened.

In his official report to General Ward, Harrison was under-standably more circumspect and cast a somewhat different light on what had happened, one that offers the distinct possibility that Harrison had misunderstood Ward's orders. At approximately 1:00 P.M., he said in this report, "and while our line was resting behind the crest of the hill," a drum roll called "Attention" to his regiment and to the regiment on his left. He said he then called to General Ward and asked what his instructions were. His reply was, "The orders are to advance." So, knowing that an assault on the rebel position in his front had been contemplated earlier in the day, "and supposing that the order involved such an assault, or at least that it involved an advance until a halt was ordered by the brigade commander, I put my regiment in march when the regiment on my left moved and passed over the crest of the hill, down its slope to a fence at its base, where I had previously instructed my officers to halt for a moment to reform their line."

It was at this point, he reported, that he asked his major to make sure the regiment on their left, the 102d Illinois, was still advancing with them. "His answer was that the regiment had halted on the crest of the hill."

Harrison made no mention in his official report about scrambling up the hill under terrible rebel fire to talk to the general. Instead, he reported, one of the general's staff officers called down to him that he should have advanced only as far as the crest of the hill and that that had been previously pointed out to him. One way or the other, it was a mix-up in which three of Harrison's men were killed and sixteen wounded.

Late that night, Harrison ordered his men to construct rifle pits along the front of his line on the crest of the hill. By daylight Sunday, he said, he had moved four companies (out of ten in his regiment) "to occupy them as sharpshooters and watch the enemy." He had no sooner done this than he was suddenly and unexpectedly relieved by another brigade, "and marched around to a new position on the left of the Fourteenth Army Corps."

In his new position, he said, he was informed that Ward's

brigade, supported by other brigades from his division, the 3d, commanded now by Daniel Butterfield, "was expected to assault the enemy's rifle pits, and without delay our brigade was formed in battalions in order of rank." The 70th, Harrison's Hoosiers, was assigned to lead the attack.

What he was facing, however, wasn't just rifle pits, it was also a rebel battery, four 12-pounder Napoleons called the Cherokee Artillery and commanded by Captain Max Van Den Corput. The guns screened one of Hood's divisions, led by Major General Carter Stevenson.

General Lew Wallace, Harrison's friend and his "official" campaign biographer in 1888, gave a nice description of the battlefront. "In front of the Confederate line," he said, "there was a hill higher than the others, and it was lodged full of sharpshooters; rearward of the line two other eminences were plain to view; and on the nearest of these a battery had been planted, masked by the woods, while the other was crowned by a redoubt skillfully constructed. Four guns looked from the redoubt down over the [Dalton] turnpike like dogs asleep in the embrasures.... These hills were the objects of attack."

Butterfield, the division commander, planned the attack. James Wood's 3d Brigade was told to take the heights on the left of the road; Ward's 1st Brigade was charged with taking the hill with the four-gun battery on the right of the road, and John Coburn's 2d Brigade was placed in reserve. (Coburn was the same fellow Garfield had sent off on a raid into rebel territory in Tennessee in 1863, leading to his humiliating capture by General Earl Van Dorn. Coburn had been exchanged and was now well on the way to rehabilitating his reputation. He was a fellow Hoosier from Indianapolis, and Harrison was fond of him.)

The boys from Indiana knew they were in for a long, hot day when the order was given to "Unsling knapsacks!" The knapsacks were placed in a pile and a detail assigned to guard them. Any lingering doubts were removed with the next order, "Fix bayonets!"

Harrison's regiment took the lead. The 70th, he reported to General Ward, "passed from the crest of an entrenched ridge, occupied by our forces, across an open field in the valley, and up a steep and thickly wooded hill to the assault of the enemy's breastworks, whose strength, and even exact location, was only revealed by the line of fire, which, with fearful destructiveness, was belched upon our advancing columns." Because of the rough terrain, Harrison had ordered all of his officers to dismount from their horses. Everyone advanced on foot, Harrison brandishing his sword.

In his letter to Carrie, he said that as his Hoosiers approached the enemy's breastworks, "I took off my cap and, waving it above my head, cheered the men on," probably shouting "Come on, boys!" Lieutenant Cox, now the regiment's acting adjutant, was there. Not one to turn away from hyperbole, he told his sister Katie that "never was a body of men in such a *hot* place as was the invincible 70th on that terrible day."

Surely it was hot enough—hotter than anything Old Tippecanoe had ever seen. Through it all, said Harrison, his men "moved on with perfect steadiness, and without any sign of faltering up the hillside and to the very muzzle of the enemy's battery, which continued to belch their deadly charges of grape and cannister." That rigid discipline he had instilled in them was paying off.

Captain Meredith of Company E, the one who had promised Harrison that he would swear off liquor and become a better officer, thought he might have been the first Yankee to jump over the parapet guarding the rebel guns. Company E, he said, "struck that battery square in the face, and ... its last discharge was right over our heads, almost in our faces." He continued:

> I remember that after the gallant Confederates had done their best, one brave fellow would neither run nor surrender, but stood there laying about him with his ramrod. I had fired the last two shots of my revolver at him and had begged him to surrender, but his only reply was a swinging sweep of his ramrod, which was

dodged. Then a hand reached over my shoulder, somebody said, "Captain, let me at him," a pistol was fired close beside me, and turning I saw [Major] Merrill [the regimental historian], smoking revolver in hand. In a few minutes the gunners were overcome, and the battery and the position were ours."

But not for long. "Behind the fort [containing the guns]," Harrison wrote, "the enemy had a line of breastworks, which were filled with 'gray-backs.' At first they retreated from their line but soon rallied and returned to the breastworks and forced us to get on the outside of the first work for cover, behind which we lay keeping the rebels from the guns."

The rebel counterattack was disturbing enough, but it was about this same time that Harrison's men came under fire from other Union soldiers making their way up the hill. Harrison sent messengers pleading with these men to cease firing. The firing didn't come to an end until Joe Hooker himself put a stop to it.

In the midst of all this confusion, someone, perhaps a rebel, shouted, "Retreat, we're being flanked!" At this, Harrison said, "many retired down the hill. I tried every way to rally them but could not do it under fire, and was forced at last to retire behind the next hill for that purpose. Here I learned that General Ward was wounded [not seriously] and that the command of the brigade had devolved upon me."

Harrison said that after he had reformed his regiments, he asked General Butterfield for permission to take them back to the hill where Harry Scott and 300 men were still holding on to those captured brass guns. Butterfield refused and instead ordered Harrison and his brigade to support Coburn's brigade that was being pressed hard by rebels on another hill.

During the night, soldiers from the 2d Division's 5th Ohio made their way up the hill to relieve the Hoosiers guarding the guns. They surreptitiously hauled the guns down the hill and to the disgust of Harrison's men tried to take credit for capturing them.

It was a hard day for Harrison and his regiment. They lost twenty-six killed, 130 wounded. The glory-grabbing 5th Ohio, Major Merrill took pains to point out, lost three killed and twelve wounded.

The enemy retreated Monday morning, and Harrison took his men up the hill to bury the dead. "We worked hard all day," he wrote Carrie, "and buried 50 dead from our Brigade, besides about 100 rebel dead. The scenes on the battlefield were of the most appalling character, and I could not have imagined that I could have witnessed them without more emotion. A fire had broken out in the woods at night and many of our dead were horribly burned, which gave additional gentleness to their stiffened corpses. We buried our own dead with every possible attention and enclosed their common grave with a fence of pine poles, marking each grave with the name of the deceased." The four rebel guns were dragged off to Resaca, along with 1,200 small arms picked up by Harrison's men on the battlefield, and were turned over to the ordnance department.

Harrison confided to Carrie that he spent some time worrying whether he might be censured for retiring, "but am pleased to find out it is regarded as a 'very brilliant charge.' General Hooker told me he so regarded it. I was exposed to death as much as a man could be and escape, and know you will unite with me in thanksgiving to God who only could have brought me safely through such dangers." He added that Carrie's brother, Harry, "behaved with *conspicuous* gallantry."

And so had Ben Harrison. His soldiers, never very warm in their feelings about their 140-pound colonel, began now to come around. They conferred an affectionate nickname on him, "Little Ben," and that's how they always remembered him.

Harrison's performance at Resaca was celebrated in the Indianapolis and Cincinnati newspapers and even drew a warm letter of praise from his father. "He seems to be very proud that I have won some distinction in my new profession," he wrote Carrie. "I am glad that I have been able to show them all that I can hold a creditable place in the army as well as in civil life, and that if not the most petted one in the family, its famous name is as safe in my keeping as that of any who now bear the name. We must not however think too much of the praises of the newspapers, nor forget that to God who sustains me belongs all the honor."

Sherman, however, was disappointed in the results at Resaca, and especially in the timid performance of one of his and Grant's favorite generals, McPherson (who died a hero outside Atlanta two months later). Sherman knew he had missed his chance to destroy Johnston.

Harrison and his brigade were back in action on May 19 at Cassville, ten miles south of Resaca, where Johnston had taken up new positions north of the town. Years later, in a speech to Union veterans, Harrison recalled the scene:

One day, when the army was advancing on Cassville, we suddenly came out [of the woods and the brush] into one of the great meadows or savannahs that stretch for miles along some of the smaller streams, and the whole great army, corps on corps, was revealed to us, banner after banner as it was kissed by the sunshine of the open field. From the center, far to the right and left, the distinctive corps, division, brigade and regimental colors appeared, and associated with each of these was the one flag that made the army whole. A mighty, spontaneous cheer burst from the whole line, and every soldier tightened his grip upon his rifle and quickened his step. There was an inspiration in it. Our faith had been strengthened by the vision of those who fought with us for the flag.

It was memories such as this one that Harrison and all these Civil War veterans, Union and Confederate, carried to their graves.

Harrison's brigade seemed to have a penchant for getting lost, and it got lost again at Cassville. The brigade was lost in an uncomfortable place too, for it was almost surrounded by rebel infantry and cavalry. "The word went like a flash along the line to throw up a barricade," Private Uriah H. Farr of Company D wrote in a memoir. "Every fence rail, log, chunk and movable thing within reach was instantly appropriated to that purpose, and then the men set to work digging dirt with the bayonet, and scooping it up with frying pans, hands, or anything that could be put to that use, while a strong force was sent out in front to level all the fencing, that the advancing enemy might have no protection in the coming contest."

Farr said that rebel infantry suddenly appeared in their front and began advancing, "in line, massed so as to crush all opposition." Harrison's skirmishers were called in, and every man was issued twenty extra rounds of ammunition, making sixty in all, and told to get ready for action. "Cartridge and [percussion] cap boxes were unclasped and slipped to the front of the body so as to be convenient; the commands were given and passed along the lines to aim accurately and reserve the fire till the enemy were close at hand."

Suddenly, Farr said, relief arrived—"column after column came marching into view, facing in the same direction as we were, their bright guns shining in the sun, the Stars and Stripes floating above them. The rebel hosts sullenly but rapidly retired to the wooded hill from whence they came, and after some fighting left Cassville in our hands."

Johnston had actually wanted to attack Sherman at Cassville, and Harrison's men may have seen a small part of that unfolding. But Hood, uncharacteristically, demurred, arguing he was threatened by Union troops that in fact were nonexistent. Polk said he wanted to retreat too. Only Hardee was in favor of an attack. Once again, Johnston decided, this time against his better judgment, to withdraw. Cassville was to Johnston what Resaca had been to Sherman—a missed opportunity.

So the two armies stumbled on, Sherman constantly trying to turn Johnston's flank, Johnston brilliantly repositioning his army to thwart his enemy's intentions. It was dreary work for the soldiers. Lieutenant Cox said that the regiment often marched twenty miles in the heat of the day, "each man being obliged to carry a heavy musket, cartridge box, 60 rounds ammunition, 3 day rations in haversack, knapsack, blanket, tent, and every thing he possesses in the army. I tell you it makes a heavy load for a man to carry, all day long on a forced march. I saw men fall in their tracks while trudging along, becoming so weak & powerless their legs would not carry them along. Then after the labor of marching all day the night is spent in building defenses and preparing for battle."

In a letter to Carrie, Harrison agreed the marching had been fatiguing. He said his health continued to be excellent, "except that I have been suffering from a *poisoned skin*. I suppose I got it from some poison vine.... It has spread all over my face and hands and down on my legs. It itches terribly." His hands were so sensitive for years thereafter that he often wore gloves as protection. His political opponents jumped on this as an affectation and called him "Kid-gloves Harrison." The fault, really, was a "poison vine," somewhere near Allatoona, Georgia.

"From Resaca on," General Wallace wrote, "they [Harrison and his troops] had scarcely a halt in the day or the night that was not marked by heavy fortification; for in truth the commands all came as near living under fire the while as soldiers ever did—not one, but all of them. While Resaca was the Colonel's first real battle it was simply an introduction to a series of others swift in coming, and each seemingly hotter than the one preceding. In one month he was engaged in more battles than his grandfather William Henry Harrison fought in his whole life—more than Andrew Jackson fought in his life."

One day, Private Farr recalled, General Hooker came riding by the Indiana boys. "Hardtack! Hardtack!" they yelled. He asked what the boys meant by that. Told they hadn't eaten anything in hours, he sent back orders to provide for the regiment, and they "were soon gladdened by the sight of commissary wagons." Lieutenant Cox wrote his sister, "I have almost fell in love with 'Old Joe.'"

Hooker was in the lead May 25 when his divisions caught up to the rebels at Pumpkin Vine Creek. He chased the rebel skirmishers until he ran into a very large concentration of rebel infantrymen. He didn't know it, but this was Hood's entire corps, marching away from Allatoona. Fighting raged around New Hope Church in a place known to these veterans ever after as the "hell hole."

The firing was fading away—just as a heavy rain began to fall—when Harrison and the 1st Brigade arrived on the battlefield, cold and shivering. In the mist of the next morning, the battle began anew. To Harrison's astonishment, the dawn of day revealed that he and his boys had gone astray, "through the failure of his guide" and that "his whole command was out in an open field. . . . Almost the first cannon shot apprised him of the mistake, and that it was of a serious nature. The guns were turned upon him and shells, grapeshot, canister, railroad spikes, and every deadly missile rained about his regiment. As best they could, hugging the half-finished earthwork before him, the ditch but a pool of muddy water, his men returned the fire. And all that day the contest continued with scarce an interruption, when a Wisconsin regiment came to his relief."

They were engaged again, at Golgotha Church, near Kenesaw Mountain, on June 15. He described what happened, not sparing the gruesome details, in a letter to Carrie:

My regiment was advanced without any support to within 300 yards of a strong rebel breastwork where they had 8 pieces of artillery in position and nicely covered and we being entirely exposed. We stood there fighting an unseen foe for an hour and a half without flinching while the enemy shells and grape fell like hail on our ranks tearing down large trees and filling the air with splinters. Two or three of my men had their heads torn off close down to the shoulders and others had dreadful wounds. We were ordered to be there till night when we would be relieved and we did, though I think few veteran regiments

would have done so. After dark we were relieved by a regiment
of Coburn's brigade, but they didn't stay there long and the
position was not held.... After we were relieved we fell back in
perfect order to the support of our own batteries, taking our
killed and wounded with us.

"It is said," Lieutenant Cox told Katie with his usual flair for
exaggeration, that "no troops were ever known to stand under such
artillery fire before. More than 50 shells exploded within 25 feet of
me and I was almost deaf when the battle was over."

The wounded were taken to a deserted house, but the regimental
surgeons were nowhere to be seen. So Harrison—in a performance
that would be celebrated in all of his political campaigns—rolled up
his sleeves and began treating the men himself.

Poor fellows. I was but an awkward surgeon, but I hope I gave
them some relief. There were some *ghastly* wounds. I pulled out
of one poor fellow's arm a splinter five or six inches long and as
thick as three fingers. Major Reagan was struck twice, once
with a musket ball which was turned aside by his spy-glass and
once by a piece of shell which bruised him badly on the side.

Harrison took a look at the battlefield again the next day, after
the rebels had evacuated their lines. "The woods," he said, "were lit-
erally torn into splinters and in looking over the ground it seems
marvelous that so few were hurt. God does mercifully preserve my
unworthy life. May it continue to be His case. Love and kisses to
my dear children and all that will admit to that familiarity among
my *female* friends." Every now and again, Harrison surprised his
friends with a touch of drollery.

He was playful in another letter to Carrie in which he described
a ride he had taken behind the lines to the supply depot "to see
what could be done by dint of my *eloquence* and popularity." He said
he succeeded in "getting a ham, some beans, and a few soda crack-

ers, not to mention a sack of corn.... This was quite a success as I know of some *generals* who have failed to get these things where I got them. I find I have quite an extensive acquaintance through the army and can get many personal favors where others fail.... General Hooker himself is very kind to me."

The amazing part of it is that for all the terrible things happening around him, Little Ben seemed to be *enjoying* himself. "I would not like to leave my Regt," he told Carrie. "I have got to love them for their bravery and for dangers we have shared together. I have heard many similar expressions from the men toward me." He probably was pleased when he succeeded General Ward in command of the 1st Brigade. That didn't mean, though, that he was yet finished with his "incubus," for Ward was named commander of the division, in place of Butterfield. The regimental historian, Samuel Merrill, now a lieutenant colonel, took command of the 70th Indiana.

Lieutenant Cox, angling for promotion to first lieutenant, got along better with Merrill than he had with Harrison. "I do not think as much of Harrison as I used to," he told his sister, "and Colonel Merrill I highly esteem—he is a good officer and a gentleman—he does not treat his inferiors like dogs as Harrison does—and he has some regard for a mans feelings."

A frustrated Sherman tried his only frontal attack on Johnston's position on June 27, sending three divisions up Kenesaw Mountain against well-entrenched rebel lines. Harrison and his men put down their shovels—as usual, they were busy digging earthworks—and watched. "All that brave men could do they [the Union soldiers] did," General Wallace said, "but there is a limit to the purest courage, a point at which it too is overtaken by the impossible. That point was at last reached," and Harrison and his brigade watched in sorrow and frustration as the Union soldiers fell back, leaving hundreds of dead and wounded on the hillside.

Harrison tried to explain to Carrie in a letter dated July 7 just how difficult it was to attack Joe Johnston's lines:

In the first place in advancing you will come at 1000 yards from the enemy's works into a "tangle," that is, all the small trees and some large ones are felled cross-wise so that you have to make your way through a *continual succession of tree-tops*. As you get nearer, say 300 yards, you come to an abatis which consists of tree-tops, bushy ends towards you, all the leaves trimmed off and every branch and twig sharpened so that it will catch in the clothes. If you succeed in getting through this, you will find about 20 yards from the [rebel] rifle pits two lines of stakes about 12 feet long, set about four feet in the ground and inclining towards you, the upper end being sharpened and the stakes set so close that a man can't pass between them. If you can stand the deadly stream of musketry fire you can dig up or cut down these stakes, you will have no other obstacle save the climbing of the breastworks and a line of bayonets jetting up inside.

He concluded his letter by criticizing armchair strategists back home who were complaining about the slow pace of Sherman's advance on Atlanta. "I should like to see a few thousand of the 'On to Atlanta' civilians of the North charging such a line of works. Most of the tender-skined [sic] individuals of this class would require help to get into the works if they were *empty*."

One of the concerns of the Lincoln loyalists in the north was the 1864 presidential election; it was fast approaching, and Lincoln's supporters worried he might actually lose to the Democrats if the Union armies didn't soon roll up some impressive battlefield victories.

Sherman was just as frustrated as anyone else. One day, observing the enemy lines through his field glasses, he saw a group of Confederate officers huddled on a hilltop observing his lines through their field glasses. He told one of his generals to order a nearby artillery battery to throw a few shells in the direction of the rebel officers. One of the shells struck General Polk, the fighting bishop, and killed him instantly.

On July 7, Harrison told Carrie that "we can see the steeples of the churches in Atlanta. We are now four miles from that city, but it will probably take up a good many days to make that distance." The weather, he said, had become unbearably hot "and on the march the men suffer terribly from the sun and cannot make any great distance in a day. The enemy has been so consistently in our front that our marches have always been short."

Harrison's brigade crossed the Chattahoochie River above Vining's Station on July 17. The next day, President Davis and his advisers in Richmond fired Johnston and replaced him with the conniving Hood. Davis wanted his Army of Tennessee to fight, not retreat. As a result, says Bruce Catton, "the South lost 20,000 good soldiers, Atlanta, the presidential election, and most of what remained of the war."

After stacking their arms near Peach Tree Creek on July 20, Harrison's men scattered, some heading for the creek, some picking ripe blackberries. "About the middle of the afternoon," Colonel Merrill wrote, "the skirmishers on the hill in front began to fire at a furious rate, and some of our men who had gone up to get a view came hurrying down the hill at breakneck speed. Everyone in our command was rushing into line, the officers calling to men, 'Fall in! Fall in!' and the men exclaiming, 'Oh God, boys, they are out of their works! We've got 'em now.'"

Hood was in charge, and he was attacking Sherman. Harrison and his men were right in the middle of it, holding what appeared to Hood to be a gap in the Union lines. This moment, finally, was Harrison's.

In his official report, Harrison said he and his brigade were ordered to occupy a ridge near a large open field. On his left was the 2d Brigade from his own division, commanded by his old friend from Indianapolis, Colonel Coburn, and on his right were elements of General John Geary's 20th Division. The opening between Coburn and Geary was so tight that Harrison had to double up his five regiments, back to back. The first line was made up of the 102d and 129th Illinois and the 79th Ohio; the second line contained the 105th Illinois and Harrison's own Hoosiers, the 70th Indiana. The idea was that when the order was given, the whole line would advance against the exposed rebel infantry.

Harrison said there "was a low ridge covered with small pines" just in front of his own line, "and still beyond this and a ravine which intervened, was a high cleared ridge, which was the line finally occupied by our troops. The ridge was the key point to the whole position." Harrison sent his own skirmishers ahead, including 100 men from the 79th Ohio and 102d Illinois, most of them armed with Spencer repeating rifles.

"I watched the enemy's advance over the crest of the higher ridge in our front and down its slope towards us, until their lines were scarcely separated by a distance of one hundred yards from ours. During this advance the artillery on the left of the second division had been pouring into the enemy quite a destructive fire of case-shot and shell, and the skirmishers on my front, re-inforced by the detail of one hundred Spencer rifles, which I had ordered forward at the beginning of the attack, were punishing the enemy severely." Harrison said he could see the enemy charge breaking up, with many of the rebels lying down and a few turning back, "while the officers, with drawn swords, were trying to steady their lines and push them forward."

Seeing this disorder, Harrison decided that it was time for his men to counterattack. One newspaper, the *Indianapolis Daily Journal*, reported years after the battle that Harrison and Coburn asked their division commander, the bibulous General Ward, for permission to advance their two brigades and to occupy the ridge. Ward refused. The newspaper said that a witness then overheard Harrison say to Coburn, "John, I am going to place my men on that ridge, if you will support me." Coburn allegedly replied, "I'll see you through."

All we can be sure of is that Harrison, with or without Ward's consent, ordered three of his regiments that were positioned to the left of the small (and unnamed) creek to advance "and attack the enemy vigorously while at the same time I brought forward the two right regiments." Coburn, at the same time, ordered his own men to advance on Harrison's left. "Our advance, though desperately resisted by the enemy, was steady and unfaltering," Harrison reported. "The fighting was hand to hand, and step by step; the enemy was pushed back over the crest in our front and the key point of the battle won."

One witness said he heard Harrison shouting these unlikely words to his men, "Come on, boys, we've never been licked yet, and we won't begin now. We haven't much ammunition, but if necessary we can give them the cold steel, and before we get licked we will club them down; so, come on."

Colonel Merrill recalled seeing Captain Meredith and the mischievous boys from Company E, including Acting Adjutant Cox, charging after the rebels. Cox, "beautiful as a girl, brave as a lion, rushes through the left of the Illinois regiment to the hilltop, his form as he reaches the crest outlined against the sky, waves his hat exultantly, and beckons a command 'Forward!' for no voice could be heard in the uproar."

"Our boys take steadier aim now and advance with enthusiasm," Private J. L. Ketcham recalled. "They [the rebels] don't retreat without giving us several volleys. We gain their hill, passing over their killed and wounded, and lie down behind some fence rails the skirmishers have thrown up and fire into them, retreating. They made several attempts to rally and recross the open field, but without success."

Private Ketcham said General Ward, a Kentuckian, appeared on the battlefield just as the rebels began running. He called out to his aide, Lieutenant Harryman, "Ha'yman, Hay'man, come hea'. Look how the First Brigade, my old brigade, goes in!"

At one point, Harrison said, his left flank was uncovered, and the enemy appeared to be taking advantage of the opening. "The danger was soon removed, as I was sure it would be," he said, "by the splendid advance of Colonel Coburn's brigade, which, after fighting its way desperately to the top of the hill, connected with me on the left."

Long after the battle ended, Coburn called Harrison "the personification of fiery valor, with voice and gesture urging on the furious charge. We could see the divisions on our right and left giving way in apparent confusion; a regiment was surprised on the right with their arms in the stack; a battery was captured, and on the left a host of fugitives scattered towards the rear. But our advance seemed to give them encouragement—they rallied and retook their lines.... I never saw on any battle-field dead and wounded in such numbers and so close together.... No man in the army that night stood higher than Harrison for heroism. Had he been a West Pointer his promotion would have been ordered by telegraph."

"We have fought *the* battle of this campaign," Acting Adjutant Cox told Katie, "and given the soundest thrashing they have yet had. It was a fair fight, neither side have breastwork and lasting five hours.... My captures are one Captain's sword marked C.S.A., Reb canteen (cedar), haversack, etc."

This time, Cox could be pardoned for exaggerating. Harrison and Coburn had performed important services at Peach Tree Creek. It was Hood's first attempt to crack Sherman's lines, and these two colonels from Indianapolis and their ten regiments had done as much as anyone to thwart it. The next morning, it is said, Fightin' Joe Hooker himself came riding along Harrison's lines, and congratulated the colonel for his day's work. "By God, Harrison," he is supposed to have said, "I'll make you a brigadier general for this fight."

It's unlikely he made those remarks the morning after the battle, but there is no doubt he was impressed with Harrison's performance. On October 31, in a letter to Secretary of War Stanton, he called for Harrison's promotion to brigadier general:

With more foresight than I have witnessed in any officer of his experience, he seemed to act on the principle that success depends upon the thorough preparation in discipline and esprit of his command for conflict, more than on any influence that could be exerted on the field itself.... When collision came, his command vindicated his wisdom as much as his valor. In all the achievements of the 20th Corps in that campaign, Colonel Harrison bore a conspicuous part.... Colonel Harrison is an officer of superior abilities and of great professional and personal worth.

A campaign biography published in 1892, when Harrison was unsuccessfully seeking reelection as president, said "a fight so stubborn [as Peach Tree Creek] has seldom been seen on earth," and attributed the victory almost entirely to Harrison's heroics. Surely it was propaganda, but there was just enough truth in it to make it almost plausible.

Harrison and the rest of Sherman's army had first spotted Atlanta's church steeples on July 7. On August 10, more than a month later, they could still see the steeples, but they were now beginning to seem evanescent. "You cannot imagine how tiresome this siege has become to me," Harrison told Carrie. "The campaign heretofore has been full of activity and movement but now we are tied to our places in the trenches, unable to leave for an hour and hearing only the monotonous cracking of the guns on the skirmish line. I am positively wearing out from staying so long in one place."

August 20 was his birthday, and he wrote a revealing letter to his wife on that day:

I am 31 years old today, and nearly eleven years of this period we have been man and wife.... I hope to be a better husband and father, a better citizen, and a better Christian in the future than I have been in the past. The reason is that my mission as a soldier will end before another birthday. Certainly my present term of enlistment will end before next Aug. 20 unless Genl. Hooker should accomplish his threat of making me a Brig.

Genl.... The very complimentary notice in which Genl. Hooker
made in his conversation with [Murat] Halstead [influential
editor of the *Cincinnati Commercial*] was, of course, gratifying to
me but, in all candor, I do think "Uncle Joe" was somewhat
extravagant and hope he will not push me *too* rapidly, as that
has been the ruin of more than one good officer in this war. On
your account and my children, I would like to wear the "lone
star," but my own ambition does not soar very high.

Little Ben *was* a modest man. And, unlike so many men who
have clawed their way to the White House, he really was telling the
truth when he confessed his ambition didn't soar very high. He simply wanted to do his job with dignity and with competence and by
doing so to avoid bringing dishonor to his family's glorious name.

"Atlanta is ours," he told Carrie on September 2. "The city surrendered to a detail from our division yesterday morning. Col.
Coburn was I believe in command of the troops that entered first.
[Harry Scott, Carrie's brother, was there too.] Our corps now
occupies the city. My brigade and two others are still back on the
river and will not move up for a time. I have been placed by Gen.
[Henry W.] Slocum in command of the post here [on the Chattahoochie River], in addition to the command of my own Brigade,
and have my hands full."

Ten days later, on September 12, he was ordered to report to
Governor Morton in Indianapolis for "special duty." Ostensibly, he
was being sent home to help in recruiting soldiers to fill the vacan-
cies in various Hoosier regiments, and in fairness, he did do some
recruiting. In fact, however, he was being sent home to campaign
for the Republican statewide ticket headed by Governor Morton.

He was on the ticket himself, having been selected by his party
to run again for supreme court reporter, the job that had been taken
away from him by the Democrats two years earlier. He had
accepted the nomination back in April, although applying some
conditions to his acceptance. In a letter to party officials, he made
his conditions as clear as a lawyer could:

While allurements of home and peaceful pursuits are not to be turned aside without an effort, yet I could not reconcile it without my own sense of duty to quit the army for *any* civil office or pursuit, unless incapacitated by disease or wounds from efficient service in the field. Should the war be ended, or virtually so, during the campaign now opening, as many hopeful ones believe, or should my usefulness in the army be, from any cause brought to an end, then I should be much gratified to resume the duties of Reporter.

He set off for home on September 12, traveling part of the way on an Ohio River steamer. Passengers had been warned that from time to time bushwhackers lined the shore and opened fire on passing steamers. It happened one afternoon while Harrison and his fellow passengers were eating dinner. "Shots from the shore came whistling through the thin sides of the dining room, and in a moment all was confusion," one of the passengers, Colonel W. T. Ritchie, recalled (his version of the events was reported somewhat breathlessly in an Indianapolis newspaper). Almost everyone in the dining room dived under the tables, but one attractive young lady, apparently unconcerned, left the cabin to see what was happening. Colonel Ritchie followed her to the hurricane deck. Colonel Harrison was already there, he said, "a revolver in each hand ... blazing away with great enthusiasm and vigor at the people on the shore." He "stood there in a storm of bullets and banged away until the boat was out of range."

The picture of Little Ben on the hurricane bridge, blazing away at the bushwhackers, became a part of his standard political hagiography.

He arrived home to a fond welcome from Carrie and the children and began stumping for votes a week later. At the same time he was canvassing the southern part of the state, Ohio Congressman James A. Garfield was speaking for the ticket in northern Indiana.

Republicans argued that a vote for Morton and Harrison was a vote for the boys at the front. Democrats—always a powerful consideration in Civil War Indiana—argued that a vote for the Republicans was, in the words of the *Daily State Sentinel,* "an endorsement of the corruptions, the frauds, the reckless extravagance, and the suicidal policy of Lincoln and his adherents."

While he was on the road, Harrison wrote Carrie that he thought the Republican newspapers "are making too much noise and parade about the treasonable designs of the Copperheads. It would be better to say less and *do* more."

But that was unfair. Democrats were having a difficult time making their case because the Republican-led Union *was* doing more. The North had won three exciting victories—Sherman at Atlanta, Admiral Farragut at Mobile Bay, and Sheridan in the Shenandoah Valley. On October 11, election day, Morton and the rest of the Indiana ticket swept to an easy 20,000-vote victory. Lincoln carried Indiana in the presidential election on November 8 by the same margin.

In his victory speech, Harrison gave a ringing defense of Lincoln and the administration's policies, including emancipation. Without black men, he said, Sherman's victory might never have happened. "Black men, in a hundred ways, did the work which would have otherwise fallen upon our brave soldiers.... Not a Negro has escaped and made his way into our camps but has brought more aid to our cause than the entire brood of whining, carping Copperheads who object, in the interest of treason, to the employment of the black men." If the Democrats should defeat Lincoln in November, he said, "the Copperheads would strip the uniforms from the backs of those dusky soldiers and send them back to slavery."

Harrison's biographer Harry Sievers calls the speech a partisan harangue. But in coming to the defense of the black man's contribution to the winning of the war, Harrison was courageously stating a proposition that many Hoosiers had trouble accepting.

After the fall of Atlanta, Sherman took off to the southeast, toward Savannah on the seacoast, and disappeared, leaving Thomas behind to deal with Hood's army. It was just the way Sherman liked it—no newspapermen (he loathed them all) and no railroad line to defend. Sherman and his "bummers" simply lived off the fat of the land.

Instead of chasing after him, Hood did something that still seems curious—he marched away in the opposite direction. His idea was to invade western Tennessee, defeat Thomas's army, and capture Nashville. Maybe Sherman would come after him, maybe not. If he didn't, he would march to Virginia and join Lee. It was a forlorn strategy, with little hope of success.

Hood made it worse by botching what could have been the last great Confederate victory of the war; he allowed General Schofield and 23,000 Yankees to slip past him at Columbia, forty miles south of Nashville. Then, in an act of unreasoned fury, he ordered a frontal assault on Schofield's well-defended lines at Franklin, eighteen miles from Nashville, on November 30 and lost 6,500 men, including a dozen generals. "Hood had wrecked his army, top to bottom, and the army knew it," Shelby Foote writes.

Harrison had hoped to rejoin Sherman and his old brigade and to take part in the march to the sea. He got as far as Dalton, Georgia. There, he discovered the railroad was torn up, making further progress for the time impossible. He was given orders to turn around and report to Brigadier General Charles Cruft (one of Grant's stalwarts at Fort Donelson) at Chattanooga, where he was put in command of a ragamuffin collection of soldiers that had been cut off from their assigned units. They were reorganized as a brigade and shipped off by rail to Nashville to take part in Thomas's defense of that city.

Harrison's brigade was something less than a well-oiled fighting machine. Of the 1,000 men serving in it, Harrison said in his official report, "quite a large number of the men ... designated as effective were, in fact, quite unfit for duty in the field—many were still suffering from wounds received in the Georgia campaign; others were fresh from the hospitals and only partly convalescent from attacks of sickness; while a still larger number were raw recruits, utterly uninstructed and not inured to hardship. The recruits represented almost every European nationality, and many of them were unable to speak or understand the simplest words of our language."

"The command [the 5,000 men making up his division] was hastily thrown together," General Crufts noted in his official report. "It was rapidly armed, and from its very composition could be illy provided with the ordinary appliances which render field service endurable. About one-fourth of the command consisted of soldiers recently from the hospital, scarcely convalescent; another fourth, of soldiers returned from furlough, and the remaining half of raw recruits of every nationality, without drill or experience of any kind, but earnest and worthy men. The officers, as a class, were good ... but they were separated from their regular commands, without their personal baggage, camp furniture, servants, change of clothing, stationery, etc., and many of them without money, or time to secure any supply of these necessities. The command left without ambulances or wagons. The medical department had not adequate supplies." The performance of his officers and men should be looked at in light of these deficiencies, he said.

Harrison, the perfectionist and rigid disciplinarian, must have hated every minute of it. It is no wonder he never wrote any glowing letters about his service at Nashville to Carrie or revealed any of the campaign's details to General Wallace, his official biographer.

His brigade with its walking hospital cases and raw recruits who couldn't speak English arrived in Nashville a few days after the rebel disaster at Franklin and was assigned to hold the left of the line defending the city. "As an attack by Hood was imminent," General Wallace wrote (even though, in fact, Hood was no longer in position to attack anybody), "the Colonel proceeded without loss of time to prepare for it. He erected a breastwork covering the entire front of his line."

Part of Harrison's line cut through the back yard of Judge

Trimble's house, Wallace said. Harrison "waited on" the judge to express his regrets about tearing up the yard. "Colonel," the judge told him, "if it is necessary for the defense of Nashville, take the bottom brick in my house."

The weather turned very cold, and men were close to freezing on the picket lines. Private Richard M. Smock, a Hoosier himself and one of Harrison's soldiers, was on picket duty on one of the coldest nights.

I saw a man approaching from the direction of the officers' quarters. I halted him, and when he gave the countersign and advanced, I saw it was General [then Colonel] Harrison. He had a large can filled with hot coffee, and when I asked him what he was doing, he said he was afraid some of the pickets would freeze to death, and he knew some hot coffee would help the men to keep alive. He was the most welcome visitor I ever met, for I really believe I would have frozen before morning had not the coffee been brought. After leaving me, the General passed on to all the other pickets to cheer them up with the beverage. His act was one of kindness.

The story appealed to Harrison's supporters because it showed the kindlier aspects of his frosty character. "Call such a man cold?" an anonymous author wrote in a campaign biography, after recounting the hot coffee story. "You might as well call a volcano cold because its sides are grey and barren. Truly, there is much of God-warmth in Ben Harrison's heart."

The day after the battle at Franklin, Schofield withdrew his 21,000 men and retired inside the Nashville fortifications. That meant that Thomas had 55,000 men defending the position, including Harrison's brigade. Hood, with only 22,000 men left from an army that once numbered 75,000, decided to advance on Nashville and to lay siege to it.

The freezing cold was followed by four days of snow and sleet.

When the sun came out again, there was mud everywhere, axle-deep, and neither army could move. It wasn't until Thursday, December 15, that Slow-Trot Thomas, under severe pressure from Washington to get moving, finally began his attack on Hood's thinly defended lines.

Steedman, on the left, opened the assault. Harrison's biographer Harry Sievers says Harrison's brigade led the charge, followed by two divisions made up of black soldiers. That was wrong: Harrison and his brigade took no part in the battle. Cruft's entire division, in fact, was held in reserve, as well it should have been. Harrison said that on Wednesday morning his brigade had been ordered to move out of the breastworks in and around Judge Trimble's back yard and to relieve a division in the 4th Army Corps. "The troops were kept in this position, under arms, during this and the following day while the battle of Nashville was progressing in their front," he wrote. "No demonstration was made upon the line held by us, nor were any of my troops engaged, though the artillery in my line opened somewhat effectively."

Thomas had intended Steedman's advance to be a feint against the rebel general Benjamin Cheatham. The main attack would come from his center and right, many of those troops commanded by General William J. Wood, the same fellow who had created the gap at Chickamauga that almost wrecked Rosecrans's army.

Steedman's troops—without Cruft and Harrison—fought for two hours but could not budge Cheatham's rebels from their well-entrenched positions. That didn't bother Thomas; after all, Steedman's attack was never intended to be much more than a feint, and he was doing valiant work by keeping Cheatham occupied while the rest of the battle unfolded elsewhere.

Hood was forced to withdraw late in the day, and the fighting resumed Friday morning. Steedman's troops again took part in heavy fighting, but again without Cruft and Harrison, and one of his colored regiments, the 13th U.S. Infantry, did lead the charge, losing 221 men. Late in the afternoon, the Union center, commanded by General Wood, seeking vindication, surged forward. The rebels—even Hood's gallant Texans—had seen enough, and the whole line collapsed. "I beheld for the first and only time a Confederate army abandon the field in confusion," Hood wrote. But, of course, Hood hadn't been there when Thomas had routed Bragg's rebel army the same way once before, at Missionary Ridge. Thomas's men killed or wounded 1,500 Confederates; captured 5,000 more, a quarter of Hood's army; and seized fifty-three guns. What was left of Hood's grand army, filled with some of the finest soldiers in the world, was a wreck, and it simply faded from the war.

It was a great victory, as complete as anything Harrison had ever seen, and he had taken no active part in it. It is no wonder he preferred to talk about his experiences on other battlefields.

He didn't say much either about his role in the pursuit of Hood's beaten and bedraggled army. "With a view to reaching the Tennessee River before Hood and cutting his pontoons and otherwise intercepting his retreat," General Wallace said, "Colonel Harrison was ordered to march to Murfreesboro, and there take trains and push forward with the utmost speed." But the rear guard for Hood's retreat was Nathan Bedford Forrest's cavalry, and he was still a terror.

"From Murfreesboro southward the Confederates had burned all the wood piles and destroyed the water tanks," Wallace said. "The delay thus caused was serious. . . . Details of ax-men chopped up rails to feed the engine; at the creeks buckets were used to fill the tanks with water."

The weather was terrible. On December 21, Harrison wrote in his official report, he loaded his men in box cars, sixty inside and twenty on top of each car. "Those on top soon found the cold unbearable, and many became so benumbed with cold that it was with great difficulty they could be got off the cars." Harrison never did catch up to any of Hood's men. The pursuit was called off on New Year's Eve, and Harrison was ordered to report to General Cruft at Chattanooga. "I must say," he told Cruft, "that the campaign, though not characterized by much fighting, was one of unusual severity and hardship."

Even so, General Cruft praised Harrison's performance in a letter to the War Department. "He has served the country, during the recent short but arduous and brilliant campaign (as commander of a Brigade in the Division under my command) most faithfully and creditably. He has proven himself on all occasions to be an excellent officer. His long and meritorious service entitles him to remembrance at the hands of the Government and to speedy promotion." Harrison learned about his promotion to brigadier general in February 1865, while he was on leave from the army, recovering from a bout with scarlet fever.

Nashville was the end of a long march for Harrison; it was his last battlefield. He had done his part, but it would be difficult to argue he had been a great regimental commander. Hayes was better. Garfield was smarter. But Harrison was competent; he molded a solid regiment, and in at least one battle, Peach Tree Creek, he and his men made a significant contribution, fighting with skill and valor. He ended the war feeling a lot better about himself. And his father, John Scott Harrison, wrote Ben to say how proud he was of him.

Chapter 12

APRIL 9, 1865

IT HAD ALL BEGUN on April 12, 1861, when Lieutenant Henry S. Farley fired the first shot at Fort Sumter, in Charleston harbor, from an old coast-defense mortar. It ended almost four years later on April 9, 1865—Palm Sunday—at Appomattox Court House. That day the tall, marvelously handsome Robert E. Lee, the fifty-eight-year-old aristocrat, surrendered what was left of his Army of Northern Virginia to the much plainer Ulysses S. Grant, the one-time clerk in his father's leather store in Galena, Illinois, eighteen days short of his forty-third birthday.

Lee arrived at Wilmer McLean's modest farm house (poor McLean had moved to Appomattox from Manassas in 1861 to get away from all the fighting) at about 1:00 P.M. on his famous gray horse, Traveler, accompanied by a single aide, Colonel Charles Marshall, grandson of the great Supreme Court chief justice. Grant arrived thirty minutes later accompanied by several aides, one of them the incomparable Phil Sheridan.

Lee was dressed in his best uniform, with a red sash around his waist, over which he had buckled a gorgeous ceremonial sword. "I thought I must make my best appearance," he had explained. Grant was dressed in what he called "rough garb," wearing "a soldier's blouse for a coat, with the shoulder straps of my rank to indicate to the army who I was." His boots were muddy, and he wore no sword. "I must have contrasted very strangely with a man so handsomely dressed, six feet high and of faultless form," he said. "But this was not a matter that I thought of until afterwards." That is almost surely not true; Grant knew perfectly well what he was doing. This was the way he wanted to look on the most momentous—the most generous—day of his life. He was still Zachary Taylor; Lee was still Winfield Scott.

They talked at first about the old days when they had served together in the War with Mexico. Lee finally had to change the subject—it was time, he said, to talk about why they were meeting in Wilmer McLean's parlor.

They discussed the wording of the terms of surrender for a few minutes. Lee said he thought something should be put down on paper. Grant called for writing materials and scribbled these extraordinary words.

> Gen. R. E. Lee,
> Comd'g C. S. A.
> GEN: ... Rolls of all the officers and men to be made in duplicate. One copy to be given an officer designated by me, the other to be retained by such officer or officers as you may designate. The officers to give their individual paroles not to take up arms against the Government of the United States until properly exchanged, and each company or regimental commander to sign a like parole for the men of their commands. The arms, artillery and public property to be parked and stacked, and turned over to the officer appointed by me to receive them. This will not embrace the side-arms of the officers, nor their private horses or baggage. This done, each officer and man will be allowed to return to their

homes, not to be disturbed by United States authority so long as they observe their paroles and the laws in force where they may reside.

Very respectfully,

U. S. GRANT,

Lt. Gen.

Grant said in his memoirs that when he put his pen to paper he "did not know the first word that I should make use of in writing the terms. I only knew what was in my mind, and I wished to express it clearly, so that there could be no mistaking it."

Lee read what Grant had written and said that his army was organized a little differently from Grant's army, that in his army all the horses were privately owned. Would it be possible for the cavalrymen and the artillerists to go home with their horses? Grant thought about that for a while and then said he would allow every man who claimed to own a horse or a mule to take the animal with him. That way, Grant said, they might be able to put in a crop to carry them through what certainly would prove to be a very difficult time.

It was a remarkable document—clear, concise, and generous. "This will have the best possible effect upon the men," Lee said. "It will be very gratifying and will do much to conciliating the people."

It was all over by 4:00 P.M. Lee mounted Traveler and slowly began to make his way back to his defeated army. Grant and his officers pulled themselves together and saluted the grand old man who had fought so valiantly for so forlorn a cause. Grant then sent a telegram to Secretary Stanton: "General Lee surrendered the Army of Northern Virginia this afternoon on terms proposed by myself."

When his own troops heard the news that it was all over, after four terrible years, they began firing a 100-gun salute. Grant told them to stop. "The Confederates were now our prisoners," he wrote in his memoirs, "and we did not want to exult over their downfall."

The key to the terms of surrender were Grant's final words, in which he pledged the United States would not disturb the Confederate veterans as long as they observed their paroles and the laws in force in the states where they resided. It meant that none of these men, as long as they kept their word, could be tried for treason. Grant was serious about that, and he stood in the way of vengeful politicians, including Andrew Johnson, who thought otherwise.

By the time the terms were agreed upon, there was nothing much left of Lee's army, perhaps fewer than 20,000 men, all of them hungry. Grant ordered his commissary wagons to supply them with rations for a good meal or two before they began the long walk back to their farms and villages.

All through these proceedings, Grant, in his rough soldier garb, clearly had been the center of attention, the man in charge. He was the victor, and there was no mistake about it. The whole nation, North and South, probably understood that as well. Next to Lincoln himself, Grant was the most important man in the United States.

Other Confederate armies were still in the field—as many as 200,000 men in all—but Lee's surrender meant the end for them too, and they all knew it. Nearly all of them surrendered in a few days.

Grant still had a job to do—he was, after all, the supreme commander of the victorious Union armies—and he headed back to Washington to begin the process of breaking up what was on April 9, 1865, the most effective fighting machine in the world. He wanted, he said, to put a stop to "the purchase of supplies, and what I now deemed other useless outlay of money." He had, after all, learned something working in his father's leather shop.

President Lincoln asked the Grants to join him at Ford's Theater the night of April 14; Grant said that he and Julia would be pleased to do so but that he expected they would be in Burlington, New Jersey, visiting their children, who were attending school there. It was on their way back to Washington that the Grants learned that the president had been assassinated.

"I knew his goodness of heart, his generosity, his yielding disposition, his desire to have everyone happy, and above all his desire to see all the people of the United States enter again upon the full privileges of citizenship with equality among all," he said. He worried that Lincoln's successor, Andrew Johnson, would be less sympathetic to the former Confederates and that the cause of reconstruction in the South would be badly damaged.

James A. Garfield had taken his seat in Congress on December 5, 1863, at thirty-two the youngest member in the chamber. He was still there when the war ended and would, in fact, serve in the House for seventeen years. He had been a preacher and a professor, and it was no surprise, then, that he loved to talk. "Some of the older and staider members smiled at his overflow and vehemence, and endless good nature," Noah Brooks, the Washington correspondent of the *Sacramento Union*, said. Garfield also demonstrated early on a contrarian disposition by voting against continuing the practice of giving bounties to encourage army and navy enlistment and then, even more dramatically, by voting against reviving the rank of lieutenant general for Grant. Grant, after all, was the man who had fired Rosecrans, and he still felt pangs of conscience about his shabby role in that. Secretary Chase took him aside and gave him an old-fashioned dressing down. You will never get ahead, he told Garfield, if you continue to act irresponsibly. Garfield was not stupid, and he caught on, slowly.

He had started out living alone in the capital, and that was not his style. He was bored and lonely, and he said he dreamed some nights of his lost little daughter, Trot. He was delighted to accept an offer from another Republican member of the Ohio delegation, Robert Schenck, chairman of the Military Affairs Committee, to share rooms with him.

Schenck, who had also seen action in the war (he was seriously wounded leading a brigade at Second Bull Run), was just as outgoing and flamboyant as Garfield. Among his many passions was draw poker, and he had written a treatise about it that attracted fans on both sides of the Atlantic Ocean, including Queen Victoria.

Garfield and Schenck turned their rooms on C Street into "a second army headquarters," Garfield's biographer, Allan Peskin, says. Lobbyists, generals, arms manufacturers, and inventors showed up at all hours of the day and night. The crowds became so thick that the two congressmen had to post guards to direct the human flow.

Garfield and Schenck had both signed on with their party's radical fringe and had become disenchanted with Lincoln's cautious, middle-of-the road policies. Jacob Dolson Cox, Garfield's old roommate in Columbus, dined with him one night and was shocked by his anti-Lincoln diatribe. Garfield even called the man thought by many to be America's greatest president a "baboon," a term of derision popular during the war among some Southern editors and politicians.

In his position as a member of Schenck's Military Affairs Committee, Garfield hobnobbed with dozens of very wealthy men. Like politicians before him and long after him, Garfield wondered why they had so much money and why he had so little. After all, he reasoned, he was just as smart and just as clever as they were. He was receptive, then, to one of his old soldiers from the Big Sandy campaign, Ralph Plumb, a hustler who proposed that they buy up hundreds of acres in the valley and explore for oil, used in those days to make kerosene for lamps.

It wasn't quite as wild a scheme as it sounded. Garfield and Plumb had spent some time when they were chasing Humphrey Marshall theorizing about the possibilities of oil bubbling beneath the valley's surface. Plumb proposed that he and Garfield and a handful of others form an "inner circle" and buy up land in the valley for pennies an acre and then sell it to outsiders for as much as $100 per acre. They would pocket the difference and become very rich. So much the better if they actually discovered oil, although that always seemed unlikely.

Garfield went along with Plumb and began looking for subscribers. Some signed on, but not very many, and in time they dropped away as it became apparent that Garfield and Plumb were up to their ears in a highly questionable real estate promotion, not a serious oil-drilling venture. Plumb reappeared a little later with a scheme to make money mining coal in a place called Scabble in Illinois. Garfield signed on to that one too but had to pull out when he couldn't come up with enough money to pay for stock in the company. Plumb struck it rich and in time became a member of Congress himself.

Garfield remembered that he had passed the bar exam back in Ohio in 1859 after spending a few idle afternoons studying in a law office. He took up lawyering during the time he was a member of Congress and soon found he could make a few honest dollars that way. In his first big case, he was paid $3,040 for successfully defending the will of Alexander Campbell, the founder of his Disciples of Christ denomination, against his children, who said their father had been mentally incompetent when he wrote it.

Garfield was easily reelected in 1864. While at home in Hiram, taking a few hours away from his campaign, his wife, the long-suffering Crete, had handed him a note saying that they had been married more than four years but had spent a total of twenty weeks together. When Garfield returned to Washington, he brought Crete and the children with him. They moved into a proper house.

Garfield was in New York City the night of April 14, 1865, when Lincoln was assassinated. The next morning, his early biographers said, as many as 50,000 people gathered in Wall Street, prepared to lynch any Southern sympathizers they could lay their hands on. Garfield, dazed by the news (whatever his opinion about Lincoln's politics), wandered aimlessly about the city before joining a number of people trying to quell the crowd gathered in front of the Exchange Building. One man was killed, Garfield's biographers said, when he shouted that Lincoln deserved to die. Others in the crowd began to chant "The World!" "The World!" The *World*, with offices nearby, was a Democratic, anti-Lincoln newspaper, and the mob seemed prepared to burn it to the ground.

"Then," writes biographer John Clark Ridpath, "a man stepped to the front of the balcony and held his arm aloft. His commanding attitude arrested universal attention. Perhaps he was going to give them the latest news. They waited. But while they listened, the voice—it was the voice of General Garfield—only said:

Fellow-citizens: Clouds and darkness are around about Him! His pavillion is dark waters and thick clouds of the skies! Justice and judgment are the establishment of His throne! Mercy and truth shall go before His face! Fellow-citizens: God reigns and the Government at Washington still lives!

The tide of popular fury was stayed, Ridpath wrote. The *World* was saved. Not just the *World*, but the entire city!

It became a part of Garfield's legend—the day he stilled the mob and saved New York City—and it is shamelessly untrue. Garfield was in New York that day; he did give one or more speeches asking for forbearance, but he never stilled a mob at the Exchange Building (and nobody was killed there either). It was a good story, and typically, he never said anything to clear it up.

The day Lee signed the terms of surrender at Appomattox Court House, Rutherford B. Hayes was preparing to lead his brigade "over awful mountain roads, through a desolate country," in an attack on rebel forces at Lynchburg, Virginia. Lee's surrender meant Hayes could cancel all his fighting plans. "I am very happy to be through with the war," he wrote his mother.

Unlike Garfield, he had always admired and respected President Lincoln, and he was devastated by news of the president's death. "I have been greatly shocked by the tragedy at Washington," he wrote Uncle Sardis. "At first it was wholly dark. So unmerited a fate for Lincoln! Such a loss for the country! But gradually, consolatory topics suggest themselves. Now the march of events will neither be stopped nor changed. The power of the nation is in our armies and they are commanded by such men as Grant, Sherman, and Thomas, instead of McClellan, Hooker, or, etc., etc. Lincoln's fame is safe. He is the Darling of History evermore. His life and achievements give him titles to regard second to those of no other man in ancient or modern times. To these, this tragedy now adds the crown of martyrdom."

On May 20, Hayes submitted his resignation as a brigadier general of volunteers and asked that it take effect as of June 8, giving him exactly four years of active service. That same day, in a letter to his mother, he said, "The soldiers are leaving for home very rapidly. They are all in excellent spirits and glad to go. I have no idea that many of them will ever see as happy times as they have had in the army."

He packed up all his uniforms and belongings and shipped them home. He took care to make sure that the regimental mascot, a stallion named Old Whitey that saw action in twenty engagements, found his way back to Uncle Sardis at Fremont, Ohio, as well.

Joined by Lucy, he traveled to Washington and watched the grand review of Union troops from seats reserved for members of Congress. Because he would not take his seat in Congress until December, he was home in Ohio a few days later.

Unlike Garfield, a student of government who would, in time, become chairman of the House Appropriations Committee, Hayes didn't really take to Washington. He was a backbencher, toeing, somewhat listlessly, the Radical Republican line and grousing constantly about all the petty demands put on him by his constituents. He was delighted to escape the capital and head home to run for governor in 1867. His Democratic opponent was Allen G. Thurman, former chief justice of the state supreme court. They were both vying to succeed General Cox, Garfield's old friend, who had refused to run for reelection because he couldn't accept the state party's call for Negro suffrage. Ohio leaned heavily to the Democrats in 1867, and Hayes's own seat in Congress went to Sam Carey, a temperance candidate. The vote for governor was so close that for a while Hayes thought that he had been defeated. Helped greatly by overpowering support from Union veterans, he carried the state by 3,000 votes in what was a striking personal victory.

"I am enjoying the new office," he wrote Uncle Sardis. "It strikes me as the pleasantest I have ever had. Not too much hard work, plenty of time to read, good society, etc." Governors in Hayes's time weren't expected to do very much; the job was partly ceremonial, partly administrative. The last thing anyone expected was aggressiveness. Even so, with these limitations, Hayes had his moments. He improved a number of state institutions (he and Lucy spent a lot of time visiting prisons), and he was the driving force in organizing what would become Ohio State University.

Hayes's friend, Major McKinley, was serving as the chief adjutant for Brigadier General Samuel Sprigg Carroll, commanding a ragtag provisional division stationed at Winchester that included the 23d Ohio, when he and the rest of his troops heard the news of Lee's surrender. The troops at Winchester fired a salute of 200 guns to mark the great event. McKinley then ordered that the City of Winchester "be thoroughly illuminated this evening" to celebrate "the crowning victory of our arms, and the prospect of a speedy peace." Residents of Winchester, deeply sympathetic to the rebel cause, probably would have preferred to wrap their homes and porches in crepe than to set off flares to celebrate Lee's defeat. Someone saved McKinley's order, and it was displayed for years thereafter in the local library.

As adjutant, McKinley officially spread the news of Lincoln's assassination and the arrest of John Wilkes Booth. Because feelings were running so high, he ordered soldiers traveling into Winchester to wear their side arms and to be back in camp by tattoo. "McKinley issued order after order to his division," biographer William Armstrong writes, "but, with the fighting over, army regulations and routine were resented more than ever." This army was basically a volunteer one, and these men—all the Union men—had heard enough orders to last them a lifetime. They wanted nothing more than to put down their arms and go home.

McKinley flirted briefly with the idea of joining the regular

army and making the military a career. But his father, arguing that
the army didn't amount to much in peacetime, talked him out of it.
It wasn't until August that Major McKinley, a twenty-two-year-old
veteran of four years of fighting, returned to Poland. "We had a
million soldiers in the field when the war terminated," he said later,
"and the highest testimony to their character is found in the fact
that when the muster hour came, and this vast army, which for
years had been accustomed to wars and carnage, returned to their
homes, they dropped into the quiet walks of citizenship, and no
trace of them was ever discernible except in their integrity of character, their intense patriotism, and their participation in the growth
and development and maintenance of the Government which they
had contributed so much to save."

He decided that instead of becoming a professional soldier, he
would become a lawyer. He began studying law in the offices of a
prominent local attorney and then studied briefly at the Albany
Law School. He opened his practice in Canton early in 1867, making him the fourth lawyer among these five future presidents.
(Grant, of course, was the lone holdout.)

That same year, McKinley made his first political speech—for
his old friend, Rutherford Hayes, running for governor. Speaking
from the top of a dry-goods box in what is now North Canton, he
reminded the voters of Hayes's gallant conduct in the war and how
he had waded, swum, and floundered across that dense marsh at
Opequon. He attacked Hayes's opponent, Judge Thurman, as a
Peace Democrat who had directed every energy of his mind against
the war measures of the Union party. It was an early example of a
campaign style—waving the bloody shirt—that would mark U.S.
elections for more than three decades. Most of the time it worked.
Hayes was elected governor, and in a year or two McKinley was
elected Stark County prosecutor.

In late March 1865, Benjamin Harrison was training new
recruits at Blair's Landing near Hilton Head, South Carolina. He
and the other commanders were ordered to round up all their soldiers, fully trained or not, and forward them to Sherman wherever

he might be found in North Carolina. Harrison told Carrie that he had made a farewell visit to one of his favorite haunts, an old tumbledown plantation house about three miles from Blair's Landing. It was early spring, and flowers were coming into bloom. He picked two rosebuds and mailed them to Carrie, telling her "to retain one of the buds yourself and imagine my whispering in your ear with the simple gift all that could be delicate and affectionate in a lover, in his first declarations."

He arrived at Wilmington, North Carolina, in his steamship, conveniently named *Champion*, on April 10 to learn that Richmond had fallen and that Lee had surrendered to Grant at Appomattox Court House the day before. Wilmington was in the midst of a wild celebration, and Harrison and the soldiers from the *Champion* happily joined the parade. "There was plenty of wine and so forth," the abstemious Little Ben told Carrie, "and we soon had a merry party. I was called out to respond to a toast to Sherman's army and after a short speech toasted the *Ladies*, two of whom ... were present. Before the party broke up I had to make another speech."

Four days later, on April 14, he was given orders to join his old command with Sherman's army at Raleigh, North Carolina. He arrived there on April 19 and was struck at first by how quiet it was. Then he learned the awful truth: President Lincoln had died four days earlier, and Sherman had just released the news to his command. Harrison was reunited with his own boys, the 70th Indiana, later that day. He gave a speech to his Hoosiers the next night in which he eulogized the president.

In a letter to Carrie, he said that after six months of effort to reach his old command, "I find myself at last able to date this letter from my old home in the army.... I found a most cordial welcome here both from my superiors and inferiors and was compelled to make them a little speech last night. They all expressed the most cordial feeling and the most enthusiastic gladness about my return. I was very grateful to know they missed me."

No one, he told Carrie, seemed happier to see him than his old nemesis, the demon-like "incubus," General Ward. "I find," he told Carrie, "he has been a very true friend to me in my absence. I shall never permit myself to say a word against him again."

Sherman's army began its march to Richmond on April 30. It arrived in the former Confederate capital nine days later and then set off for Washington, marching across some of the war's most wrenching battlefields, Chancellorsville and Spotsylvania among them. The ground was still strewn with what was left of the dead, Union and Confederate.

On May 23, the Army of the Potomac, the eastern army, paraded down Pennsylvania Avenue in the Grand Review, battle flags flying, thousands lining the sidewalks, with President Andrew Johnson taking its salute in his box near the White House. This was the army everyone in Washington knew; they had seen it come and go all these years. They had heard about the western armies, but they had never actually seen any of these tough, long-striding soldiers. They had their chance the next day when Sherman's Army of the Tennessee came swinging down the avenue. Harrison rode in the parade, just behind General Ward, in front of the boys from his brigade, including the regiment that was closest to his heart, the 70th Indiana. Grant, at the president's side, and Hayes and Garfield in the congressional stands watched them file by, in perfect step.

"The review was a good thing for Sherman's army," Little Ben told Carrie. "We took the shine off the Army of the Potomac and the marching *altogether* exceeded them."

A mature, battle-tested Harrison, his discharge papers in his pocket, arrived home with the boys from the 70th Indiana early in June. They took part in a huge welcome-home demonstration on June 16, at which Harrison was called upon to give a speech. It is a good example of Harrison's oratorical style:

I well remember three years ago, under the shade of these trees, when I made my first appeal to the men of Marion County.

Now we are here again, sheltered by these same trees, but oh! how much brighter the skies.... Many who went out with us are not here. We buried them in Southern soil, but thank God the secession flag does not fly over them. They sleep in the soil of the great Republic.

Then he spoke to his own men:

Do you remember the enclosure, my Comrades, at the foot of the hill at Resaca, up which we made that fearful charge? How we gathered their torn blankets around them, and tenderly composed their limbs for their last sleep, casting branches of evergreen in their graves! They lie there still, and along by the wayside lie others. They were not permitted to return with us, but they left behind them honorable records. I almost feel that I would rather lie within that little mound at the foot of the hill than to have had no participation in this struggle. These brave men lived to accomplish more for the good of their country than most men who go down silvered to the grave.

Harrison rejoined his old law firm and resumed his duties as supreme court reporter; he managed to put out three more profit-making books before collapsing from overwork. He took his first long vacation—fishing, hunting, and thinking about his future—and decided to resign his reporter's job, to hire two clerks to help at his law office, and to spend more time with his family. Harrison was probably the most successful lawyer of all these future presidents; his law practice thrived. So did Harrison himself, in body and spirit.

He dabbled in Indiana politics and campaigned for every Republican candidate for president. He did his party a great service when he represented Union generals in a civil suit arising out of a Supreme Court decision, *Ex Parte Milligan*. In that decision, the justices said that Lambdin P. Milligan, a civilian, had been illegally tried and sent to prison by a military—instead of, properly, a civilian—tribunal. With that decision in hand, Milligan was suing for damages. Harrison's job was not to win the case—that was impossible—but to limit the damages. The jury returned a $5 award for Milligan, and Harrison, in the words of one historian, "became an instant favorite of the Republican faithful."

What the faithful did know—especially the ones who were politically active—was that Harrison, this quiet, austere man, was a terror in the courtroom and on the stump. In his stump speeches for his party's candidates, he always invoked the memories of his service in the war, and this feeling, it was said, "transfused his speeches with a moving, even poetic feeling."

It is easy to write off Harrison as a cipher—most historians do. But he reached the White House because he possessed remarkable abilities as a lawyer and as a campaigner.

It wasn't until 1876, the year Hayes was elected president, that Harrison ran for office again. He was hastily thrown into the governor's race when his party's candidate, former Congressman Godlove S. Orth, was forced to resign from the ticket because of his involvement in a swindle ring in Venezuela. The Democratic candidate was James D. Williams, better known as "Blue-Jeans" or "Uncle Jimmie." Nothing ever came easily to Little Ben; he lost the election to Williams, who didn't mind being called "this horny-handed son of toil," by 5,000 votes.

It wasn't really Harrison's fault. The scandals in his own party, running from Congressman Orth all the way up to the Grant White House, had been too much to overcome.

The next year, when railway workers went on strike and Governor Williams refused to do very much about it, Harrison led a privately organized committee on public safety that brought the protest in Indiana to a peaceful conclusion. Harrison's performance was widely applauded, and he was seen from then on as one of the two or three leading figures in the Republican Party in Indiana. He would even serve a term in the U.S. Senate.

In 1878, he and the rest of his family buried his father, John

Scott Harrison, in the family plot at North Bend, Ohio. They noticed that a nearby burial plot of a young man they all had known named Augustus Devin had been disturbed. Further examination revealed that the body had been stolen. Harrison and Carrie went home the next day, but Harrison's younger brother, John, deeply disturbed by the grave robbing, began poking around the Ohio Medical College in nearby Cincinnati. A constable accompanying Harrison and some of his friends spotted a rope stretching down into a dark shaft. It was suspiciously taut. They hauled at the rope and brought up from the bottom of the shaft what appeared to be a body wrapped in cloth, the rope tied around its neck. They put it down on the floor and lifted the cloth from the dead man's face. "My God!" shouted John, "that's my father!" And so it was. Body snatchers had stolen John Scott Harrison and delivered him to the college too.

In the end, the "Harrison Horror," a sensational story all across the nation, led to reforms in the ways medical colleges secured cadavers for students to dissect. The whole distastefully gothic episode also managed to win some sympathy for Little Ben and the Harrison family. Things like that shouldn't happen to the son and the grandson of a president of the United States, almost everyone agreed.

Chapter 13

THE WHITE HOUSE IN THE
GILDED AGE

IN A SATIRICAL WORK published in 1873, Mark Twain and his next-door neighbor, Charles Dudley Warner, gave the era the name it deserved—the Gilded Age. "What's the chief aim of man?" Twain once asked. "To get rich. In what way? Dishonestly if we can; honestly if we must."

The Gilded Age lasted for thirty-six years, from Lincoln's assassination in 1865 to McKinley's assassination and the rise of Theodore Roosevelt and the progressive era in 1901. It was a time of gross excess. The rich were stinking rich, and the poor were desperately poor. Corruption flourished everywhere, from Grant's White House to almost every machine-controlled city and precinct in the country. New York City's boss William Marcy Tweed spent $13 million to build a court house that had been originally budgeted for $250,000. The court house, critics pointed out, cost the taxpayers almost twice as much as Alaska.

It was also a time of sweeping change, surging growth, brilliant inventions, and striking artistic and literary accomplishments. In

1865, the United States was largely a rural country, with villages and towns and only a few large cities. By 1901, it was an industrial giant, producing almost as much in goods and products as Great Britain, France, and Germany combined. Population, fueled by immigration, grew at an astonishing rate, from 36 million in 1865 to 78 million in 1901. Thomas Alva Edison, one of the greatest inventors who ever lived, was creating the incandescent light bulb and the phonograph. (President Hayes got his wife out of bed in 1878 to hear a midnight demonstration by the great man himself.) Alexander Graham Bell was perfecting something called the telephone. Twain was writing *Tom Sawyer* and *Huckleberry Finn*; Henry James was writing *The Portrait of a Lady*. Thomas Eakins was working in Philadelphia, painting oarsmen on the Schuylkill River and surgical operations in Dr. Gross's clinic; Winslow Homer was working in Boston, painting fishing boats and fishermen. Louis Henry Sullivan was designing and building his first skyscrapers in St. Louis and Chicago.

The Republicans ruled in Washington through most of these tumultuous years. They were, first of all, the party that had won the war and that had saved the Union. They were also the party that had freed the slaves. All of that was high-minded and admirable. On the other hand, they were the party that favored high tariffs to protect U.S. industry from foreign imports, raising the cost of all kinds of goods for American consumers. They believed, in fact, that business and industry should be allowed to do just about anything they wished. That wasn't so admirable.

The Republicans won seven of the nine presidential elections that took place during the Gilded Age, and they did it each time with a Civil War veteran. Grant was elected in 1868 and 1872; Hayes in 1876; Garfield in 1880; Harrison in 1888; and McKinley, the last of the line, in 1896 and 1900.

In all seven of these Republican victories, the boys in blue—the Civil War veterans, one-and-a-half million of them—played a key role. Most of them voted Republican because they could never forgive the Democratic Party for opposing Lincoln's war policies.

By 1868, almost everyone had seen enough of President Andrew Johnson. A racist and a crude, unlettered man, he had been impeached by the House of Representatives and escaped conviction in the Senate by a single vote. Grant was the obvious choice to succeed him. As General Logan placed his name in nomination at the Republican National Convention, the stage curtain rose, revealing an immense backdrop covered with a mural of Grant and the Goddess of Liberty. Grant's father, Jesse, was there, a special guest, and no one in the hall could have been more stunned—Ulysses and a goddess!—by the display.

The Democrats chose as their standard-bearer the former governor of New York, Horatio Seymour, whose war record was just questionable enough to allow his enemies to declare he had been sympathetic to the rebel cause. (Among other things, he had called draft rioters in New York City in 1863 "my friends.") That set the stage for the first of the "bloody shirt" campaigns in which the Republicans charged the Democrats with treason.

Veterans were organized in clubs, most of them drawing their membership from the Grand Army of the Republic; they campaigned enthusiastically for Grant and his running mate, Schuyler Colfax. They called themselves the Boys in Blue. "Fall in!" one of the Boys in Blue leaders said. "Soldiers, it is the old cause and the hosts are again preparing for the conflict.... Grant again heads the column."

Songs, telling a simple story, were the precursors of the thirty-second TV ads of a later time. One of them, "Come on, Boys in Blue" went this way:

We will vote as we battled in many a fight,
For God and the Union, for Freedom and Right.
Let our ballots secure what our bullets have won—
Grant and Colfax will see that the work is well done.

We whipped them before, we can whip them again.
We'll wipe treason out as we wiped slavery's stain;

For traitors and slaves we've no place in our land—
As true, loyal men to our colors we stand.

"The Boys in Blue," historian Mary Dearing writes, "became a veritable army as the campaign progressed." In Pennsylvania, it was said, the Boys in Blue had organized so many veterans for the Republican ticket that almost nobody was left for the Democrats. It was pretty much the same everywhere else in the North. They wore their own distinctive uniforms and marched in parades and torchlight processions. They packed the seats at mass meetings and gave a distinctive, dramatic, and patriotic edge to Republican rallies. Horace Greeley's *New York Tribune* boasted, "Over 500,000 Veteran Boys in Blue, clad in Grant and Colfax caps, are nightly swinging their lanterns and rending the sky with cheers for their old leader."

Democratic newspapers, led by the *New York World*, tried to argue that Grant's blundering during the war had led to the loss of the lives of thousands of soldiers whom a better, more humane general would have saved. Rumors even circulated—it was a favorite device during the Gilded Age—that Grant had fathered an illegitimate child with an American Indian woman at Fort Vancouver.

Democrats organized their own veterans' clubs, called, embarrassingly, the "White Boys in Blue." The clubs were openly racist, parading with signs reading "White Supremacy" and "No Nigger Voting." But their cause was seriously damaged by the refusal of their two best-known generals, George McClellan and Winfield Scott Hancock, to participate in the campaign in any meaningful way.

With the help of Negro votes in the South, Grant easily won the electoral vote, 214 to 80. The popular vote was Grant, 3,014,000; Seymour, 2,709,000.

Sometimes great generals do make great or at least successful presidents. George Washington was both a great general and a great president. Andrew Jackson and Dwight Eisenhower were successful in both jobs. Grant, a great general, was not a great, or even a successful, president.

He wanted to be president because he felt he deserved to be president. He had won the war, and he wanted to crown those years with the presidency. He had no idea what he would do once he entered the White House. Being a general seemed so simple—find the enemy and destroy him—but who was the enemy now? In the army, he had surrounded himself with men of great talent and skill—men to begin with such as Foote and old C. F. Smith, later with such truly great military leaders as Sherman and Sheridan. But that's all they understood too—winning battles.

In the White House, he allowed himself to be surrounded by men of great wealth or, at least, men who hoped one day to accumulate great wealth. He had been poor as a boy and as a young man, and he always had felt a little insecure in whatever he was doing. These men impressed him, and the fact that most of them were at least a little bit crooked didn't seem to bother him very much.

In the spirit of the times, he believed in the old Whig notion that the president was basically an administrator, in charge of carrying out the laws passed by the Congress. This notion, of course, was exactly wrong. With the country in turmoil, with race issues unsettled in the South, with Native Americans making their last stand in the west, with venal men prowling the corridors of every agency in Washington, what the country needed was a supreme politician.

Grant, however, was hopelessly naïve; nothing underscored that more than his conviction that the United States could solve much of its race problem by annexing Santo Domingo (the Dominican Republic) and exporting thousands of newly freed slaves to settle there. Lurking in the background were a number of greedy men who hoped to make a killing in the resettlement. A treaty was even drawn up, only to be shot down in the Senate.

Consider, too, the Gilded Age's biggest rascals, Jay Gould and James "Jubilee Jim" Fiske. By 1869, they had become rich by taking control of the Erie Railroad, then looting it for their own benefit. Their next move was much more ambitious; they took steps to corner the nation's gold supply. Grant didn't actually join in on the plot—he was always an honest man—but he allowed himself to be seen frequently in the company of the two pirates. When he belatedly realized his two companions were trying to bamboozle him, he ordered his treasury secretary to start selling gold, driving the price down and setting off the Black Friday panic that bankrupted thousands of investors. Grant's action put an end to Gould and Fiske's venture, but at a fearsome price.

To top it all, stories about the Credit Mobilier scandal began to break just as Grant was completing his first term. Credit Mobilier was a construction company organized to build the Union Pacific Railroad. Eleven members of Congress and Grant's own vice president, Schuyler Colfax, accepted Credit Mobilier stock in return for exerting political influence on the company's behalf. Congressman Garfield admitted he had come close to the action himself.

Little things hurt too. Grant had never been much for councils of war, and now he wasn't much in favor of meetings and conferences. He made decisions without consulting politicians. In one of them, he appointed a postmistress in Garfield's congressional district without consulting the prickly congressman himself. Garfield fumed about it for years.

What sustained Grant through all his tribulations were the veterans, most of them still young and virile, many of them still armed. For all the scandals and all the corruption, these men cared deeply about the political process, and the man they felt most comfortable with, scandals or no, was their old commander. Nothing could change that.

In the face of all of Grant's problems, Democrats should have been able to put together a competitive ticket in 1872. But in an act of sheer madness that knows no parallel in the history of U.S. party politics, they chose a founder of the Republican Party, Horace Greeley, editor of the *New York Tribune* and one of the most eccentric men in the United States, as their standard-bearer. Grant won easily.

The 1872 election, biographer Jean Edward Smith writes, "marked the high point of Grant's presidency." But, Smith pointed out, landslides sometimes can be dangerous. Franklin Roosevelt stumbled after his landslide victory in 1936; so did Ronald Reagan after his big win in 1984. And so did Grant. Hubris—that old bugbear—set in, and a smug and satisfied Grant did little or nothing as his corrupt underlings and associates pocketed the spoils of victory.

The economy, swept by panic, collapsed in 1873 and did not fully recover until six years later. Democrats scored a landslide victory in the congressional elections in 1874, picking up eighty-five seats in the House and giving them control of that chamber. At the same time, the administration's reconstruction program was falling apart. To his dying day, one critic said, Grant never understood why the South defied the law. He was just as confused by the attitude of northern voters, who had supported his reconstruction ideas in 1872 but who were now criticizing them with mounting distaste. Grant caved in, gradually withdrawing most of the Union troops that had been sent to protect the newly freed slaves and to ensure their newly acquired civil rights. "By the summer of 1876," William McFeely says, "there was no one around the White House who gave a damn about the black people."

With all the lurid tales of corruption in high (and low) places, with Reconstruction collapsing in the South, and with the economy still struggling, 1876 should have been a banner year for Democrats seeking to return to the White House. Standing in their way was an unlikely obstacle, Rutherford B. Hayes.

Hayes was Ohio's favorite-son candidate at the Republican convention in Cincinnati. On the first ballot he had sixty-one votes. House Speaker James G. Blaine, still trying to shake off charges of corruption, led the parade, with 285 votes. In second place was Indiana Senator Oliver P. Morton, the wartime governor who had talked Benjamin Harrison into joining the army. Before the fifth ballot, Morton withdrew his name and turned his Indiana delegates over to Governor Hayes, figuring this was the only way to stop

Blaine. New York and Pennsylvania switched on the sixth ballot to give Hayes the nomination.

The Democrats chose Governor Samuel J. Tilden of New York, a reformer who had played a key role in wrecking the Tweed Ring. They chose another politician without a war record, Governor Thomas A. Hendricks of Indiana, as his running mate.

That meant the Republicans, in the absence of very much positive to say about their record in office, could once again wave the bloody shirt. And wave it they did. Harrison, running (unsuccessfully, it turned out) for governor of Indiana, set the tone. "I am willing to take as our ensign the tattered, worn-out old gray shirt, worn by some gallant Union hero, stained with his blood as he gave up his life for his country.... When they [the Democrats] purge their party of the leprosy of secession, we will bury the 'bloody shirt' in the grave with the honored corpse who wore it, and not before." The *Indiana Journal* was so taken with Harrison's rhetoric that it ran the passage at the top of the editorial page throughout the campaign.

Garfield told a rally of Republican veterans that the Democratic Party represented "secession, disunion, slavery and all that went to make disunion and slavery horrible in the eyes of men and in the eyes of God." Colonel Robert G. Ingersoll, one of the great orators of his time, took the Republicans' bloody shirt argument about as far as it could go. "Every man that endeavored to tear the old flag from the heaven that it enriches was a Democrat," he told Union veterans. "Every man that tried to destroy this nation was a Democrat. The man that assassinated Abraham Lincoln was a Democrat.... Soldiers, every scar you have on your heroic bodies was given you by a Democrat."

The election ended in an unholy mess, matched in U.S. history only by the George W. Bush/Albert Gore election in 2000. Just like Gore, Tilden won the popular vote by almost a quarter-million votes. And on election night, Hayes went to bed convinced that Tilden had won the electoral vote as well. His only regret at losing, he said, was the fate of "the poor colored men of the South."

But General Daniel E. Sickles, an important figure in the party, wasn't ready to concede. He stopped in at Republican National Headquarters in New York City late that night and discovered that votes were still being counted on the West Coast and in some of the southern states. Over the signature of Zachariah Chandler, the party's national chairman, he telegraphed leading party war-horses in South Carolina, Louisiana, Florida, and Oregon to hang on. "With your state for Hayes, he is elected. Hold your state."

Republican Party leaders hurried south—Garfield went to Louisiana—to make sure the count in the three key southern states went Hayes's way. The country was in a nasty crisis, with a lot of talk about using armed veterans to guarantee one outcome or another. With all the contested states returning two sets of vote counts—one for Hayes, one for Tilden, and with the Senate in Washington controlled by Republicans, and the House by Democrats—it was no wonder that some rational Americans worried if the impasse could ever be resolved.

Hayes took little or no active part in the crisis, spending his time quietly with his family at home in Ohio. One evening, a bullet shattered a parlor window, whizzed through two rooms, and buried itself in a wall in the library. Hayes told his family not to say anything about it.

Hayes probably won South Carolina fairly and squarely. Florida was a lot closer, with Tilden leading in one unofficial count by ninety-four votes. That, Republican leaders knew, could be fixed in their favor relatively easily. Louisiana was toughest of all, for Tilden seemingly had carried the state by more than 6,000 votes.

The voting in all the states in dispute involved outrageous fraud—stuffed ballot boxes, repeat balloting by voters paid for their trouble, and party ballots marked with the other party's symbol to confuse illiterate voters. Lew Wallace, sent to Florida to help Hayes, told his wife that "if we win, our methods are subject to impeachment for possible fraud; if the enemy win, it is the same thing—doubt, suspicion, irritation go with the consequence whatever it might be."

Congress decided the only way to resolve the issue was by appointing a commission, composed of five senators, five representatives, and five Supreme Court justices, of whom eight were Republicans and seven Democrats. On February 16, on a straight party-line vote, the commission awarded Louisiana to Hayes. The fix was in, and the other disputed states soon fell to the Republicans as well. Hayes was declared the winner at 4:10 A.M. on March 2, 1877, with 185 electoral votes to Tilden's 184.

Southern Democrats ultimately accepted the decision because Hayes's handlers, with Garfield taking a significant role, had cut a deal. For their silence, the new Republican administration would remove the remaining federal troops in the South and would allow self-rule, meaning all-white rule.

It was a sellout but perhaps not quite as egregious as it sounds. The fact is, serious efforts at reconstruction, enforced by the army, had collapsed during Grant's second term. More than most of his contemporaries, Hayes was sympathetic to abused minorities (including frontier American Indians and Chinese railroad workers), but, like Grant before him, he sensed the nation was exhausted and no longer had the will to impose black equality on the South by force of arms.

Garfield, typically, was all for making the deal. In a letter to Hayes dated December 12, he said, "It would be a great help if, in some discreet way, those Southern men who are dissatisfied with Tilden and his violent followers could know that the South was going to be treated with kind consideration by you."

Hayes and Garfield believed there was a middle way to reconcile the South without turning it over wholesale to the white supremacists. What they had in mind was, of all things, a resurrection of the Whig party in the South. They contended that there were enough important men in Dixie still nursing warm affection for the Whigs to win elections and to seize power. Hayes would help the new party along by appointing some of these old Whigs to his Cabinet and would sweeten the pot by supporting a number of railroad and canal projects dear to entrepreneurs in the region.

The retrofitted Whigs would represent "intelligent white rule" in the South, one proponent of the idea said, and as intelligent white men they would replace what was left of the odious carpetbagger organizations. Blacks would be given a subordinate status along the lines of the white working class in the North.

It was a crazy idea, but no crazier than Grant's plan to settle thousands of ex-slaves in Santo Domingo. The flaw in Hayes and Garfield's reasoning was their belief that some sensible compromise could be reached with racist southern white males who were well on their way to reestablishing a system in which they would once again rule supreme. The white racists succeeded, and the system endured for another 100 years.

Hayes kept his word, however. He appointed one of the Southern Bourbons, David M. Key, a former rebel officer, as postmaster general. Then he withdrew federal troops from South Carolina and Louisiana.

Hayes had been a good colonel and suspected he would not have been a very good general. By the same token, he had been a good governor, and now it was quickly becoming apparent he would not be a great president. Sometimes, especially in extraordinary times, it is not enough just to be good.

He did what he could. He beat back a crippling railroad strike with federal troops, halted bandit raids on the Mexican border, and pushed for a larger navy. He supported hard money and vetoed bills that tried to flood the country with greenbacks. He campaigned, without much success, for civil service reform, angering the corrupt wing of his party, known as the "Stalwarts" and led by Senator Roscoe Conkling of New York. At one point, he showed considerable courage by firing one of Conkling's chief cronies, Chester A. Arthur, who held the biggest patronage-dispensing job in the country, collector of customs in New York. He beat back repeated efforts by the Democrats (who gained control of the Senate in 1878) to revoke laws allowing federal troops to supervise elections in the South.

To Lucy's delight, he also stopped serving wine and hard liquor at the White House. Garfield, among many others, didn't think much of that. "Attended a State dinner at the President's wet down with coffee and cold water," he wrote in his diary on January 8, 1880.

Unlike Grant, who had never been very interested in veterans' issues, Hayes showed a passion for the cause. He signed one pension bill introduced by Democrats and explained afterward that he had signed it because "it was right. It was a measure necessary to keep good faith with the soldier.... We could not afford—we ought not—to haggle with them."

Already, with greedy claims agents scouring the country in pursuit of soldiers who hadn't filed for benefits (they took part of the payments for their services), fraud was beginning to be a problem. It was Hayes's position—and it would be Harrison's too when pension fraud became a national scandal—that this was the price the country had to pay to give the honest soldiers what they deserved.

By the end of his term, with the economy in recovery, Hayes's standing with the public was probably at its highest point. "I am now experiencing one of the *ups* of political life," he wrote in his diary. Some of his friends urged him to run for a second term, even though he had vowed when he had first run for president that he would serve only one term.

But the party chieftains had seen enough of Hayes and all his talk about reform. They wanted someone a lot more pliable. That was all right with Hayes. He had been president for four years, and that was quite enough. "He had really wanted not so much to *be* president as to *have been* president," one observer said.

But, if not Hayes, then who? Grant had spent most of his time out of office making an extended world tour, with Julia at his side; they were greeted enthusiastically everywhere they went. The longer he stayed away, one observer said, the better he looked to the demoralized Republicans. Conkling and the Stalwarts eagerly pushed his name forward for the 1880 election, and Grant seemed ready and willing to return to the White House for a third time. He came home in the fall of 1879 and lost a certain aura that distance had provided. Opposition began to gather, and one of the names put forward was James A. Garfield's.

By 1880, Garfield had been a member of Congress for seventeen years. Unlike Hayes, he liked the job and had become a powerful member of the Republican leadership.

The party was divided into three factions—Conkling's patronage-hungry Stalwarts; the Reformers, liberals in favor of civil service reform and free trade; and the "Half-Breeds," moderates who walked the line between the two other factions. The Stalwarts favored a third term for Grant, the Half-Breeds at first favored James G. Blaine, and the Reformers supported Senator George Edmunds of Vermont.

Grant would have won the nomination if the unit rule had remained in force. Under that rule, a candidate winning a majority of a state's delegates won them all. Because opposition to Grant was scattered and divided, the anti-Grant forces would have been wiped out in a number of states. Garfield, as chairman of the convention's Rules Committee, was one of the leaders in the fight against the rule that went on for two days. In the end, the rule was rejected, and Grant's chances for the nomination went down with it.

The balloting went on and on, through thirty-five ballots. On the thirty-sixth ballot, several states switched their votes and Garfield, the dark horse, won the nomination. It was at that moment, one Washington newspaper reported, that an eagle landed on the roof of Garfield's house in Washington. Second place on the ballot went to Chester Arthur, the very same Conkling crony whom Hayes had fired for incompetence and corruption.

Garfield was not a household name in 1880, but his name was known to almost everyone taking a serious interest in national affairs. Most of these people knew that he had served in the Civil

War—he preferred to be called General Garfield—and that he had earned a reputation as an expert on the budget and the appropriations process during his time in Washington.

Arthur had worn a uniform in the Civil War too, although only as a member of New York's state militia. As quartermaster general, with the rank of brigadier general, he had been responsible for enlisting and feeding and clothing the dozens of regiments New York sent off to war. He became an expert on stockings, blankets, canteens, underwear, tents, and rations, and by all accounts he did a decent job. The closest he ever came to battle was during the spring of 1862 when he traveled to the South to inspect New York troops, taking time out to make sure Union soldiers hadn't damaged property owned by his wife's family in Virginia. He resigned his post in January 1863, when a Democrat replaced his chief political sponsor, Governor Edwin D. Morgan.

Garfield and Arthur were a curious pair, but at least they could argue that they had served their country, and campaign posters showed them both in full dress uniform, swords and all.

The Democrats finally got around to nominating a war hero of their own, General Winfield Scott Hancock, and hoped that by doing so they would put an end to those terrible Republican attacks on their patriotism. But the Republicans would have none of it. They simply argued that Hancock was the dupe of party leaders who had opposed Lincoln's war.

"A thousand Union generals ... could not palliate ... the terrors and the torture, the bloodshed and massacre, with which the Democratic Party has prepared, and again sets in the field, a Solid South against the Soldiers and Sailors of the patriotic North," one circular said.

Mention of the "Solid South" was instructive, for Republicans could no longer count on very many black votes in any of the eleven states of the old Confederacy. The Bourbons had reclaimed the South and had extinguished the voting rights of most of the African Americans. The South would remain solid for Democrats until the national party, under Franklin Roosevelt and Harry Truman and their successors, took up the African American cause.

Garfield won the electoral count, 214 to 155. The popular vote could hardly have been closer, 4,446,000 votes for Garfield, 4,444,000 votes for Hancock. Garfield made up for the loss of the Solid South by carrying all of New England, New York and Pennsylvania, and most of the Midwest. No one could say the soldier vote wasn't important in 1880, for, in an election that close, every vote is important.

In office, Garfield was in something of a bind. He had carried New York, and won the election, because of Boss Conkling, and now Conkling wanted his reward—patronage jobs. Instead, prodded by his secretary of state, James G. Blaine, Garfield named New York's leading Half-Breed as collector of customs. Conkling became so enraged he resigned, thinking his loyal constituents would rally around and send him back to Washington, stronger than ever. But there was no rallying around, and Conkling drifted off into retirement and political obscurity.

By July 1881, Garfield had had enough of all the party infighting and the humid weather in the capital and had decided to get away for a vacation. His only companion in the carriage that took him to the Baltimore & Potomac Railroad station the morning of July 2 was Secretary Blaine. A deranged job-seeker, Charles J. Guiteau, watched as the carriage drew up to the station. He said later that Garfield and Blaine were "just as chatty and hilarious as two schoolgirls."

Guiteau, loaded pistol in his pocket, had been stalking Garfield for weeks. Now was his chance. "Guiteau came up from behind the President, extended his pistol at arm's length and fired into Garfield's back from less than a yard away," biographer Allan Peskin wrote. The president cried, "My God, what is this?" Guiteau took two steps forward, shouted that he was a Stalwart, "and fired once more as Garfield was half twisting and half falling. With the second shot the President crumpled to the carpet and Guiteau wiped off his pistol and put it back in his pocket." He was captured by a police officer, Patrick Kearney, as he tried to make his escape.

In today's emergency rooms, the two wounds wouldn't be life threatening. One bullet had grazed his arm, and the other had entered his body a few inches to the right of his spine. But doctors, in seeking to remove the bullet, botched the job—they never did find it—and blood poisoning set in. The soldier who had faced enemy fire on the battlefield died September 19, the eighteenth anniversary of the great battle at Chickamauga, seventy-nine days following the assassination.

What would a Garfield presidency have been like? It's an intriguing question, for Garfield was the smartest, the most devious, and the most political of all these Civil War presidents. He was not the sort of man who would have accepted the conventional wisdom in the Gilded Age that presidents really were better off seen and not heard. The question, with Garfield, was always one of character. Still, he was aggressive, ambitious, and knowledgeable. He had *possibilities.*

Arthur was a party hack, and his behavior as vice president—he had roomed with Boss Conkling throughout the showdown with Garfield—had been notorious. But he was a different man as president—a little better at his job than anyone had anticipated. He actually signed the Pendleton Act in 1883, establishing competitive examinations for civil service jobs. He began rebuilding the antiquated navy, vetoed pork-barrel legislation, pushed for lower tariffs, and appointed responsible people to high positions. "Overall," one historian says, he "conducted a responsible, if undistinguished (and unimportant), presidency."

He also brought the good times back to the White House, opening a popular bar in the billiards room. There, the smartly dressed widower—he really looked like a president in the Gilded Age ought to look—gave lively supper parties with plenty of wine and whiskey.

The Republicans met in Chicago in 1884 in the same hall in

which they had chosen Garfield. Arthur had hoped to win the nomination, but Republicans weren't interested. They gave the prize—finally—to Blaine. It was the first time since the Civil War that the Republicans had chosen a candidate who had not seen service as a general in the Union Army. Blaine, the "Plumed Knight," had paid a substitute to take his place. Senator Benjamin Harrison, one of the delegates at the convention, was worried. The most fervent defender of the soldiers' cause, he said it was important that the party "should have some regard to the wishes of the soldier in our nomination, and in our platform. They are numerous and, as my correspondence shows, are a little restive." To placate the restive soldier vote, the party chose Black Jack Logan as Blaine's running mate.

The Democrats chose Grover Cleveland, the reform-minded governor of New York, to head their ticket, and Governor Thomas A. Hendricks of Indiana, Tilden's old running mate, once again brought up the rear. That the two men came from the two most important swing states in the nation was not coincidental.

Neither of the Democrats had seen service in the war either. Cleveland, like Blaine, had paid a substitute, a Polish seaman named George Brinske, $150 to take his place. Brinske spent most of the war working as an orderly in a soldiers' hospital in Washington, D.C.

Cleveland, in his bachelor days in Buffalo, had been something of a man-about-town, and he had fathered an illegitimate child with a widow of questionable morality named Maria Halpin. That set his critics to singing their favorite campaign chant, "Ma, ma, where is my Pa, Up in the White House, darling, Making the Laws." The Democrats came back with a somewhat weaker attack—that Blaine's first child was born only six months after he and his wife were married. They did a little better with their own favorite ditty, "Blaine, Blaine, James G. Blaine, the Continental liar from the State of Maine." The election began to move in Cleveland's favor after Blaine failed to speak out against one of his supporters who had

called the Democrats the party of "rum, Romanism, and rebellion."
It was, all in all, one of the two or three dirtiest presidential campaigns in American history.

There wasn't a whole lot of waving of the bloody shirt this time,
for the simple reason that both leading candidates had bought their
way out of serving their country. In the end, when all the dirt had
settled, Cleveland emerged as a narrow winner, with 4,875,000
votes (and 219 electoral votes) to 4,848,000 voters (and 182 electoral votes) for Blaine, leading the Democrats back to the White
House for the first time since the incompetent James Buchanan
served there on the eve of war.

Cleveland, an honest and practical man, hated to see taxpayers'
dollars being wasted. Nothing irked him more than the fact that
members of Congress kept sending him private bills authorizing
pensions for soldiers he believed hadn't earned them. Republicans
defended the bills, with Harrison explaining that "the soldiers are
getting old, and many of them are unable to make the strict proof
required at the Pension Office." By the middle of the 1880s, the
House, with its eighty-two Union veteran members, was meeting
once a week just to consider private pension bills for men who said
they were veterans and who had already lost their claims at the Pension Bureau. In his first term, Cleveland vetoed 228 of the private
pension bills, providing the Democrats with 228 poisoned arrows.

Cleveland might have gotten away with rejecting the bills if it
hadn't been for his language; it was frequently heavily laden with
sarcasm. Rejecting one bill, in which a claimant insisted he had
been ill for five of the seven weeks he served in the army, Cleveland
said, "Fifteen years after this brilliant military service and this terrific encounter with the measles, the claimant discovered that his
attack of the measles had some relation to his army enrollment and
that this disease had 'settled in his eyes, also affecting his spinal
column.'"

Making things worse, Cleveland went fishing on Decoration
Day and refused to give a speech at the Gettysburg battlefield. He

vetoed a bill granting $12 monthly pensions to veterans who had served in the army or navy for at least ninety days and who were no longer able to work, even if their disability had no connection to their military service. Veterans' organizations, led by the Grand Army of the Republic (GAR), furiously battled to overturn the veto but failed by a small margin. But they were not unhappy, for they had created a working issue for the next presidential campaign.

But that was nothing compared to the storm that broke over some captured rebel flags that had been collecting dust in the basement of the War Department building for years. In April 1887, Adjutant General R. C. Drum told the secretary of war, William C. Endicott, that "it would be a graceful act to anticipate future requests of this nature" and return the flags to the states whose troops had carried them during the war.

Drum offered the flags to the southern state governments in a circular letter in June. General H. V. Boynton, correspondent for the *Cincinnati Commercial Journal*, a Republican newspaper, read the letter and immediately realized its possibilities. He wired his editors an account of what was occurring, along with a list of the flags in Washington that Ohio troops had captured.

Governor Joseph B. Foraker, who had served as a private in the Union Army, read the newspaper account and exploded in calculated pyrotechnics that might have had something to do with the fact that he was facing a difficult reelection campaign. He sent a telegram to Boynton to begin legal proceedings to make sure the flags didn't leave Washington. Boynton, quick to take orders, hired two prominent lawyers to prepare the case. Newspapers picked up the story, and Union veterans reacted predictably. One of them wired the governor, "The old soldiers of Hillsboro hope you will not give up any captured flags.... Intense feeling here among the boys who wore the blue." Foraker, understanding he was on to a very good thing, wired back, "No rebel flags will be surrendered while I am governor." Then, in a message to President Cleveland, he said, "The patriotic people of this state are shocked and indignant beyond anything I can express. I earnestly request you to revoke the order that has given such unqualified offense." His fiery response to the challenge earned him a nickname he carried proudly for the rest of his life—"Fire-Alarm Foraker."

The head of the GAR, Lucius Fairchild, spluttered when he heard the news. "May God palsy the brain that conceived it," he roared, "and may God palsy the tongue that dictated it!"

With the country in an uproar and his own political future in peril, Cleveland revoked the order, saying "the return of these flags in the manner thus contemplated is not authorized by existing law nor justified as an Executive act." He passed the buck by saying that in the future Congress should deal with the flags. Fire-Alarm Foraker, riding the flag issue for all it was worth (he was easily reelected), gloated that the president "quailed like a whipped spaniel."

On July 4, Cleveland said he wouldn't be attending the GAR's grand encampment in St. Louis because of "threats of personal violence and harm in case I undertake the trip in question." In his handling of the flag fiasco, Cleveland had inadvertently provided the issue—a "wedge issue," in modern campaign terminology—for the next presidential campaign. General Sherman said it was now even more crucial that the Republicans pick "some good Union Soldier who fought the four years of the war," and that the single issue in the 1888 campaign "should be was that war right or wrong."

Cleveland, running on a platform calling for tariff reductions to help reduce a burgeoning budget surplus, was easily renominated at his party's convention. Chosen as his running mate was Allen G. Thurman, the same fellow who had run against Hayes for governor of Ohio in 1867.

The Republicans met in Chicago, looking for a war hero and a high-tariff man. Harrison was one of the possibilities. On the face of it, though, Harrison's record in public office didn't have much to recommend it. He had been elected twice as reporter for the Indiana supreme court, but when he ran for governor in 1876 he had been defeated by "Blue Jeans" Williams. He had also served one term in the Senate, but he didn't do much in Washington except champion almost every veteran who came to him for help in securing a pension. In one case, he supported a private bill to assist a veteran who had been discharged from the army for drunkenness. His alcoholism, Harrison said, grew out of the stress he had endured as a soldier. He lost his senate job when Democrats took control of the state legislature and elected one of their own.

But Harrison was a survivor. He and his troops had had that annoying habit of becoming lost in the midst of the smoke of the Civil War, but they had always recovered and gone on to victory. He had survived Democratic attempts to steal away his job as court reporter. He had been defeated for governor by a "horny-handed son of toil" and had lost his job as senator to the same kinds of Democrats who had thwarted him so often in the past. But he was still highly regarded by party leaders in Indiana and elsewhere. One of the reasons was his work in a courtroom in which he spared the party and old Union generals a great deal of grief by making sure none of them would have to pay very much in damages for illegally prosecuting civilians in military tribunals during the war. He had also been the epitome of the loyal party man, campaigning relentlessly for Republican candidates.

To Harrison, the Republican Party—his party—was the party that had fought treason in the Civil War, and nothing else was so important as that. In a speech in Chicago, he summed it up this way:

> We took the ship of state when there was treachery at the helm, when there was mutiny on the deck, when the ship was among the rocks, and we put loyalty at the helm; we brought the deck into order and subjection. We have brought the ship into the wide and open sea of prosperity.... I believe that the great party of 1860 is gathering together for the coming election with a force and a zeal and a resolution that will inevitably carry it to victory in November.

Ohio's Senator John Sherman, the general's brother, led the first ballot with 229 votes, with Harrison trailing in fifth place with eighty. Votes began to shift to Harrison on the fourth ballot, and, with the help of Pennsylvania party boss Matthew Quay, he wrapped up the nomination on the eighth ballot.

The Republican platform called for the maintenance of high tariffs, which was fine by Harrison. He had once explained that he refused to sympathize "with this demand for cheaper coats, which seems ... necessarily to involve a cheaper man and woman under the coat." The platform also promised that no veteran "should become an inmate of an almshouse, or dependent upon private charity," and that was fine by Harrison too. Republicans said the huge budget surplus, $140 million and growing, would be in large part dedicated to veterans' benefits.

Democrats, with their pledge to eliminate most of the surplus by the imposition of lower tariffs (bringing in less revenue to the treasury), were distressed. They could talk about what they had done for veterans, but they couldn't promise very much in the future because they wouldn't have all that money in the surplus to give away.

Cleveland very carefully spelled out why he had vetoed so many of the private pension bills. Those bills, he said, were "unreasonable, unfair, and reckless," and his vetoes of them were "the best service I can render to the veterans."

But logic was wasted in the face of Republican demagoguery. Every Republican orator, every Republican editor denounced Cleveland, the man who paid someone to take his place in the army, as the "great vetoer" of legislation aimed at improving the lives of those boys who had marched off to war. Thousands of circulars were distributed in which veterans pledged to oppose any politician who had ever failed to support any measure supporting veterans' benefits.

Harrison's only worry was that he and his party might promise too much. He called for the most "grateful liberality" in dealing with the veterans, but he stopped short of supporting calls for giving pensions to all Union veterans, even those who had never heard a shot fired in anger.

The campaign songs, once again, played their part. In 1888, Republicans dealt with the flag issue this way:

> *And Grover C. will sorry be, and sorely rue the day*
> *He undertook to give the rebel-flags away.*
> *Yet Grover he will sorry be, and lament long I say,*
> *The fact he a'fishin' went on Decoration Day.*
> *And Grover C. and Allen T. will find, as all men do,*
> *How vain it is to "buck again" the boys who wore the blue.*

By 1888, the Grand Army of the Republic had reached a position of such power and influence that Republicans hardly needed to organize any more Boys in Blue organizations. The GAR, still technically neutral but firmly aligned with the Republicans, did the job. All their reunions and encampments were turned into rallies for Harrison and the rest of the Republican ticket. Thousands of veterans traveled to Indianapolis to pay their respects. To one of these groups, Harrison spoke from the heart. "The comradeship of the war will never end until our lives end," he said, for "the fires in which our friendship was riveted and welded were too hot for the bond ever to be broken."

These Gilded Age elections were so close that almost any blooper could tip the scales. The "Rum, Romanism, and Rebellion" gaffe had severely damaged Blaine's chances against Cleveland in 1884. Now, four years later, it was Cleveland's misfortune to be badly damaged by a dirty trick. A California Republican named Charles Murchison wrote a letter to the British minister in Washington, L. S. Sackville-West, saying he was a naturalized American citizen of English birth and wanted the minister's advice on how he should vote in the election. Sackville-West was taken in and foolishly replied that Murchison should vote for Cleveland, because the

Democrats, with their low tariffs, would be more favorable to British interests. The letter was leaked to the newspapers and caused a flurry among Irish-American voters, who had their own reasons for distrusting the British.

Harrison attributed his victory in 1888 to "divine intervention." Boss Quay said it was just as well Harrison didn't know "how close a number of men were compelled to approach the penitentiary to make him president." Still, it was a personal triumph for Harrison, who had run a very credible campaign himself (he gave almost 100 speeches to an estimated 300,000 visitors from his front stoop and never stumbled once). Although he lost the popular vote, with 5,444,000 votes to 5,534,000 for Cleveland, he carried the electoral college 233 votes to 168, taking the states of New York, Cleveland's home state, and Indiana. Moreover, his party, for the first time since 1880, found itself in control of both houses of Congress.

As president, however, Harrison was a failure, the least successful of all the Civil War veteran presidents. He managed to puzzle almost everyone. First, in naming his cabinet, he virtually ignored all the party leaders who had secured the nomination and election for him. But then, he allowed the people running the Post Office Department to clean out the place—"decapitating a fourth-class postmaster every five minutes," according to one observer. More than 30,000 postal workers were fired to make way for Republican Party hacks.

He named James Tanner, a Civil War corporal who had lost both his legs in battle, as pension commissioner. Tanner took up his job with a zeal that might have shocked even Harrison, who always believed there wasn't much the veterans didn't deserve. In one speech, Tanner said he would "drive a six-mule team through the Treasury." In another, he said, "God help the surplus."

It was a scandal, and Democrats didn't take long to seize upon it. It was too much even for the Republicans, and Tanner was replaced after six months. Still, the spending continued, until the surplus was eliminated. The money had been spent on pensions for the veterans and pork-barrel river and harbor projects for the politicians. Voters were not pleased, and Democrats made substantial gains in the off-year elections in 1890. Farmers and working people began grumbling, and a populist revolt seemed to be in the making. But Harrison was such a political partisan—blind to anyone else's ideas—that his own confidence in what he and his party were doing remained unshaken.

One of the bills passed in 1890 was the McKinley Tariff Act, written by the major himself, at the time a congressman from Ohio, which gave a huge boost to tariff rates. It was widely blamed for the financial panic that followed in 1893 and for the depression that swept the country a little later.

Harrison won renomination at the party's convention in Minneapolis in 1892 simply because his opposition within his party was so fragmented it couldn't unite behind anyone else. Blaine, the one real threat, had pulled out of the race, and McKinley, elected governor of Ohio in 1891 after losing his congressional seat the previous year, was still untested. Delegates chose one of the Civil War's greatest reporters, Whitelaw Reid, editor and proprietor of Greeley's old paper, the *New York Tribune*, for second place on the ticket. The Democrats turned to Cleveland again, and second place went to Adlai Stevenson of Illinois (grandfather of the Democratic presidential candidate in 1952 and 1956).

The newly organized Populist Party, feeding off agrarian unrest and a visceral reaction to the Gilded Age's greedy excesses, nominated James B. Weaver for president. The party called for the direct election of senators and a graduated income tax.

The McKinley tariff, and the turmoil that had followed its enactment, was the key issue in the campaign. But not far behind was a widespread feeling that Harrison and the Republicans had gone too far in driving that truck through the Treasury to reward the veterans. The Grand Army of the Republic, voters were told, had become greedy and overbearing in its demands.

It was a bad time all around for Harrison. The campaign stumbled from the start, and he was forced to take time to deal with the serious illness of his wife, Carrie, to whom he had written all those warm and tender letters during the time he was in the army. She died two weeks before election day.

Cleveland won the election handily, by Gilded Age standards. The Populists came in a surprisingly strong third, carrying four western states. Harrison returned to Indianapolis, married Carrie's first cousin, thirty-eight-year-old Mary Dimmick, and outraged most of his relatives and children by fathering another child when he was sixty-three years old.

In his second term, Cleveland tried, without much success, to deal with a severe depression and labor unrest that spilled over into violence during the Pullman strike. Troubles piled up on his doorstep when James B. Coxey's little army of the unemployed marched on Washington in the spring of 1894; most of the marchers were arrested for trespassing on the Capitol lawns. In the fall, Republicans swept aside Democrats and Populists to regain control of both houses of Congress.

A stubborn man, Cleveland returned to the pension fight that had caused him so much trouble earlier. By 1894, his Pension Bureau had cut off pensions to 2,266 veterans and had reduced the pensions of another 3,343. William McKinley joined a chorus of Republican condemnation, attacking the administration's "universal indictment against pensioners."

With Cleveland declining to run for another term, the Democrats tried something new in 1896. Meeting in Chicago, they succumbed to the demands of farmers and Westerners for the free coinage of silver and nominated Nebraska's William Jennings Bryan, a former congressman, as their presidential candidate. He had stampeded the convention earlier with his "cross of gold" speech, the most celebrated speech in the history of American party conventions. In it, he attacked Republicans for standing by the gold standard. "You shall not press down upon the brow of labor this crown of thorns," he bellowed. "You will not crucify man upon a cross of gold." Most voters understood that his call for unlimited coinage of silver promised monetary inflation that would make it easier for farmers and others to pay their debts.

The Republicans chose McKinley, with Fire-Alarm Foraker putting his name into nomination. "God lives," Fire-Alarm shouted, "the Republican Party is coming back to power, and William McKinley is to be President of the United States." Thirty-four free-silver delegates bolted from the hall after the convention adopted a platform plank calling for support of the gold standard.

McKinley was no political genius, but he had one working for him—industrialist Mark Hanna, the first thoroughly modern campaign manager. Hanna made sure voters knew that the major had seen action in the Civil War; most important, he made sure they knew that McKinley had joined the Union Army as an eighteen-year-old private. He and his campaign workers sent trainloads of veterans off to visit McKinley at his home in Canton, Ohio. At the same time, the major stopped by a number of army encampments and reunions.

Hanna decided there was no longer a need to wave the bloody shirt thirty-one years after Appomattox. What he and McKinley did was a lot subtler—they argued that free coinage of silver would mean the payment of every pension at 53 cents to the dollar. The *Chicago Tribune* said the South (whose Confederate veterans didn't receive pensions) would be delighted to see pension payments to the Yankee soldiers cut in half.

It was a clever, if specious, argument, and it seemed to work everywhere except in the West. "Have a little mercy on our debt-ridden veterans out west," one old soldier wrote.

Hanna responded to the rumblings of discontent by putting together a train called the "Patriotic Heroes Battalion," loading it up with old campaigners and sending it out on tour. It was a startling sight, the GAR historian Mary Dearing says. "The engine was bedecked with bunting, flags, and mottoes, as was also the 'famously stocked' Pullman dining car. Then followed General [Russell]

Alger's two private cars, and after those, two sleeping coaches. All were covered with portraits and such inscriptions as '1896 as Vitally Important as 1861' and 'For the Honor of Our Country.' Back of the observation car was a flatcar fitted with a portable platform, two thirty-foot collapsible flag poles, and a cannon."

"It is not doubted," the *Chicago Tribune* said, "that this special train with its soldier orators, its two thousand yards of bunting, its flags and cannon, will make something of a stir along its journey." Make a stir it did. The cannon would be fired to announce the train's arrival, and then the speaking would be turned over to that one-legged rogue General Sickles, the one-armed General Oliver O. Howard, and the legless Corporal Tanner, the man who had done so much to empty the Treasury. As the train pulled out of the station, a bugler would sound taps. Everywhere it went, the generals and Corporal Tanner drew huge crowds. The tour started in Illinois and rattled on—cannon firing, flags flying, and old generals haranguing huge, enthusiastic crowds—through Wisconsin, Minnesota, South Dakota, Iowa, Nebraska, Kansas, Indiana, Kentucky, and Ohio.

Hanna's campaign stunts may not have won the election, but they certainly forced Bryan to spend most of his time defending his free-silver crusade. The result was that McKinley won a decisive victory, the biggest since Grant skunked Greeley in 1872.

In office, McKinley became the only one of the soldier-presidents to serve as a wartime commander-in-chief, leading the nation to victory in the Spanish-American War in 1898. McKinley was reelected in 1900, defeating Bryan again, but he was fatally shot by Leon Czoglosz, an anarchist and unemployed mill worker, at the Pan-American Exposition in Buffalo, New York, on September 6, 1901. He died eight days later, on September 14, the 39th anniversary of the battle at South Mountain. Rutherford Hayes had died in 1893, but his sons, Webb and Birchard, attended the funeral in Canton, along with tearful veterans from the 23d Ohio, carrying the regiment's tattered battle flags. They were joined by Confederate veterans from Atlanta, Georgia, wearing their old uniforms.

McKinley's vice president, Theodore Roosevelt, the great "bully pulpit" president, succeeded him in office. Roosevelt cracked down, selectively, on giant corporations, reformed the way meat and other foods were inspected, built the Panama Canal, mediated an end to the war between Japan and Russia, sent a great white fleet of battleships around the world to demonstrate his country's growing naval strength, and began the preservation of the nation's unprotected natural resources. (His first secretary of the interior was James R. Garfield, the martyred president's son.) In essence, Roosevelt grabbed hold of the withered powers of the presidency and boldly reasserted them, bringing a merciful end to the Gilded Age. He was a successful chief executive and one of the most entertaining figures in all of U.S. presidential history.

But he always said nothing in his life was so exciting as his brief time in combat with his Rough Riders in Cuba. "I killed a Spaniard with my own hand, like a jack rabbit," he said. "Oh, but we had a bully fight!"

Much has been made of Roosevelt's bully performance against teenaged conscripts in the War with Spain. Not long ago, Congress even voted him, posthumously, the Medal of Honor. But his wartime experience pales in comparison to the experiences of the five presidents who fought in the Civil War.

Starting with Belmont and Forts Henry and Donelson, Grant led his troops in some of the bloodiest battles in history—Shiloh, Vicksburg, Chattanooga, the Wilderness, Spotsylvania, and Cold Harbor. Garfield defeated Humphrey Marshall in the Big Sandy Valley and stood at George Thomas's side at Chickamauga. Hayes fought a dozen or more engagements and battles, at Carnifex Ferry, Princeton, South Mountain, Opequon, Fisher's Hill, and Cedar Creek, and was wounded four times. A young McKinley served with him in all those battles, galloping across hotly contested battlefields, and was a hero to his men at Antietam. Harrison marched with Sherman to Atlanta and fought with skill and valor at Peach Tree Creek.

They all fought in battles so desperate and bloody we can barely comprehend them. It is no wonder that Grant, Garfield, Hayes, McKinley, and Harrison were touched with a fire that only death could extinguish.

Acknowledgments

I'm not sure it's possible to express thanks to anything as elusive as the Internet. But, in researching this book, I have spent a lot of time in cyberspace. Let me give just two examples of what was out there for me. All of Rutherford B. Hayes's Civil War diary entries and letters (all of his wife Lucy's letters too) can be found on the website of the Rutherford B. Hayes Presidential Center. The library's web address is http://rbhayes.org. Second, all 128 volumes of the most important Civil War source, the *Official Records of the Union and Confederate Armies*, are floating out there in cyberspace too. I used the Cornell University website, http://cdl.library.cornell.edu.

For all the wonders of the new information age, it is still essential to spend time inside libraries with books and manuscripts, and I hope it always will be. It is my good fortune to live eight miles from that immense treasure trove, the Library of Congress, and its magnificent reading room. I have also spent many rewarding hours in the Kate Waller Barrett Library in my hometown, Alexandria,

Virginia, and in a wonderful little library in Dundee, New York, not far from my summer cottage. I spent a number of profitable days at the Hayes Center in Fremont, Ohio; it is a gem we should all cherish. Everyone there was helpful, especially Nan J. Card, the enthusiastic curator of manuscripts.

Once again—it's three times now—I would like to acknowledge the good work of my agent, David Black. My publisher, Peter Osnos, generously supported the whole notion of this book from the beginning; my editor, Paul Golob, has been eagle-eyed. Finally—I have always wanted to say this—I did my own research and typed the manuscript on my own computer.

Bibliography

STANDARD WORKS

Battles and Leaders of the Civil War. Edited by Robert Underwood Johnson
and Clarence Clough Buel. 4 vols. New York, 1884–1887.
Confederate Military History. 17 vols. Wilmington, N.C.: Broadfoot Pub-
lishing, 1988.
The Rebellion Record: A Diary of American Events. Edited by Frank Moore.
7 vols. New York: D. Van Nostrand, 1864.
*War of the Rebellion: A Compilation of the Official Records of the Union and
Confederate Armies.* 128 vols. Washington, D.C., 1880–1901.
*War of the Rebellion: A Compilation of the Official Records of the Union and
Confederate Navies.* 30 vols. Washington, D.C., 1894–1922.

MANUSCRIPTS AND PAPERS

Papers of Ulysses S. Grant. Edited by John Y. Simon. 14 vols. Carbondale,
Ill.: Southern Illinois University Press, 1972.
James A. Garfield Papers. Washington, D.C.: Library of Congress.
Benjamin Harrison Papers. Washington, D.C.: Library of Congress.
Rutherford B. Hayes Papers. Fremont, Ohio: Rutherford B. Hayes Presi-
dential Center. Also available on the library's website, rbhayes.org.

William McKinley Biographical File. Fremont, Ohio: Rutherford B.
Hayes Presidential Center.
A Civil War Diary of William McKinley. Edited by H. Wayne Morgan. *Ohio Historical Quarterly* July 1960.
Lucy Webb Hayes letters. Fremont, Ohio: Rutherford B. Hayes Presidential Center. Also available on the library's website.
Russell Hastings Papers. Fremont, Ohio: Rutherford B. Hayes Presidential Center.
Confederate Military History. 17 vols. Wilmington, N.C.: Broadfoot Publishing, 1988.
Colonel James M. Comly diary. Fremont, Ohio: Rutherford B. Hayes Presidential Center.
Humphrey Marshall Papers. Louisville, Ky.: Filson Historical Society.

BOOKS AND ARTICLES

Alger, Horatio. *From Canal Boy to President, or the Boyhood and Manhood of James A. Garfield.* New York: John Anderson, 1881.
Anderson, Bern. *By Sea and By River: The Naval History of the Civil War.* New York: Knopf, 1962.
Andre, Richard, Stan Cohen, and Bill Wintz. *Bullets and Steel: The Fight for the Great Kanawha Valley.* (Pictorial Histories). Charleston, W.Va.: Pictorial Histories, 1995.
Andrews, J. Cutler. *The North Reports the Civil War.* Pittsburgh: University of Pittsburgh Press, 1955.
Armstrong, William H. *Major McKinley: William McKinley and the Civil War.* Kent, Ohio: Kent State University Press, 2000.
Arthur, E. C. "The Dublin Raid." *The Ohio Soldier* January–April 1889.
Barnard, Harry. *Rutherford B. Hayes and His America.* Indianapolis, Ind.: Bobbs-Merrill, 1954.
Bond, Otto F., editor. *Under the Flag of the Nation: Diaries and Letters of Owen Johnston Hopkins, a Yankee Volunteer in the Civil War.* Columbus, Ohio: Ohio State University Press, 1998.
Boritt, Gabor S., editor. *Lincoln's Generals.* New York: Oxford University Press, 1994.
Brown, John T., editor. *Churches of Christ.* 1904.
Bundy, J. M. *The Life of James A. Garfield.* New York: A. S. Barnes, 1881.
Burt, Silas W. *My Memories of the Military History of New York During the War for the Union.* Albany, N.Y.: 1902.

Carrington, Henry. *Ohio Militia and the West Virginia Campaign 1861.* Boston: R. H. Blodgett, 1904.

Cashman, Sean Dennis. *America in the Gilded Age: From the Death of Lincoln to the Rise of Theodore Roosevelt.* 3d ed. New York: New York University Press, 1993.

Catton, Bruce. *The Coming Fury.* New York: Doubleday, 1961.

————. *Never Call Retreat.* New York: Doubleday, 1965.

————. *Terrible Swift Sword.* New York: Doubleday, 1963.

————. *This Hallowed Ground: The Story of the Union Side of the Civil War.* New York: Doubleday, 1956.

————. *U.S. Grant and the American Military Tradition.* New York: Grosset & Dunlap, 1954.

Coffin, Charles Carleton. *The Life of James A. Garfield.* Boston: James H. Earle, 1881.

Coles, Henry L. *Ohio Forms an Army.* Columbus, Ohio: Ohio State University Press, 1962.

Conger, A. L. *The Rise of U.S. Grant.* New York: Da Capo Press, 1996.

Connely, Thomas Lawrence, and Archer Jones. *The Politics of Command: Factions and Ideas in Confederate Strategy.* Baton Rouge, La.: Louisiana State University Press, 1973.

Cook, Roy Bird. "The Battle of Carnifex Ferry." *West Virginia Review* November 1931.

————. "William McKinley: The Soldier in West Virginia." *West Virginia Review* March 1924.

Cooling, Benjamin Franklin. *Forts Henry and Donelson: The Key to the Confederate Heartland.* Chattanooga, Tenn.: University of Tennessee Press, 1987.

Coulter, E. Merton. *The Civil War and Readjustment in Kentucky.* Chapel Hill, N.C.: University of North Carolina Press, 1926.

Cox, Charles Harding. "The Civil War Letters of Charles Harding Cox." Edited by Lorna Lutes Sylvester. *Indiana Magazine of History* August 1962, December 1963, March 1972.

Cox, Jacob Dolson. *Military Reminiscences of the Civil War.* New York: Scribner's, 1900.

————. *Sherman's Battle for Atlanta.* New York: Da Capo Press, 1994.

Cozzens, Peter. *George Crook and Rutherford B. Hayes: A Friendship Forged in War.* Fremont, Ohio: Rutherford B. Hayes Presidential Center. (no date).

Crook, George. *General George Crook: His Autobiography.* Edited by Martin F. Schmitt. Norman, Okla.: University of Oklahoma Press, 1946.

Curry, Richard O., and F. Gerald Ham. "The Bushwhackers' War: Insurgency and Counter-Insurgency in West Virginia." *University of Iowa Quarterly* December 1964.

Davis, Harold E., editor. *Garfield of Hiram: A Memorial to the Life and Service of James Abram Garfield.* Hiram, Ohio: Hiram Historical Society, 1931.

Davis, William C., and Meredith L. Swentor, editors. *Bluegrass Confederate: The Headquarters Diary of Edward O. Guerrant.* Louisiana State University Press, 1999.

Davison, Kenneth E. *The Presidency of Rutherford B. Hayes.* Westport, Conn.: Greenwood Press, 1997.

Dearing, Mary R. *Veterans in Politics: The Story of the G.A.R.* Westport, Conn.: Greenwood Press, 1974.

Duncan, Richard L. *Lee's Endangered Left, the Civil War in Western Virginia, Spring of 1864.* Louisiana State University Press, 1998.

DuPont, Henry A. *The Campaign of 1864 in the Valley of Virginia.* New York: National Americana Society, 1925.

Eaton, Clement. *A History of the Southern Confederacy.* New York: Macmillan, 1954.

Eisenschiml, Otto. *The Celebrated Case of Fitz John Porter, an American Dreyfus Affair.* Indianapolis, Ind.: Bobbs-Merrill, 1950.

Fellman, Michael. *Citizen Sherman: A Life of William T. Sherman.* New York: Random House, 1995.

Foote, Shelby. *The Civil War, A Narrative.*

———. *Fort Sumter to Perryville.* New York: Vintage Books, 1958.

———. *Fredericksburg to Meridian.* New York: Vintage Books, 1963.

———. *Red River to Appomattox.* New York: Vintage Books, 1974.

Fuller, Corydon E. *Reminiscences of James A. Garfield.* Cincinnati: Standard Publishing, 1887.

Gallagher, Gary W., editor. *Struggles for the Shenandoah, Essays on the 1864 Valley Campaign.* Kent, Ohio: Kent State University Press, 1991.

Garfield, James A. "My Campaign in East Kentucky." *North American Review* December 1886.

Geer, Emily Apt. *First Lady: The Life of Lucy Webb Hayes.* Fremont, Ohio: Rutherford B. Hayes Presidential Center, 1995.

Goebel, Dorothy Burne, and Julius Goebel Jr. *Generals in the White House.* New York: Doubleday, 1945.

Grant, Ulysses S. *Personal Memoirs and Selected Letters.* New York: Library of America, 1990.

Hamilton, James J. *The Battle of Fort Donelson*. South Brunswick, N.J.: A. S. Barnes, 1968.

Hayes, Rutherford B. "Incidents at the Battle of Cedar Creek." *Ohio Commandery* March 1889.

Henry, Frederick A. *Captain Henry of Geaugu: A Family Chronicle*. Cleveland: Gate Press, 1942.

Hirshson, Stanley P. *Farewell to the Bloody Shirt*. Gloucester, Mass.: Peter Smith, 1968.

Hoogenboom, Ari. *Rutherford B. Hayes: "One of the Good Colonels."* Abilene, Tex.: McWhiney Foundation Press, 1999.

————. *Rutherford B. Hayes: Warrior and President*. Lawrence, Kans.: University Press of Kansas, 1995.

Howarth, Stephen. *To Shining Sea. A History of the United States Navy, 1775–1991*. New York: Random House, 1991.

Hughes, Nathaniel Cheairs. *The Battle of Belmont*. Chapel Hill, N.C.: University of North Carolina Press, 1991.

Jeffers, H. Paul. *An Honest President: The Life and Presidencies of Grover Cleveland*. New York: William Morrow, 2000.

Johnson, Patrick Givens. *The United States Army Invades the New River Valley 1864*. Privately published, 1986.

Joseph, Alvin M. *The Civil War in the American West*. New York: Knopf, 1991.

Lamers, William M. *The Edge of Glory: A Biography of William S. Rosecrans*. Baton Rouge, La.: Louisiana State University Press, 1989.

Le Duc, William G. *Recollections of a Civil War Quartermaster*. St. Paul, Minn.: North Central Publishing, 1963.

Leech, Margaret. *In the Days of McKinley*. Norwalk, Conn.: Easton Press, 1986.

Lewis, Lloyd. *Captain Sam Grant*. Boston: Little, Brown, 1950.

————. *Sherman· Fighting Prophet*. New York: Harcourt, Brace, 1932.

Lewis, Thomas A. *The Guns of Cedar Creek*. New York: Harper & Row, 1988.

————. *The Shenandoah in Flames*. Alexandria, Va.: Time-Life Books, 1987.

Lives of General Benjamin Harrison and Whitelaw Reid. (no author). Political Publishing Company. (no date).

Lowry, Terry. *September Blood: The Battle of Carnifex Ferry. Pictorial Histories*. Charleston, W.Va.: 1985.

Maclay, Edgar Stanton. *A History of the United States Navy from 1775 to 1890*. 2 vols. New York: D. Appleton, 1898.

Marcus, Robert D. *Grand Old Party, Political Structure in the Gilded Age, 1880–1896.* New York: Oxford University Press, 1971.

Mason, F. H. *The Forty-Second Ohio Infantry: A History.* Cleveland: Cobb, Andrews, 1876.

Mayer, George H. *The Republican Party, 1854–1964.* New York: Oxford University Press, 1971.

McConnell, Stuart. *Glorious Contentment: The Grand Army of the Republic. 1865–1900.* Chapel Hill, N.C.: University of North Carolina Press, 1992.

McKinley, William. "Personal Recollections of Rutherford B. Hayes." *The Chautauquan* April 17, 1893.

McKinney, Francis F. *Education in Violence: The Life of George H. Thomas and the History of the Army of the Cumberland.* Detroit, MI.: Wayne State University Press, 1961.

McManus, Howard Rollins. *The Battle of Cloyds Mountain: The Virginia and Tennessee Railroad Raid.* Lynchburg, Va.: H. E. Howard, 1989.

McPherson, James. *Battle Cry of Freedom: The Civil War Era.* New York: Oxford University Press, 1988.

———. *"To the Best of My Ability": The American Presidents.* London: Dorling Kindersley, 2000.

Merrill, Samuel. *The Seventieth Indiana Volunteer Infantry in the War of the Rebellion.* Indianapolis, Ind.: Bowen-Merrill, 1900.

Moore, George Ellis. *A Banner in the Hills: West Virginia's Statehood.* New York: Appleton-Century Crofts, 1963.

Morgan, H. Wayne. *From Hayes to McKinley, National Party Politics, 1877–1896.* Syracuse, N.Y.: Syracuse University Press, 1969.

———. *William McKinley and His America.* Syracuse, N.Y.: Syracuse University Press, 1963.

Morris, Roy, Jr. *Sheridan: The Life and Wars of General Phil Sheridan.* New York: Crown, 1992.

Niven, John. *Salmon P. Chase, A Biography.* New York: Oxford University Press, 1995.

Northrop, Henry Davenport, and James Bergen. *The Life and Public Services of General Benjamin Harrison.* Boston. (no date).

Patrick, Rembert W. *The Reconstruction of the Nation.* New York: Oxford University Press, 1967.

Perry, James M. *A Bohemian Brigade: The Civil War Correspondents, Mostly Rough, Sometimes Ready.* New York: Wiley, 2000.

Peskin, Allan. *Garfield.* Kent, Ohio: Kent State University Press, 1978.

———. "Garfield and Hayes: Political Leaders of the Gilded Age." *Ohio History.* 1968.

————. "The Hero of the Sandy Valley: James A. Garfield's Kentucky Campaign of 1861–1862." *Ohio History* January and April, 1963.

————. "The 'Little Man on Horseback' and the 'Literary Fellow': Garfield's Opinion of Grant." *Mid-America Magazine* October 1973.

Porter, George H. *Ohio Politics During the Civil War.* New York: AMS Press, 1968.

Preston, John David. *The Civil War in the Big Sandy Valley of Kentucky.* Baltimore: Gateway Press, 1984.

Priest, John Michael. *Before Antietam: The Battle for South Mountain.* New York: Oxford University Press, 1992.

Reid, Whitelaw. *Ohio in the War: Her Statesmen, Her Generals and Soldiers.* 2 vols. Cincinnati: Moore, Wilstach and Baldwin, 1868.

Ridpath, John Clark. *The Life and Work of James A. Garfield.* Cincinnati: Jones Brothers, 1881.

Russell, John W. "McKinley at Antietam." *Munsey's Magazine* March 1909.

Scalf, Henry P. *Kentucky's Last Frontier.* Pikeville, Ky.: Pikeville College Press, 1972.

Schuster, Richard. *The Selfish and the Strong.* New York: Random House, 1958.

Sears, Stephen W. "Fire on the Mountain." *Blue & Gray Magazine.* December/January, 1986–1987.

Secrist, Philip L. *The Battle of Resaca—Atlanta Campaign 1864.* Macon, Ga.: Mercer University Press, 1998.

Shaw, John, editor. *Crete and James: Personal Letters of Lucretia and James Garfield.* Lansing, Mich.: Michigan State University Press, 1994.

Sherman, William T. *The Memoirs of General William T. Sherman, by Himself.* Bloomington, Ind.: Indiana University Press, 1957.

Sievers, Harry J. *Benjamin Harrison: Hoosier President, the White House and After.* Indianapolis, Ind.: Bobbs-Merrill, 1968.

————. *Benjamin Harrison: Hoosier Statesman, from the Civil War to the White House, 1865–1888.* New York: University Publishers, 1959.

————. *Benjamin Harrison: Hoosier Warrior, Through the Civil War Years, 1833–1865.* New York: University Publishers, 1952.

Smith, Edward Conrad. *The Borderland in the Civil War.* New York: Macmillan, 1927.

Smith, Jean Edward. *Grant.* New York: Simon & Schuster, 2001.

Smith, Theodore Clarke. "General Garfield at Chickamauga." *Proceedings of the Massachusetts Historical Society* February 1915.

Stampp, Kenneth M. *Indiana Politics During the Civil War.* Bloomington, Ind.: Indiana University Press, 1978.

Stackpole, Edward J. *Sheridan in the Shenandoah, Jubal Early's Nemesis.* Harrisburg, Pa.: Stackpole Books, 1992.

Stanley, David S. *Personal Memoirs of Major-General D.S. Stanley.* Cambridge, Mass.: Harvard University Press, 1917.

Strayer, Larry M., and Richard A. Baumgartner. *Echoes of Battle: The Atlanta Campaign.* Huntington, W.Va.: Blue Acorn Press, 1991.

Stutler, Boyd B. *West Virginia in the Civil War.* Charleston, W.Va.: Education Foundation, 1963.

Taylor, James E. *With Sheridan up the Shenandoah Valley in 1866, Leaves from a Special Artist's Sketchbook and Diary.* Cleveland: Western Reserve Historical Society, 1989.

Taylor, John M. *Garfield of Ohio: The Available Man.* New York: W. W. Norton, 1970.

Trefousse, Hans L. *The Radical Republicans: Lincoln's Vanguard for Racial Justice.* New York: Knopf, 1969.

Walker, Gary C. *The War in Southwest Virginia, 1861–1865.* Roanoke, Va.: Curtner Printing, 1985.

Wallace, Lew. *Life of Benjamin Harrison.* Philadelphia: Hubbard, 1888.

Wert, Jeffry D. *From Winchester to Cedar Creek: The Shenandoah Campaign of 1864.* New York: Simon & Schuster, 1987.

Wiley, John Bell. *The Life of Billy Yank: The Common Soldier of the Union.* Baton Rouge, La.: Louisiana State University Press, 1952.

Williams, Charles R. *The Life of Rutherford Birchard Hayes.* New York: Da Capo Press, 1971.

Williams, Frederick D., editor. *The Wild Life of the Army: Civil War Letters of James A. Garfield.* Lansing, Mich.: Michigan State University Press, 1964.

Williams, Kenneth P. *Grant Rises in the West.* Lincoln, Nebr.: University of Nebraska Press, 1997.

———. *Lincoln Finds a General: A Military Study of the Civil War.* 5 vols. New York: Macmillan, 1959.

Williams, T. Harry. *Hayes of the Twenty-Third: The Civil War Volunteer Officer.* New York: Knopf, 1965.

Wills, Garry. *Cincinnatus: George Washington and the Enlightenment.* New York: Doubleday, 1984.

Woodward, C. Vann. *Origins of the New South, 1877–1913.* Baton Rouge, La.: Louisiana State University Press, 1951.

Index

INDEX 325

PublicAffairs is a publishing house founded in 1997. It is a tribute to the standards, values, and flair of three persons who have served as mentors to countless reporters, writers, editors, and book people of all kinds, including me.

I.F. STONE, proprietor of *I. F. Stone's Weekly*, combined a commitment to the First Amendment with entrepreneurial zeal and reporting skill and became one of the great independent journalists in American history. At the age of eighty, Izzy published *The Trial of Socrates*, which was a national bestseller. He wrote the book after he taught himself ancient Greek.

BENJAMIN C. BRADLEE was for nearly thirty years the charismatic editorial leader of *The Washington Post*. It was Ben who gave the *Post* the range and courage to pursue such historic issues as Watergate. He supported his reporters with a tenacity that made them fearless and it is no accident that so many became authors of influential, bestselling books.

ROBERT L. BERNSTEIN, the chief executive of Random House for more than a quarter century, guided one of the nation's premier publishing houses. Bob was personally responsible for many books of political dissent and argument that challenged tyranny around the globe. He is also the founder and longtime chair of Human Rights Watch, one of the most respected human rights organizations in the world.

For fifty years, the banner of Public Affairs Press was carried by its owner Morris B. Schnapper, who published Gandhi, Nasser, Toynbee, Truman, and about 1,500 other authors. In 1983, Schnapper was described by *The Washington Post* as "a redoubtable gadfly." His legacy will endure in the books to come.

Peter Osnos, *Publisher*